Frommer's®

# SCOTLAND'S BEST-LOVED DRIVING TOURS

BICENTENNIAL 1807 WILEY 2007 BICENTENNIAL

Wiley Publishing, Inc.

Written by David Williams

First published 1992
Revised second edition 1996, published in this format 1998
Revised third edition published 2000
Revised fourth edition published 2003
Revised fifth edition published 2005
Revised sixth edition published 2007

Edited, designed and produced by AA Publishing.


Published by AA Publishing

Published in the United States by John Wiley & Sons, Inc.
111 River Street, Hoboken, NJ 07030

Find us online at Frommers.com



ISBN 978-0-470-10571-9

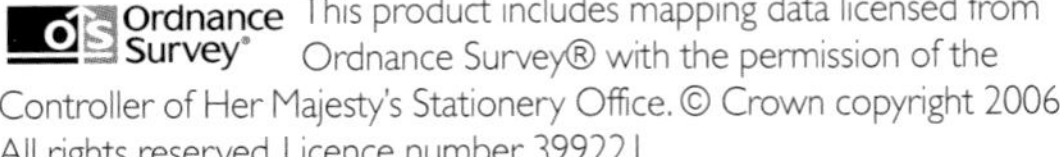


Color separation: Daylight Colour Art, Singapore

Printed and bound by G. Canale & C. S.P.A., Torino, Italy

A02697

# CONTENTS

# ABOUT THIS BOOK

This book is not only a practical guide for the independent traveller, but is also invaluable for those who would like to know more about the country. It is divided into four regions, each containing between five and seven tours that start and finish in the towns and cities which we consider to be the best centres for exploration. Each tour has details of the most interesting places to visit en route. Panels catering for special interests follow some of the main entries – for those whose interest is in history, wildlife or walking, and those who have children. There are also panels highlighting scenic stretches of road and which give details of special events, gastronomic specialities, crafts and customs. The simple route directions are accompanied by an easy-to-use map at the beginning of each tour, along with a chart showing intermediate distances in miles and kilometres. These can help you decide where to take a break and stop overnight, for example. (All distances quoted are approximate.)
Before setting off it is advisable to contact the information centre at the start of the tour for recommendations on where to break your journey, for more information on what to see and do, and when best to visit. Addresses for centres along the way are given at the end of town entries (see *i* symbol).

**Business hours**
Banks: open Monday to Friday 9.30–5, but times do vary depending on the bank and the place. Some close for lunch.
Post offices: generally open Monday to Friday 9–5.30, Saturday 9–noon. Times and days vary from place to place.
Shops: are usually open Monday to Saturday 8.30–1.30, 3.30–7.30. Many are closed on Monday mornings, and food shops are often closed on Thursday afternoons. Times may vary in busy tourist areas.

**Credit Cards**
All major credit cards are widely accepted throughout Scotland.

**Currency**
The unit of currency is the pound (£), divided into 100 pence (p). Coins are in denominations of 1, 2, 5, 10, 20 and 50 pence, and one and two pounds; Scottish notes are in denominations of £1, 5, 10, 20, 50 and 100. Bank of England notes are also legal tender, as well as euros, at the management's discretion.

**Customs Regulations**
For goods bought outside the EU, you can import, duty free, 200 cigarettes or 100 cigarillos or 50 cigars or 250g of tobacco; one litre of alcohol over 22 per cent volume or 2 litres of alcohol not

Shaggy Highland cattle

**Tour Information**
See pages 180–91 for addresses, telephone numbers, websites and opening times of attractions mentioned in the tours, including the telephone numbers of tourist offices.

**Accommodation and restaurants**
See pages 165–77 for a list of recommended hotels for each tour. Also listed are restaurants where you may like to stop for a meal.

over 22 per cent volume or fortified or sparkling wine, plus 2 litres of still table wine; 60ml of perfume, 250ml of toilet water and £145 worth of other goods. If goods are bought, duty paid, within the EU, you can import, additional tobacco, alcoholic drinks, gifts and other goods for personal use.

### Emergency Telephone Number
Police, fire, ambulance, tel: 999.

### Entry Regulations
Passports are required by all visitors, including citizens of EU countries. Visas are not required for entry into Britain by American citizens, nationals of the British Commonwealth and most European countries. Visa regulations can change – check before you travel.

### Health
Inoculations are not required for entry to Britain. Health insurance is recommended for non-EU citizens.

### Motoring
See pages 158–9.

### Public Holidays
1–2 January: New Year
Good Friday/Easter Monday
First Monday in May: May Day
Last Monday in May: Spring Bank Holiday
First Monday in August: Summer Bank Holiday
25–26 December: Christmas

### Route Directions
Throughout the book the following abbreviations are used for Scottish roads:
A – main roads
B – local roads
unclassified roads – minor roads (unnumbered).

### Telephones
Insert coins after lifting the receiver; the dialling tone is a continuous tone.
Useful numbers:
Operator – 100
Directory Enquiries – 118500 (BT), 118111 (One.Tel)
International Directory Enquiries – 118505 (BT), 118211 (One.Tel)
International Operator – 155
IDD code for Scotland – 44.
To make an international call, dial 00, then the country code, the area code, omitting the first zero, then the local number.

### Time
The official time is Greenwich Mean Time (GMT). British Summer Time (BST) begins in late March when clocks are put forward an hour. In late October, the clocks go back to GMT. The official date is announced in the daily newspapers, and is always at 2am on a Sunday.

### Tourist Office
VisitScotland, 94 Ocean Drive, Leith, Edinburgh EH6 6JH. Tel: 0131 472 2222.

# SOUTHERN SCOTLAND

Southern Scotland is dominated by the grand mass of the Southern Uplands, the great band of hills that stretches right across the width of the country. For a long time it was easier to sail along the coastline than cross the hills, so the two coastal fringes were settled first. These narrow, fertile strips are still among the most populated parts of the region, with the best land devoted to cereals and herds of prime dairy cattle. Inland, the rolling uplands are home to the countless sheep which form the basis of the prosperous woollen and knitwear industries of the Borders.

The many castles and fortified houses found in the region are reminders of the centuries of border warfare that have shaped the history of the whole of southern Scotland. Cattle-raiding, pillaging, looting and burning were commonplace, but perhaps the most poignant reminders of those turbulent days are the great Border abbeys of Melrose, Kelso, Jedburgh and Dryburgh, which were mercilessly attacked and eventually destroyed by the English. Fortunately for us, their splendid ruins still survive to conjure up the past.

Boat showing the blue and white St Andrew's flag in Eyemouth harbour

The region is much more peaceful now, and most of today's 'invaders' come armed with a bucket and spade or a set of golf clubs. The eastern side of the country, with its beaches, seaside resorts, fishing villages and busy mill towns, has been a tourist area for some time, with many of its best-known places made famous by the region's best publicist, Sir Walter Scott. The west coast's literary figure, Robert Burns, is highly regarded as 'a man of the people', and his special place in the hearts of Scots can be judged by the number of memorials, plaques and statues that mark his journeys through the country.

The region can never match the grandeur of the western Highlands or the great museums and palaces of central Scotland, but it does offer a relaxed way of life in an area imbued with tradition. Its people are proud of that fact. They are keen not to lose the unique flavour of their local culture and any visitor who witnesses a Border town's rugby match will soon learn how independent the spirit is here.

The cycle museum at Drumlanrig Castle in Dumfries & Galloway

**Tour 1**
The journey along the Clyde coast is one of the finest in this part of Scotland, with glorious views over the Firth of Clyde to Arran and the smaller islands of the Clyde. With such views, it is no wonder that many Scots retire to this area. For the visitor, this scenery provides the backdrop to many places associated with Robert Burns, the national poet and the Scots' favourite literary figure.

**Tour 2**
Many visitors overlook this far southwestern corner of the country, but there is a wealth of picturesque villages, historic buildings, sandy beaches and other attractions in this almost 'forgotten' land. It is mainly agricultural and the great absence of industry and big towns has meant that many antiquities have been preserved and older building styles have survived. This is one of the warmest and driest parts of Scotland, factors that have helped foster agriculture – and palm trees!

**Tour 3**
The muddy creeks on the northern shore of the Solway Firth were havens to smugglers bringing contraband into Scotland. Given such a tradition, it comes as no surprise that the area's most famous figure was an exciseman – none other than Robert Burns, who spent his final years in the Dumfries area. The castles and granite towns of the coast contrast with large forests and rolling farmland inland.

**Tour 4**
Although the Clyde is normally thought of as an industrial river, the upper reaches are thronged with orchards and market gardens. Add a few castles and an impressive canyon and the Clyde Valley soon becomes one of the most surprising areas in this part of Scotland. The moors and hills above the valley are no less interesting and they have been home to Iron-Age people, Romans and farmers – and weekend gold prospectors!

**Tour 5**
The tour follows many important river courses as they wind their way through the hills of the Southern Uplands, the land of the shepherd and the forester. Although the area's population has never been large, it has certainly seen many visitors. Some were unwelcome as they came to raid and plunder; others, the early tourists, came to sample the peaceful countryside and the delights of two of the country's most southerly spas.

**Tour 6**
The name of Sir Walter Scott is writ large in this area. He lived and worked here and also became one of Scotland's greatest novelists, to the extent that the Waverley novels gave their name both to a local railway line and to Edinburgh's main railway station. This is also the land of the ruins of the great Border abbeys, impressive medieval buildings that stand as monuments to man's craftsmanship – and powers of destruction.

**Tour 7**
The Border Country, of which this is part, has long seen the coming and going of armies and the number of castles found here is a measure of how dangerous an area this once was. Much of the coastline is rugged, and the cliff scenery quite spectacular, though in the north of the region the coastal scenery becomes gentler, giving way to fine beaches and grassy links that are ideal for golf. Inland, the rich agricultural district of the Merse supports many pretty villages, most of which nestle under the shelter of the Lammermuirs.

TOUR 1

# The Land O' Burns

This tour starts in Ayr, once the chief port of western Scotland but now more famous for its associations with Robert Burns. And, indeed, throughout this tour the name of Scotland's most famous son keeps cropping up...

ITINERARY

| | |
|---|---|
| **AYR** | ▶ **Alloway (3m-5km)** |
| ALLOWAY | ▶ **Electric Brae (8m-13km)** |
| ELECTRIC BRAE | ▶ **Culzean Castle (5m-8km)** |
| CULZEAN CASTLE | ▶ **Turnberry (5m-8km)** |
| TURNBERRY | ▶ **Kirkoswald (3m-5km)** |
| KIRKOSWALD | ▶ **Maybole (4m-6km)** |
| MAYBOLE | ▶ **Mauchline (18m-29km)** |
| MAUCHLINE | ▶ **Kilmarnock (9m-14km)** |
| KILMARNOCK | ▶ **Irvine (8m-13km)** |
| IRVINE | ▶ **Largs (19m-31km)** |
| LARGS | ▶ **Troon (26m-42km)** |
| TROON | ▶ **Ayr (8m-13km)** |

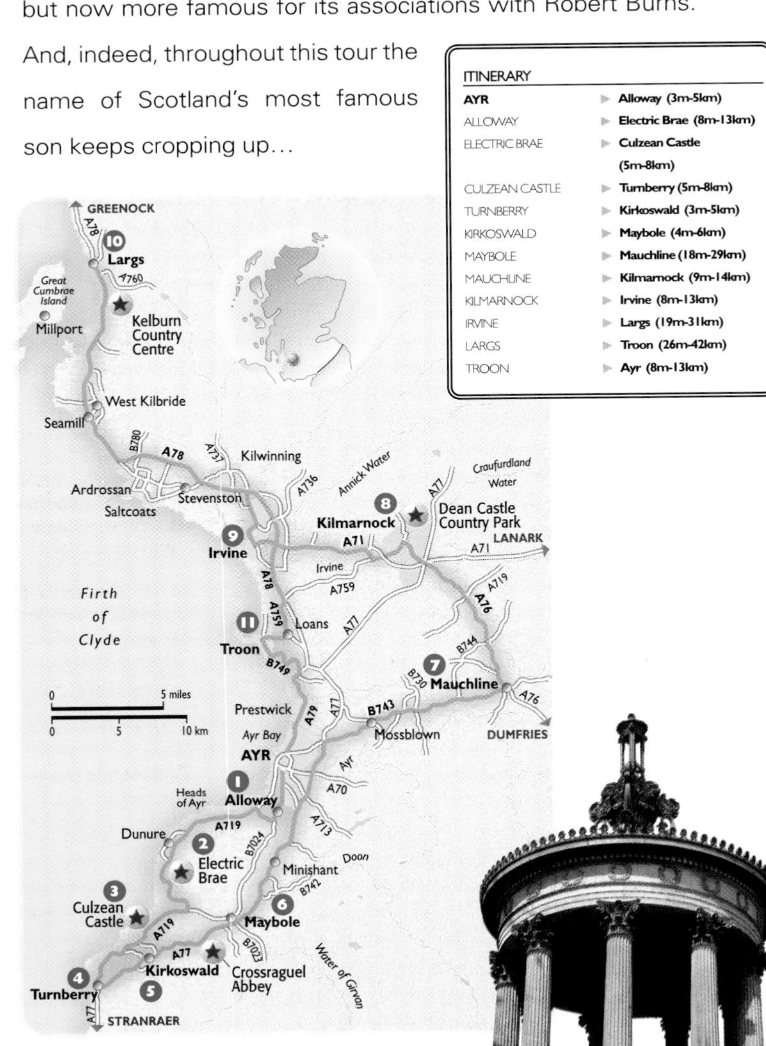


1/2 DAYS • 116 MILES • 187KM

The Burns Monument and Brig o'Doon in Alloway

[i] *22 Sandgate, Ayr*

*Take the* **B7024** *from Ayr for 3 miles (5km) to the village of Alloway.*

**SPECIAL TO...**

There are a number of celebrated golf courses along the Clyde. The links courses along the coastline are ideally suited to the game, and are littered with challenging bunkers. Most towns have courses, and the most renowned ones are to be found at Ayr, Troon, Turnberry and Prestwick. They must surely rank as some of the most attractively located courses in Britain.

**1 Alloway,** South Ayrshire
The Burns National Heritage Park was established here as this was where Robert Burns spent his early years. Burns was born in 1759 and he is regarded not only as Scotland's national poet but as one of her greatest literary figures. Although lionised by the predominantly Edinburgh-based literary celebrities of his day, he never abandoned his roots in the west and continued to work as a small farmer, and later as an exciseman. Like many great artists, he was never fully appreciated until well after his death, but now there are hundreds of Burns Societies all over the world, each year celebrating the poet's birthday (26 January) with such well-known favourites as *To a Haggis, Holy Willie's Prayer* and, probably his best-known work, *Auld Lang Syne.*

Opposite the park is the old ruined kirk where Burns' father is buried. This was a ruin even in Burns' day and it was here that Tam, in the poem *Tam o' Shanter*, saw warlocks, witches and Auld Nick (the devil). Also near by is the ancient and very beautiful Auld Brig o' Doon over which Tam escaped from the witches. Towering above the river is the Burns Monument, which is set in a very pleasant garden.

Burns was born in the little thatched cottage now known as Burns Cottage. His father, William Burnes, built it around 1757 and it has been well preserved, not only as a memorial to the poet, but as a good example of local village architecture of the time. This type of two-roomed cottage is known as a 'but and ben', with the kitchen in the front room and the living room/bedroom at the back ('ben'). The neighbouring museum holds a vast amount of Burns memorabilia.

*Continue on the* **B7024** *for a short distance. Just after crossing the River Doon, turn right on an unclassified road to Doonfoot. Turn left when the coastal road (***A719***) is met; 8 miles (13km).*

**2 Electric Brae,** South Ayrshire
After the A719 passes Dunure and turns inland at Culzean Bay, the road goes 'up' the Electric Brae, a well-known and mind-boggling optical illusion. A car might appear to be travelling downhill, but drivers who come to a halt will find the car rolling backwards! On pleasant summer afternoons, there can be quite a queue of cars on this stretch of road trying to roll 'uphill'.

*Continue on the* **A719** *for 5 miles (8km) to Culzean Castle.*

**3 Culzean Castle,** South Ayrshire

The present building is based on a medieval tower house that was later developed as a massive country house set within extensive parkland. It is now the National Trust for Scotland's most popular attraction and its country park has gardens, a nursery, a swan pond and a deer park.

In the late 18th century, Robert Adam started work on remodelling the house. The interior decoration has since been painstakingly restored to his original designs to the extent that this is now the Scottish showpiece of Adam's work. The most outstanding features are the magnificent Oval Staircase and the Round Drawing Room.

The extensive grounds, a continuing exercise in large-scale conservation, include woodlands, a walled garden, a swan pond and deer park.

**BACK TO NATURE**

The coastline of Culzean has many different things to look for and is certainly worth exploring. You may find agates on the pebble beach and the rock pools have a wide variety of life in them, including sea anemones, sea urchins and butterfish. During the summer there are many seabirds, while during the winter great northern divers might be seen offshore.

*Continue southwards on the **A719** for 5 miles (8km) to Turnberry.*

**4 Turnberry,** South Ayrshire

This famous golfing centre is dominated by the Turnberry Hotel. The golf course sometimes plays host to the British Open.

The remains of the castle, which stands by the lighthouse, may have been the birthplace of Robert Bruce. In 1307 Bruce was lured across the Clyde from Arran by a mystic fire and defeated the English force that was occupying the castle, leaving the buildings in ruins in the process.

*Leave by the **A77** and follow it northeast for 3 miles (5km) to Kirkoswald.*

**5 Kirkoswald,** South Ayrshire

Kirkoswald has a number of connections with Robert Burns as his mother's family came from the village. Burns' characters of Tam and Kate from the poem *Tam o' Shanter* came from Kirkoswald and Souter Johnnie's Cottage is on the main road. This thatched house of 1786 was the home of John Davidson, the local 'souter' (local term for shoemaker), and is now a museum furnished in the style of Burns' day. Burns would have attended the old Kirkoswald Church, now a picturesque ruin within a graveyard in which the poet's grandparents and great-grandparents are buried.

*Continue on the **A77** for 4 miles (6km) to Maybole.*

Culzean Castle, commanding a fine position above Culzean Bay

**6 Maybole,** South Ayrshire
Many substantial buildings line the narrow main street, the most striking of which is 17th-century Maybole Castle (not open). The castle is featured in the ballad *The Raggle Taggle Gypsies*, in which the King of the Gypsies, Johnnie Faa, persuaded a Countess of Cassillis to elope with him. Unfortunately he was caught and hanged, while the countess was imprisoned in the castle, in the room with the little oriel window that faces up High Street.

Maybole has a long history and its oldest building is the roofless Collegiate Church. Most of the remaining parts, although built in the 15th century, are in the style of the 13th and 14th centuries.

Crossraguel Abbey is met a little before Maybole. This relatively small Cluniac monastery (it only had 10 monks in the 15th century) was built in the mid-13th century. It was very badly damaged in the Wars of Independence (1296–1357) and had to be rebuilt. Although roofless, the walls that remain indicate the scale of the establishment. The tall tower house is a particularly unusual building for an abbey.

The ruined Baltersan Tower is on the roadside between the abbey and the village.

▶ *Continue on the* ***A77****, then turn right at the* ***B743*** *to Mauchline, 18 miles (29km).*

FOR HISTORY BUFFS

Driving from Ayr, it is worth remembering that the 'tarmacadam' surface was named after local man, John Loudon MacAdam (1756–1836), who revolutionised road-building in this country. He introduced new ways of building roads by using layers of sucessively smaller stones, topped by a binding mixture of crushed stone and gravel, cambered to disperse rainwater.

**7 Mauchline,** East Ayrshire
This little town is yet another in the area which has a number of associations with Robert Burns – not surprising, in view of the fact that he lived at the farm of Mossgiel, just to the north of Mauchline. The most outstanding building is the National Burns Memorial, which was constructed in 1896.

The church stands near the centre of the town and in its graveyard lie many people associated with Burns, including several of his children. Burns featured some of the locals in his poems, like the clockmaker John Brown ('Clockie Brown' in *The Court of Equity*), and a rogue cattle dealer called McGavin who was referred to as 'Master Tootie, alias Laird McGaun' in *To Gavin Hamilton, Esq*.

By the churchyard stands the Burns House Museum, where Burns and his wife set up house in 1788; this also has an interesting collection of local historical material.

Opposite the church stands Poosie Nansie's Inn, which provided the setting for *The Jolly Beggars*.

▶ *Leave by the* ***A76*** *and follow it to Kilmarnock, entering the town by the* ***A735****.*

Dominating the town: the National Burns Memorial Tower at Mauchline, built in 1896

**8 Kilmarnock,** East Ayrshire
This industrial town, which is bigger than Ayr, built its affluence on the making of such diverse goods as whisky, carpets and various engineering products. Although much of the heart of the town has been changed by the building of modern shops, there are still some very fine buildings, many of them highly ornamented red or white sandstone structures, erected to reflect the wealth and aspirations of their builders.

The Dean Castle Country Park is on the northeast outskirts of the town. The attractive castle was a seat of the Boyds, lords of Kilmarnock, and was carefully restored in the 20th century. It houses a collection of arms, armour, tapestries and early musical instruments. The 200-acre (80-hectare) grounds offer many opportunities for walks.

Kay Park, which is on the eastern side of the Craufurdland Water, has as its centrepiece the tall red sandstone Burns Monument, which was erected in 1879. In 1786 Burns' first work was published and his *Poems chiefly in the Scottish Dialect*, usually known as the *Kilmarnock Edition*, brought him great fame – and the sum of £20.

FOR CHILDREN

The town's Galleon Centre offers many sporting facilities, including a crèche, a pool and an ice rink. Five miles (8km) east of Kilmarnock, along the A71, is Loudoun Castle Family Theme Park, including thrill rides and entertainment.

*Leave by the **A759**. On reaching the **A71**, go to Irvine.*

**9 Irvine,** North Ayrshire
Irvine has many attractions, but the modern shopping centre, which crosses the River Irvine, dwarfs the old town and spoils Irvine's riverside location. The town prospered as a busy industrial centre and was Glasgow's main port before Port Glasgow was developed.

The Scottish Maritime Museum provides a fine introduction to this heritage. Among the exhibits are boats tied alongside the old harbour wall including a 'puffer' (a small cargo boat that served the west coast and its islands), the world's oldest remaining sea-coaster and a number of other craft, including lifeboats. The museum has exhibitions and displays of various shipbuilding crafts. The prize exhibit is the Victorian engine-shop from Stephen's Linthouse yard in Glasgow, which has been re-erected here. This superb tall brick building is supported by the original cast-iron structure

The attractive exterior of Dean Castle – museum and country park

Boats moored at the Scottish Maritime Museum include a 'puffer'

that was quite revolutionary when it was constructed in 1872. But industrial museums are not just about factories and their products: they are about the people who made this possible, and the museum has restored a shipyard worker's 'room and kitchen' tenement house to what it would have looked like in 1910.

Harbour Street leads to the river mouth and the Pilot House, erected in 1906 with an automatic tide-signalling device which hoisted balls on top of the building to indicate the depth of the water.

The old part of the town is on the other side of the river. Robert Burns came here in 1781 to learn the trade of flax dressing (called 'heckling') and stayed at No 4 Glasgow Vennel, now a museum. He worked in a 'heckling shop' at No 10; 'hecklers' tended to be politically argumentative types, hence the modern usage of the word. Other places worth looking at include the conservation area of Hill Street, the Burns Club and Museum, and Cunninghame House, which houses the priceless Eglinton Trophy, 8 feet (2.4m) high and exquisitely intricate, given as the prize for a famous mock-medieval tournament staged in 1839 at Eglinton Castle.

**FOR CHILDREN**

**Irvine's Magnum Centre is one of Scotland's most popular attractions. It has a swimming pool, ice rink, soft play area, children's fitness centre and facilities for sports such as squash and table tennis. The Clyde Coast is well known for its beaches, including Turnberry, Ayr, Prestwick, Troon, Irvine, Saltcoats and Ardrossan.**

▶ *Leave by the **A737**, then join the **A78** (towards Greenock). Follow this to Largs.*

**10 Largs,** North Ayrshire

This popular seaside town has a long and attractive promenade giving fine views of the Firth of Clyde. Largs has many distinctive sandstone buildings, especially along its front. One unique structure that is hidden away and tends to be forgotten is the 1636 Skelmorlie Aisle, originally part of the parish church. Inside is an ornate Renaissance-style monument in the form of an archway, which has a mass of fine detail carved in locally quarried sandstone. Above it is a painted ceiling which has survived remarkably well. The burial ground also

The round tower of Bowen Craig to the south of Largs, nicknamed The Pencil, commemorates the defeat of a Viking fleet here in 1263

contains the vault of a local family by the name of Brisbane, one of whose members, Sir Thomas Brisbane, gave his name to the state capital of Queensland, Australia.

At the southern end of the town, a walk along the coast leads to The Pencil, a tall monument that celebrates the Battle of Largs of 1263. A Viking fleet under King Haakon of Norway was driven ashore here and roundly defeated by the Scots, led by Alexander III. This battle ended the Vikings' occupation of Scotland and the lively Vikingar is a major exhibition celebrating Scotland's Viking heritage using models, impressive audiovisual effects and authetically hairy actors to re-create the Viking world. It's great fun for adults, as well as children.

A regular car ferry service crosses over to Great Cumbrae Island. The island's 'capital', Millport, has a pretty location looking across the water to Little Cumbrae Island, and the beach is popular with families. Walking right round the island or across its top is a favourite outing and from the roadside Glaid Stone, at the summit of the island, there is a wonderful panorama over the Firth of Clyde.

### SCENIC ROUTES

The journey along the Clyde Coast offers very fine views of the shoreline and islands. On the southern part of the route, the view is dominated by the dome-shaped island of Ailsa Craig, often called 'Paddy's Milestone' as it lies halfway between Ireland and Clydeside. On the northern part of the route, the coastal road offers excellent views of the island of Arran.

Although usually yellowish in colour, Highland cattle are sometimes red or black

*Return south along the **A78** past Irvine, turning off right on the **A759** to Loans and Troon.*

### 11 **Troon,** South Ayrshire

This is a pleasant seaside resort, with good beaches and renowned golf courses, one of which has hosted the British Open. The wide esplanade offers splendid views across the Firth towards the island of Arran. Troon developed as a port in the 19th century in order to ship out coal from the Kilmarnock coalfield. The quayside wagons were initially hauled by horses, but in 1816 a Stevenson steam locomotive was used, showing how the railways could be used to transform the country's transport system.

The inner harbour has now been turned into a marina and there is a good viewpoint close by on top of the Ballast Bank. This tall artificial mound was built up over a long time, partly by ballast unloaded from coal boats returning from Ireland.

*Leave by the **B749**. Turn right when the **A79** is met and follow this back to Ayr, 8 miles (13km).*

### RECOMMENDED WALKS

The parks in Ayr, Culzean and Kilmarnock all offer level walking that is eminently suitable for pushchairs and wheelchairs. There is also a large network of paths in Eglinton Park at Irvine, where walkers have opportunities to see swans, roe deer and mink.

# Galloway & The Covenanters

**2 DAYS • 159 MILES • 255KM**

Gentle scenery dominates this corner of the Scottish coast, while the mild weather ensures that plenty of people flock to its sandy beaches in the summer. Newton Stewart, the starting point on this tour, is a pleasant town on the River Cree, with few modern intrusions to spoil its charm.

ITINERARY

| | |
|---|---|
| **NEWTON STEWART** | ▸ **Wigtown (7m-11km)** |
| WIGTOWN | ▸ **Whithorn (11m-18km)** |
| WHITHORN | ▸ **Isle of Whithorn (4m-6km)** |
| ISLE OF WHITHORN | ▸ **Monreith (9m-14km)** |
| MONREITH | ▸ **Glenluce (16m-26km)** |
| GLENLUCE | ▸ **Port Logan (16m-26km)** |
| PORT LOGAN | ▸ **Portpatrick (16m-26km)** |
| PORTPATRICK | ▸ **Stranraer (9m-14km)** |
| STRANRAER | ▸ **Girvan (30m-48km)** |
| GIRVAN | ▸ **Glen Trool (27m-43km)** |
| GLEN TROOL | ▸ **Newton Stewart (14m-23km)** |

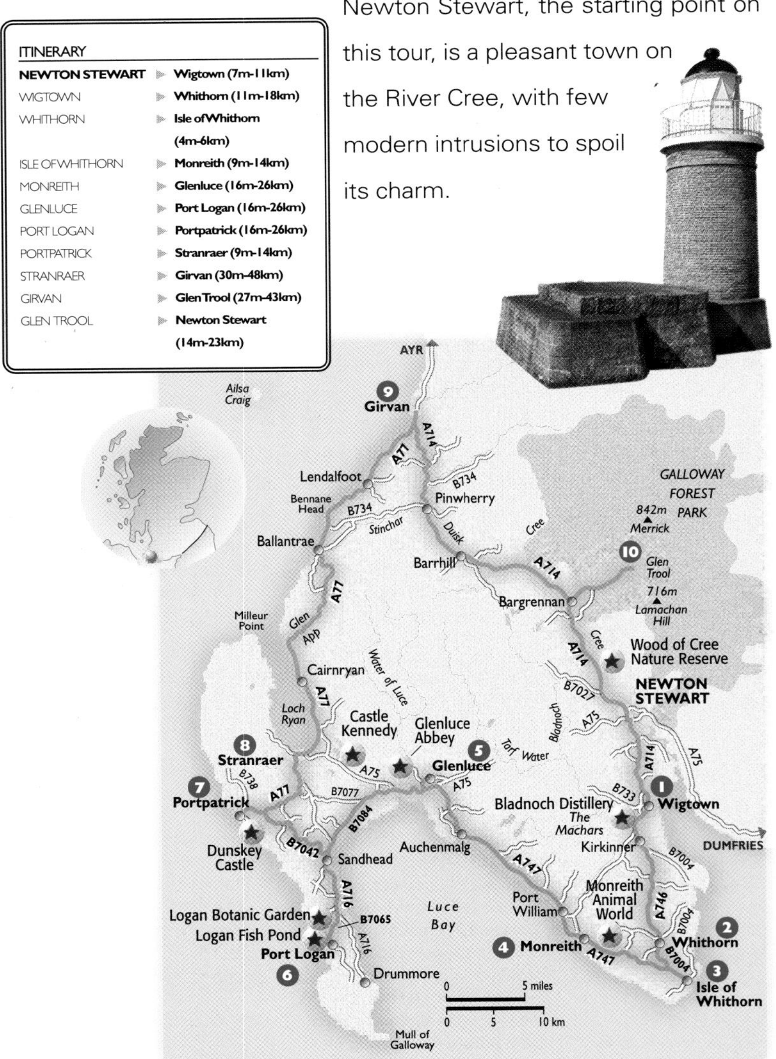

The quayside at Wigtown, on the estuary of the River Bladnoch

[i] *Dashwood Square (seasonal)*

▶ *Leave by the **A714** and head southwards to Wigtown.*

**1 Wigtown,** Dumfries and Galloway

This was formerly the county town of Wigtownshire, with an attractive central square lined by fine Georgian dwellings and an imposing civic building. Local government reorganisation sent it into decline, but its designation as Scotland's Book Town has reversed this. Many buildings on the square now house bookshops. Run down shops and hotels have been refurbished and a degree of prosperity has returned.

The tall monument seen on entering the town commemorates the local Covenanters who were executed for their beliefs. The best-known local martyrs were Margaret Wilson and Margaret MacLachlan, who were executed by drowning in the River Bladnoch in 1685. The women's graves can be seen beside the parish church.

Just south of the town is Bladnoch Distillery, which offers tours and tastings.

▶ *Continue on the **A714**, then turn left on to the **A746** to Whithorn, 11 miles (18km).*

**2 Whithorn,** Dumfries and Galloway
Whithorn has been a notable goal for travellers ever since pilgrims started to visit its important religious buildings. The religious settlement dates from the 5th century, when St Ninian established a mission, and this is the site of the first recorded Christian church in Scotland. Later, an important priory church was built, but this was demolished during the Reformation and the prosperity of the village consequently declined.

Today, the old buildings are in ruins but a Romanesque doorway in what was the priory indicates the fine style of architecture in which they were built. Archaeologists have excavated the ground in front of the priory and have uncovered valuable evidence of the buildings that stood here. They have also unearthed hundreds of skeletons as they dug down through the ancient cemetery. These skeletons have provided fascinating clues to the life, health and death of the local people. The continuing investigations, known as the Whithorn Trust, have unearthed many interesting artefacts and these are now on display at the site's Discovery Centre, which is certainly worth a visit.

*i The Whithorn Trust (seasonal)*

*Leave on the **A746**, then bear left at the **B7004**. Follow this to the Isle of Whithorn.*

**3 Isle of Whithorn,** Dumfries and Galloway
This picturesquely sited village is not in fact an island at all, but it does have a well-sheltered harbour which provides a haven for fishing boats and many pleasure craft.

Just beyond the harbour is a grassy promontory with a lookout tower, and on a fine day Ireland, the Isle of Man, England and possibly even the hills of Wales can be seen. On the seaward side of the village stand the remains of St Ninian's Chapel, which dates from the 14th century.

*Return along the **B7004**, bear left along a minor road, then follow the **A747** to Monreith, 9 miles (14km).*

**SCENIC ROUTES**

The coastal roads near the Isle of Whithorn and from Monreith to Glenluce have extensive views over the Solway Firth and the northern reaches of the Irish Sea. Keep binoculars handy in order to see the English and Irish coasts and the Isle of Man.

**4 Monreith,** Dumfries and Galloway
Just before the village is reached, a road (left) to the St Medan Golf Club leads to a memorial to Gavin Maxwell (1914–69). This is in the form of a bronze otter – Maxwell was a writer and naturalist whose book about otters, *Ring of Bright Water*, was made into a film. A prehistoric spiral 'cup and ring' mark is plainly visible just below the memorial.

*Continue on the **A747**, then turn left at the **A75** (then right at the **A747**) to reach Glenluce, 16 miles (26km) away.*

**FOR CHILDREN**

Monreith Animal World, on the A747, keeps mainly small animals in large natural enclosures. There are goats, Shetland ponies, otters, beavers, reptiles, Highland cattle and a small Gavin Maxwell museum.

The picturesque harbour of the Isle of Whithorn

The remains of 12th-century Cistercian Glenluce Abbey

**5 Glenluce,** Dumfries and Galloway

The village, developed as a staging post on the busy Stranraer to Carlisle road, is now a pleasant centre for exploring this corner of the southwest. For those who like adventure, Scotland's Outdoor Centre is close by, providing off-road driving, clay-pigeon shooting and many other activities.

Glenluce Abbey, to the northwest of the village, is an impressive ruined Cistercian monastery that was founded around 1190. Its best-preserved structure is the chapter house, which has part of the original tiled floor still extant. One of the abbey's interesting architectural details that might be overlooked is the survival of the water-supply system, which still has the original jointed earthenware pipes and lidded junction boxes.

*Rejoin the **A75** and head towards Stranraer. Bear left at the **B7084**, then follow the **A716** towards Drummore. Turn right at the **B7065** to reach Port Logan.*

**6 Port Logan,** Dumfries and Galloway

Port Logan is a planned village originally laid out in 1818, with a little pier that has an attractive lighthouse at its end. On the other side of Port Logan Bay, a small cluster of buildings marks the location of the Logan Fish Pond Marine Life Centre, one of the most surprising places in this corner of the country. This is a natural rock pool some 30 feet (9m) deep and 53 feet (16m) in diameter which holds mainly cod and pollack. It was established in 1800 as a fresh seawater 'larder' for nearby Logan House but is now a tourist attraction that will fascinate visitors, especially as the fish will take food from the keeper's hand. Logan Botanic Garden lies beyond Port Logan Bay. This is an outstation of the Royal Botanic Gardens of Edinburgh and it has a marvellous collection of plants, especially in the well-sheltered walled garden.

The warm Gulf Stream keeps the local climate exceptionally mild so many exotic plants such as tree ferns and palms are able to flourish here.

▶ *Return along the **B7065** and **A716** to Sandhead, then turn left at the **B7042**. Turn left at the **A77** to reach Portpatrick.*

> **SPECIAL TO...**
>
> Galloway is a good farming area and many farms have fine herds of dairy cows. Much of the milk is processed in local creameries so look out for local cream, cheese and other dairy products. To keep children amused while driving along country roads, get them to look out for 'Belties', the distinctive black and white Belted Galloway cattle. The area's gardens benefit from the warmth of the Gulf Stream, hence the cabbage palms and other southern hemisphere plants growing here.

### 7 **Portpatrick,** Dumfries and Galloway

One of the most attractive of Scotland's small seaside resorts, Portpatrick has a well-sheltered harbour ringed by colourful stone-built houses and hotels. Portpatrick is the nearest Scottish harbour to Ireland and it was once an important base for ferries, fishing boats and troop ships, but today it is mainly pleasure boats that tie up in the harbour.

Although the village is far from the Galloway Hills, many walkers arrive here as this is the start of the Southern Upland Way, a long-distance walk of over 200 miles (320km) that stretches right across southern Scotland and ends at Cockburnspath near Dunbar. The Way begins at the back of the harbour.

The ruins of Old Portpatrick Parish Kirk stand behind the seafront houses and its most notable feature is its four-storey circular tower. This was probably both a belfry and a beacon for the harbour. Steps from the seafront lead southward to the 16th-century Dunksey Castle. This was built around 1510 but was a ruin less than two centuries later. The walk to the castle gives splendid views of the coastline, especially if the day is fine.

▶ *Return along the **A77** and follow it for 9 miles (14km) to Stranraer.*

Ferry departing for Ireland from Stranraer harbour

### 8 **Stranraer,** Dumfries and Galloway

Stranraer is the centre for shopping and services in this part of the country, and is also part of an important transport centre. It has a rail link direct to Glasgow, and a busy ferry service to Belfast and Larne in Ireland. Near the ferry terminal stands the North West Castle Hotel, the former home of Sir John Ross, who gained fame exploring the Arctic in search of the Northwest Passage, the sea route north of Canada, in 1817. Permanent displays on his exploits form part of the local history museum. Stranraer's

### FOR HISTORY BUFFS

Castle Kennedy stands beside the village of the same name, east of Stranraer. It was built by the 5th Earl of Cassillis, a Kennedy, whose family in the 15th and 16th centuries was very powerful in this part of Scotland. Burnt down in 1716, the gaunt ivy-clad tower is surrounded by pleasant gardens, laid out by William Adam, in which there is a fine collection of rhododendrons and azaleas.

main antiquity is the Castle of St John, which is right in the centre of town. This dates back to 1510 and was later used as a gaol. Its rooftop exercise yard gives a fine view of the local scenery. Inside there are displays on castle and prison life, and the Covenanters.

*i* *28 Harbour Street*

### BACK TO NATURE

South of Bargrennan, a road goes left to the Wood of Cree Nature Reserve, which is under the care of the RSPB. The Wood of Cree is one of southern Scotland's best broadleaved woodlands and is sited by the marshy River Cree. Numerous birds may be seen, including the great spotted woodpecker and the tawny owl in the woods; snipe and water rail in the marshes; and tree pipit and redstart in the scrubland. The reserve has two marked walks: a woodland trail and a scrubland trail.

▶ *Continue on the **A77** to Girvan.*

**9 Girvan,** South Ayrshire
Girvan is a little seaside town whose pretty, sandy beach is popular with families during the summer. It has a busy harbour, probably the best place from which to view the rugged island of Ailsa Craig. The island is made from a fine-grained granite which was quarried for the making of curling stones. The island has a massive colony of gannets with over 10,000 pairs breeding there during the summer. Girvan's McKechnie Institute features exhibitions on the town and Ailsa Craig.

▶ *Leave by the **A714** and at Bargrennan turn left on to the unclassified road to Glen Trool.*

**10 Glen Trool,** Dumfries and Galloway
Glen Trool is one of Scotland's most scenic places, with access to the Merrick, the highest mainland peak in southern Scotland, and the Southern Upland Way. There is a visitor centre, and Bruce's Stone, at the end of the road by the loch, commemorates the famous king's victory over the English in 1307.

▶ *Return along the unclassified road to Bargrennan, then turn left on to the **A714** to return to Newton Stewart.*

The wide, open beach of Girvan, with views to Ailsa Craig

# Queen of the South

Dumfries' attractive setting on the banks of the River Nith has earned it the title 'Queen of the South'. This is the region's main town and its fine public buildings reflect the history and prosperity of the area. Inland from the 'granite towns' along this coast is a landscape dominated by farms and forests.

**1/2 DAYS • 118 MILES • 193KM**

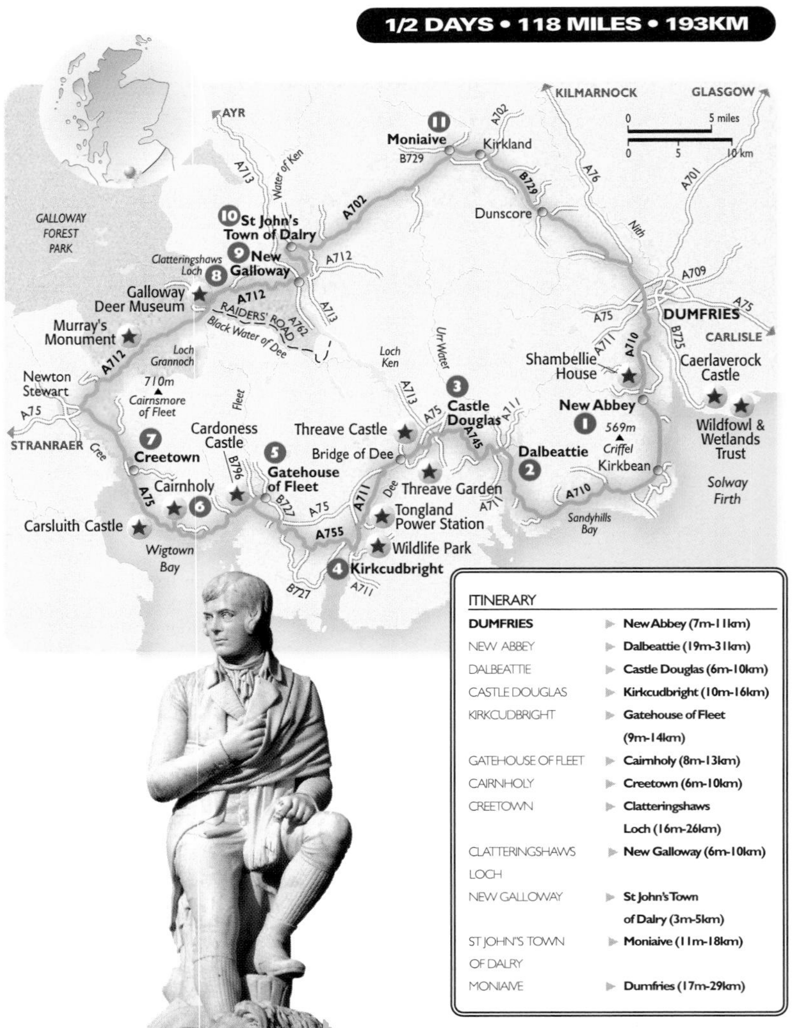


**ITINERARY**

| | |
|---|---|
| **DUMFRIES** | ▶ **New Abbey (7m-11km)** |
| NEW ABBEY | ▶ **Dalbeattie (19m-31km)** |
| DALBEATTIE | ▶ **Castle Douglas (6m-10km)** |
| CASTLE DOUGLAS | ▶ **Kirkcudbright (10m-16km)** |
| KIRKCUDBRIGHT | ▶ **Gatehouse of Fleet (9m-14km)** |
| GATEHOUSE OF FLEET | ▶ **Cairnholy (8m-13km)** |
| CAIRNHOLY | ▶ **Creetown (6m-10km)** |
| CREETOWN | ▶ **Clatteringshaws Loch (16m-26km)** |
| CLATTERINGSHAWS LOCH | ▶ **New Galloway (6m-10km)** |
| NEW GALLOWAY | ▶ **St John's Town of Dalry (3m-5km)** |
| ST JOHN'S TOWN OF DALRY | ▶ **Moniaive (11m-18km)** |
| MONIAIVE | ▶ **Dumfries (17m-29km)** |

Devorgilla's Bridge, crossing the River Nith, and Caul from the Whitesands

[i] *Whitesands*

▶ *Leave by the **A710** (the Solway Coast Road) and follow it to New Abbey.*

BACK TO NATURE

The National Nature Reserve at Caerlaverock, southeast of Dumfries, is managed to provide ideal feeding for thousands of birds that come here during the migrating season and the remainder of the year. Over 12,000 barnacle geese, plus many other birds such as pink-footed and greylag geese, whooper and Bewick's swans and various species of duck are regular visitors.
The centre has hides and an observation tower, and friendly, knowledgeable wardens lead free wildlife safaris.

FOR HISTORY BUFFS

Caerlaverock Castle was started in the 13th century and is the most important castle in the area. Unusually, it is triangular in shape and is protected by a double-towered gatehouse and a water-filled moat. Both the Scots and the English had a hand in reducing the walls, but substantial parts of the castle remain and there are some nice interior buildings.

**1 New Abbey,** Dumfries and Galloway

The village is best known for the ruins of Sweetheart Abbey, or New Abbey, founded in the 13th century as a Cistercian establishment. It is regarded as one of Scotland's most beautiful monastic ruins and, although roofless, it still has massive walls and a fine rose window. The abbey was founded by Devorgilla, wife of John Balliol, whose son became king of Scotland in 1292. After her husband died, Devorgilla carried his embalmed heart around with her until she died some 22 years later! She and the heart were buried in front of the high altar – hence the name of the abbey. Devorgilla also founded Balliol College in Oxford and named it after her husband.

The 18th-century corn mill in the village has been restored to working order and is open to the public. It is one of the finest mills of its type in Scotland. Just outside the village is Shambellie House, where the National Museum of Scotland has a museum of costume.

Threave Castle was built in the 14th century by Archibald the Grim

### SCENIC ROUTES

The route between Dumfries and Dalbeattie follows the Solway Coast Heritage Trail, which affords excellent views over the Solway Firth towards England. The Solway has huge areas of mudflats and saltmarshes which are fascinating to see but also very dangerous, especially when the tide comes in.

▶ *Continue along the **A710** for 19 miles (31km) to Dalbeattie.*

**2 Dalbeattie,** Dumfries and Galloway

Dalbeattie was established to exploit the local granite which was quarried at the nearby Craignair quarry. Many of the town's buildings are made from this bright grey stone, which sparkles in the sunlight. While some of the stone was used locally, great quantities of it were exported to construct such buildings as London's Bank of England, Liverpool's Mersey Docks, the Eddystone Lighthouse off Plymouth and the Grand Harbour at Valetta, on the Mediterranean isle of Malta.

Dalbeattie makes a good base for further exploring the coastline.

### BACK TO NATURE

The Colvend Coast, south of Dalbeattie, is one of the most attractive sections of shoreline in the region. There are fine beaches at Sandyhills Bay and secluded Rockcliffe, an oak woodland nature reserve at Southwick, and Rough Island bird sanctuary. At low tide, there are old 'smugglers' caves to explore around Portling and Port O'Warren.

▶ *Leave by the **A711**, then turn right at the **A745** to Castle Douglas, 6 miles (10km).*

**3 Castle Douglas,** Dumfries and Galloway

The town was originally called Carlingwark after the local loch, but was renamed in 1792 by a Sir William Douglas after he had acquired the land. Castle Douglas was then developed into an important market town and its horse and cattle fairs helped attract the wealth that built the spaciously laid-out town centre. Now it's a 'Food Town' and major shopping hub for the surrounding area.

The NTS's extensive Threave Garden is on the outskirts and it is particularly well known for its spring displays of nearly 200 varieties of daffodils. Threave Castle stands on an islet in the River Dee. Its four-storey tower was built in the 14th century and it is surrounded by an outer wall of about a century later. One rather unusual feature is that it has a near complete medieval riverside harbour.

[i] *Markethill Car Park, Castle Douglas; Threave Gardens (both seasonal)*

▶ *Leave by the **B736** and turn left when the **A75** is met. Turn left at the **A711** and follow this to Kirkcudbright.*

**4 Kirkcudbright,** Dumfries and Galloway

Kirkcudbright's broad streets are a delight to stroll along as many old public buildings, such as the 17th-century Tolbooth, now an Art Centre, still stand. The mercat (market) cross of 1610 is on the Tolbooth steps. MacLellan's Castle, built in the late 16th century, stands near the harbour and dominates this part of the town.

The town has had a long and colourful history, including many connections with sea trading and piracy. In the late 16th century the pirate Leonard Robertson captured an English merchant vessel and sold its cargo to local lairds. When Queen Elizabeth I of England complained to King James VI he promised to investigate the

matter, which he did by appointing a commission manned by the very lairds who had bought the stolen goods. Such was justice!

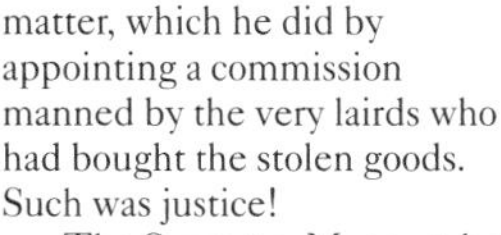

The Stewartry Museum has a good collection of local material and a section on John Paul Jones. He joined the Union navy and fought against the British during the American War of Independence; his daring exploits included attacks on the British coast. During a 'quiet' time he had the audacity to visit this area in secret. Broughton House, in High Street, was the home of E A Hornel and is run by the NTS as a museum dedicated to the artist, who died in 1933.

Tongland Hydroelectric Power Station stands on the River Dee, to the north of Kirkcudbright. This is just one of the power stations in the Galloway Hydroelectric Scheme and visitors are offered organised tours around the buildings. Downstream of the station is the attractive Tongland Bridge built by Thomas Telford in 1805.

**FOR CHILDREN**

The Kirkcudbright Wildlife Park has a wide collection of animals, including wildcats, Arctic foxes, racoons, pygmy goats and owls.
There are good beaches at Sandyhills Bay, southeast of Dalbeattie, and swimming pools at Dumfries, Castle Douglas and Newton Stewart.

i *Harbour Square (seasonal)*

► *Leave by the **A755** and turn left at the **A75**. Turn right at the **B796** to reach Gatehouse of Fleet.*

### 5 Gatehouse of Fleet, Dumfries and Galloway

This was once a prosperous spinning and weaving village but it is now more peaceful. There are numerous hotels, one of which, The Murray Arms, was where Robert Burns wrote *Scots Wha Hae*.

Cardoness Castle, outside the village, was built by the McCullochs in the 15th century, in a prominent position above the Water of Fleet.

i *Car Park (seasonal)*

► *Return along the **B796** and turn right at the **A75**. Follow this towards Creetown. Turn right at a narrow signposted road to Cairnholy, 8 miles (13km).*

### 6 Cairnholy, Dumfries and Galloway

There are two monuments at Cairnholy. These were used well over 3,000 years ago as burial sites and for ceremonies

MacLellan's Castle, an impressive 16th-century building which dominates Kirkcudbright

of some kind. Cairnholy I is particularly impressive, with its pillared façade and two tombs. The tombs would originally have been covered by a massive cairn of boulders, but these were later removed, probably by farmers seeking easily obtained building stones.

► *Return to the **A75** and turn right. Leave the **A75** on the right at the signposted road to Creetown.*

### 7 Creetown, Dumfries and Galloway

Creetown is another 'granite town' with many of its buildings made of the local grey stone. The Gem Rock Museum is sited in a former school and has a marvellous collection of minerals, fossils and many other exhibits from all over the world. The Exhibition Centre features a display on life in Creetown with wartime memorabilia, as well as local history and nature, kiltmaking and arts and crafts. Carsluith Castle is on the left before entering Creetown. This started off as a rectangular tower in the 15th century but

Prehistoric chambered tomb at Cairnholy I

later additions gave it an L-shape and a balcony. It fell into ruins after 1748.

► *Rejoin the **A75** and turn right. Turn right at the **A712** to the Clatteringshaws Forest Wildlife Centre near Clatteringshaws Loch (Galloway Forest Park).*

### 8 Clatteringshaws Loch, Dumfries and Galloway

This artificial loch is surrounded by moorlands and conifers and is within the boundary of the Galloway Forest Park. The park is home to many animals and there are herds of wild goat and deer on the southern shore of the loch. The Clatteringshaws Visitor Centre has lots of information on the wildlife,

geology and history of the area and close by it is a reconstructed Romano-British hut from around AD 200–300, which is worth a look.

Close to the Loch is Bruce's Stone, a memorial to Robert the Bruce, the Scottish king who, so legend says, learned a lesson in persistence from a spider. This marks the spot where he allegedly rested after defeating English soldiers, commanded by Sir Aymer de Valence, at the battle of Glentrool.

Near the centre, the Raiders' Road goes off to the right through the forest and follows an old cattle rustlers' route. Different breeds of deer

#### RECOMMENDED WALKS

There are a great number of walks in the Galloway Forest Park, including forest strolls and more strenuous walks on to the rugged hills. Criffel (1,867 feet/569m), southwest of New Abbey, is the highest of the coastal hills. It offers tremendous panoramic views over the Solway Firth towards the Lake District.

can be seen here and you may be lucky enough to see otters; buzzards, sparrowhawks and ravens have also been spotted.

▶ *Continue on the* ***A712*** *for 6 miles (10km) to New Galloway.*

**9 New Galloway,** Dumfries and Galloway
This quiet little village stands above the Water of Ken, a 9-mile (14.5-km) loch, created by the Hydro, and now both scenic and recreational.

▶ *Leave by the* ***A712****, then turn left at the* ***A713*** *to reach St John's Town of Dalry.*

**10 St John's Town of Dalry,** Dumfries and Galloway
The main street in this pleasant village is lined with white-washed cottages, and at the top of the street is a peculiar little stone seat known as St John the Baptist's Chair. There is no evidence that he ever sat upon it, but one of Sir Walter Scott's acquaintances found the legend intriguing enough to try to take it away. The Southern Upland Way follows the main street and passes the chair on its long coast-to-coast journey between Portpatrick and Cockburnspath. The church, which was erected in 1831, has several interesting gravestones. The most notable is the horizontal Covenanters' stone (to the Auchencloy Martyrs) in the corner of the churchyard, inscribed with the story of their shooting by the Earl of Claverhouse.

▶ *Leave by the* ***A702*** *and follow it for 11 miles (18km) to Moniaive.*

**11 Moniaive,** Dumfries and Galloway
Moniaive is best remembered for being the birthplace of James Renwick, the last Covenanter, who was hanged in Edinburgh in 1688. A monument commemorating him has been erected at the edge of the village.

To the east, beyond Kirkland, stands Maxwelton House, the birthplace and home of Annie Laurie, about whom a famous ballad was composed. The original song was written around 1700, although a later version was penned in 1835. The house was built on to a 14th-century castle.

▶ *Continue on the* ***A702****, then turn right at the* ***B729****. Turn right at the* ***A76*** *to return to Dumfries.*

**SPECIAL TO...**

**The relaxed style of living in the area has attracted many craftsmen and women. The amazing variety of crafts includes engraving, pottery and jewellery-making as well as more unusual ones like the production of embroidered landscapes, willow furniture and even clogs.**

The Robert Bruce memorial by the shores of Loch Trool in the Galloway Forest Park

**1/2 DAYS • 119 MILES • 190KM**

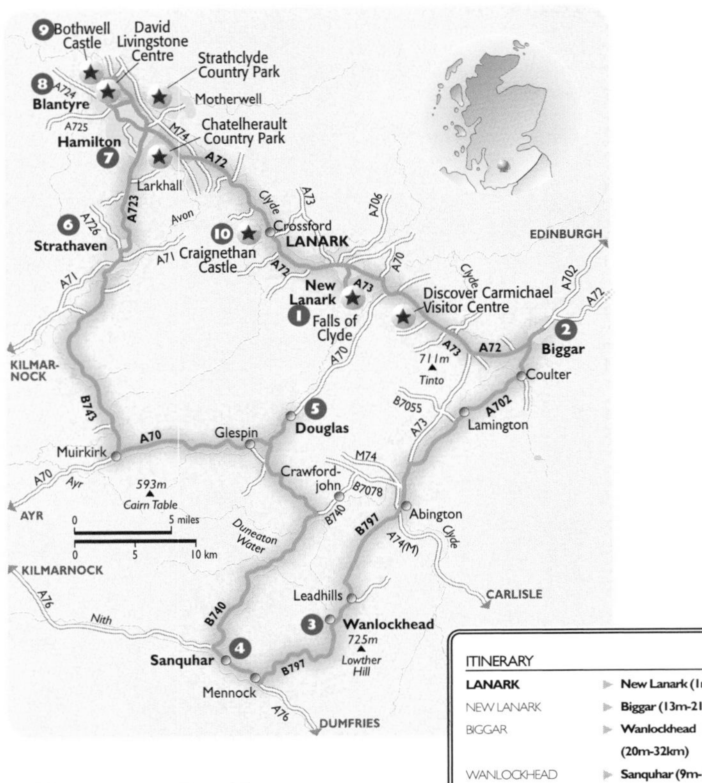


# Seeking Gold

| ITINERARY | |
|---|---|
| **LANARK** | ▶ **New Lanark (1m-2km)** |
| NEW LANARK | ▶ **Biggar (13m-21km)** |
| BIGGAR | ▶ **Wanlockhead (20m-32km)** |
| WANLOCKHEAD | ▶ **Sanquhar (9m-14km)** |
| SANQUHAR | ▶ **Douglas (19m-31km)** |
| DOUGLAS | ▶ **Strathaven (24m-37km)** |
| STRATHAVEN | ▶ **Hamilton (7m-11km)** |
| HAMILTON | ▶ **Blantyre (3m-5km)** |
| BLANTYRE | ▶ **Bothwell Castle (4m-6km)** |
| BOTHWELL CASTLE | ▶ **Craignethan Castle (13m-21km)** |
| CRAIGNETHAN CASTLE | ▶ **Lanark (6m-10km)** |

This tour starts in Lanark, home to another Scottish hero, William Wallace, who is thought to have lived in nearby Castlegate before being caught up in the struggle against the English. A statue of him now stands above the door of the 18th-century Church of St Nicholas. Lanark makes a good base from which to explore the surrounding hills and valleys of the Clyde Valley.

[i] *Horsemarket, Ladyacre Road*

*Follow the signs from the market for 1 mile (1.5km) to the village of New Lanark.*

RECOMMENDED WALKS

From New Lanark, it is possible to walk up the Clyde Gorge to the dam at the waterfall of Bonnington Linn. This magnificent gorge, formed about 12,000 years ago after the last Ice Age, has a number of fine waterfalls, notably Corra Linn. The water is used to power a hydroelectric power station, but on certain holiday weekends the station is closed down and the falls are at their most impressive.

The dramatic Falls of Clyde, well worth a walk from New Lanark

**1 New Lanark,** South Lanarkshire

The village, a World Heritage Site and a major tourist attraction, is set in the magnificent wooded gorge of the Clyde. It was founded during the 18th century by David Dale, who harnessed the power of the Clyde, and by 1820 the cotton mills supported a population of 2,500. But it was Dale's son-in-law, Robert Owen, who made New Lanark famous as a model community.

A pioneer of social reform, Owen established an enviable standard of living for his workforce and their families, with benefits such as reduced hours of work, free medical care, education and cultural activities for all. The buildings were well constructed and spacious (for that time) and he took on pauper apprentices and housed and educated them. He also built the Institute for the Formation of Character. His ideas, including his refusal to use child labour, were revolutionary, and it astounded other mill owners that his mills were efficient and profitable.

Fewer than 200 people live here now, many of them employed in the award-winning heritage sites. These include a restored millworkers' house, a period-style shop, Robert Owen's house, various exhibitions and working textile machines, and an audio-visual ride, the New Millennium Experience.

*Return to Lanark, then leave by the* ***A73****. Turn left at the* ***A72*** *and the* ***A702*** *and follow this to Biggar, 13 miles (21km).*

FOR CHILDREN

The Discover Carmichael Visitor Centre lies between Lanark and Biggar. As well as numerous animals and outdoor activities, there is also a collection of wax models of historical Scots figures. Biggar Little Theatre has a complete Victorian theatre in miniature which is used for puppet plays. There is also a puppet exhibition and a chance to try your hand at outdoor Victorian games.

## FOR HISTORY BUFFS

Iron Age people built a number of hillforts overlooking the Clyde Valley and these often have ramparts and ditches that were used as defensive structures. The locations were chosen for their lofty positions and good views of potential attackers. Notable ones include Arbory Hill (east of Abington) and Quothquan Law (west of Biggar).

Wanlockhead lead mine – once a major mining centre but now closed down, although it's possible to take a tour of Loch Nell Mine

### 2 Biggar, South Lanarkshire

Biggar's main street is even wider than Lanark's, a fact that may have encouraged the saying 'Lanark's big, but Biggar's Biggar!'

For such a compact place, Biggar has a remarkable number of interesting places to visit. The oldest is Boghall Castle, now a ruin but once a substantial fortification that was besieged by both Regent Moray and Oliver Cromwell. The most unusual building in the village houses the Biggar Gasworks Museum, the only surviving rural gasworks in the country, built in 1839.

The Gladstone Court Museum (off High Street) contains a number of replica shops, a schoolroom, a bank and a post office, scenes which portray life in Victorian Biggar. Further down the street can be seen the small footbridge called the Cadgers Brig. Legend has it that William Wallace crossed this in 1297 disguised as a cadger (a pedlar) to spy on the English army that was camped near by.

On one of the higher parts of the village stands St Mary's Church, founded in 1545, and the last pre-Reformation church in Scotland. Opposite this is the Moat Park Heritage Centre, which has displays covering 6,000 years of history in Clydesdale. Behind it lies a small valley in which runs the Biggar Burn and this can be followed upstream to Greenhill, a farm that was relocated here, stone by stone, from south of Tinto. This is a Covenanting museum, with relics and mementoes of the 17th century.

Scotland's only surviving rural gasworks houses the Biggar Gasworks Museum

## SCENIC ROUTES

The route after Abington climbs through moorland into the Lowther Hills and after Wanlockhead the road descends to meet Nithsdale; this latter part, through the Mennock Pass, can be very beautiful in late summer when the heather and bracken are changing colour.

[i] *155 High Street (seasonal)*

▶ *Leave by the **A702**, going southwest, and follow this to Abington. Turn off at the **B797**, which leads to Wanlockhead, 20 miles (32km).*

### 3 Wanlockhead, Dumfries and Galloway

Sitting at an altitude of 1,533 feet (467m), this is Scotland's highest village. With neighbouring Leadhills, Wanlockhead was once a major lead mining centre, hence all the piles of debris that have been left here. Lead was probably mined here in Roman times, but the modern history of the mines started in about 1675 and the industry managed to keep going until the 1950s. Gold has also been excavated in the area; the largest piece found was nearly 7oz (200g) in weight and is now in the British Museum. Gold-panners sometimes come to the district to try their luck and skill in winning a few flakes from the streams.

A number of buildings associated with the mines, complete with mining equipment, have been preserved as the Museum of Leadmining, and these include the Pates Knowes Smelt Mine, Wanlockhead Beam Engine, Loch Nell Mine (guided tours), miners' cottages and the miners' library. The history of the mines and of the district is told in the Visitor Centre.

*i* *Welcome Break Service Area, M74 northbound, Abington*

**RECOMMENDED WALKS**

Wanlockhead is on the Southern Upland Way and the Way's route can be followed from the village to the summit of Lowther Hill. The strange-looking 'golf ball' building on top of the hill houses radar equipment.

*Continue on the **B797** and turn right at the **A76** to Sanquhar.*

**4 Sanquhar,** Dumfries and Galloway

Although there is a great deal of agricultural land around Sanquhar, it has the air of an industrial town, and is situated on the edge of the district's coal mining area.

The ruins of Sanquhar Castle lie on the outskirts. The castle was built by the Ross family but sold to the Douglases of Drumlanrig in 1639. One of that family, the 1st Duke of Queensberry, built the mansion of Drumlanrig but spent only one night there and then retired to Sanquhar Castle.

The finest building in the village is the Tolbooth, a splendid Georgian building topped by an octagonal cupola, a clock tower and a weathercock. A double-sided staircase leads to a first-floor entrance.

The busy main street boasts the oldest post office in the world (1763) and a tall granite obelisk erected to commemorate the two Sanquhar Declarations. These were issued by the Covenanters in defiance of Charles II and James VII (II of Great Britain).

*Continue on the **A76** and turn right at the **B740**. Turn left at an unclassified road before Crawfordjohn; this road leads to Glespin, Douglas and Muirkirk. When this road meets the **A70**, turn right and follow it to Douglas, 19 miles (31km).*

**5 Douglas,** South Lanarkshire

The village is named after the Douglas family, the most famous member of whom was the 'Good' Sir James, so-called by the Scots because it was he who attempted to carry out Robert the Bruce's wish to have his heart taken to the Holy Land. Unfortunately he never got there, as he was killed in Spain. The English, however, knew him as 'Black Douglas' because he was such a ferocious fighter. His most barbaric act took place here in 1307 when he destroyed his own castle, then occupied by English troops. In a gruesome act that became known as the 'Douglas Larder', he made a great pile of

Crumbling stonework marks the site of the Castle of Sanquhar

all the food in the captured castle, poured on all the wine, killed all his prisoners and threw their bodies into the mix and set fire to it!

The 14th-century St Bride's Church, which has an attractive 16th-century octagonal clock tower, has a mausoleum in which lie the remains of the Good Sir James. The clock tower is the oldest working town clock in the country and was supposedly a gift from Mary, Queen of Scots in 1565. However, don't set your watch by its chimes because they sound three minutes before the hour, keeping faith with the Douglas family motto 'Never behind'.

▶ *Return along the **A70** and continue on it to Muirkirk. Turn right at the **B743** and follow this to Strathaven.*

### 6 **Strathaven,** South Lanarkshire

Strathaven is the site of the 15th-century Avondale Castle. Beside it stands the Town Mill which continued to grind flour until as recently as 1966, but now serves as the local theatre and arts centre. The town built its prosperity on the weaving industry and the John Hastie Museum contains displays on weaving and ceramics together with mementoes of the Covenanting times and the Radical Rising of 1820, one of whose leaders was a local man, James Wilson.

▶ *Take the **A723** for 7 miles (11km) to Hamilton.*

### 7 **Hamilton,** South Lanarkshire

Although Lanark was the county town of the former Lanarkshire, Hamilton became its administrative centre and its fine public buildings reflect its importance. The town's Muir Street Museum, which is housed in a 17th-century coaching inn, has a very good transport section.

The parkland lying between the town and the motorway used to be the site of Hamilton Palace, which had to be demolished in 1927 as the extensive coal mine workings that honeycomb the land had weakened its foundations. However, the splendid 19th-century Adam-built Hamilton Mausoleum still stands here. When having a look around, it's worth noting the fine cupola and ornate carvings. Inside the building its 15-second echo is the longest of any building in Europe, a fact that put paid to its original purpose as a chapel. William Adam also designed the Duke of Hamilton's hunting lodge, Chatelherault, and this magnificent building overlooks the district. The wooded gorge of the River Avon is impressive and beyond it are the remains of Cadzow Castle and some very ancient oaks.

Formerly the Duke of Hamilton's hunting lodge, Chatelherault is today an impressive country park

*i* *Road Chef Services, M74 northbound*

### BACK TO NATURE

Chatelherault has a herd of white cattle which are the remnants of a very ancient breed. They may be linked to the Celtic Shorthorns or even to a breed brought here by the Romans. Although they look very docile they are well-known for their wildness and there are stories of people seeking refuge from them up trees! The park also has some ancient oaks which were planted around the middle of the 15th century.

### FOR CHILDREN

Strathclyde Country Park, between Hamilton and Motherwell, has land and water sports, including boats for hire. An even greater draw is M & D's Scotland's Theme Park, with over 25 exciting rides and amusements, many of them under cover.

*Leave by the A724 and follow this to Blantyre.*

**8 Blantyre**, South Lanarkshire
Blantyre was the home of the explorer David Livingstone and the David Livingstone Centre relates his exploits, which included the 'discovery' of the Victoria Falls and Lake Nyasa. The centre is based in the row of 18th-century tenements where he was born, and includes an animated display in the Africa Pavilion, an art gallery, themed garden, African playground and riverside walks.

*Return along the **A724**, turn left at the **A725** and join the **B7071** to Bothwell. Bothwell Castle is signposted from the town.*

**9 Bothwell Castle,** South Lanarkshire
The outstanding castle, which stands on a rocky promontory above the River Clyde, was partially completed before the outbreak of the Wars of Independence and was twice besieged and deliberately dismantled to deny it to the English. Later rebuilding in the late 14th and 15th centuries turned it into an impressive structure and the castle's donjon has walls 15 feet (5m) thick.

*Return along the **B7071**, heading towards Hamilton. Follow the **A724**, then the **A72** to Crossford. In the village, a signposted road on the right leads to Craignethan Castle, 13 miles (21km).*

**10 Craignethan Castle,** South Lanarkshire
Craignethan Castle, a stronghold of the Hamiltons, was built in the 15th and 16th centuries when developments in artillery had made the defence systems of many castles obsolete. Its new strategies included a caponier, consisting of a low chamber constructed across a ditch, which allowed the defenders within to protect the vulnerable base of the castle walls from attack.

*Return to Crossford and turn right. Continue on the **A72** for the 6-mile (10km) return to Lanark.*

### SPECIAL TO...

Although Lanarkshire is the industrial heartland of western Scotland, the Clyde Valley is renowned for its orchards. Plums, damsons, raspberries and other soft fruits are grown here and the route along the river is particularly pretty during blossom time. In the fruit-picking season, look out for 'pick your own' notices.

Painting from the David Livingstone Centre, showing the explorer being attacked by a lion

# Taking the Waters

Water is an important feature of this tour, which, for some of the way, follows the course of the Tweed, one of Scotland's greatest trout and salmon rivers. The tour starts in the village of Moffat, which in the 17th century gained importance as a spa after the discovery of suphurous springs there.

**1/2 DAYS • 120 MILES • 194KM**

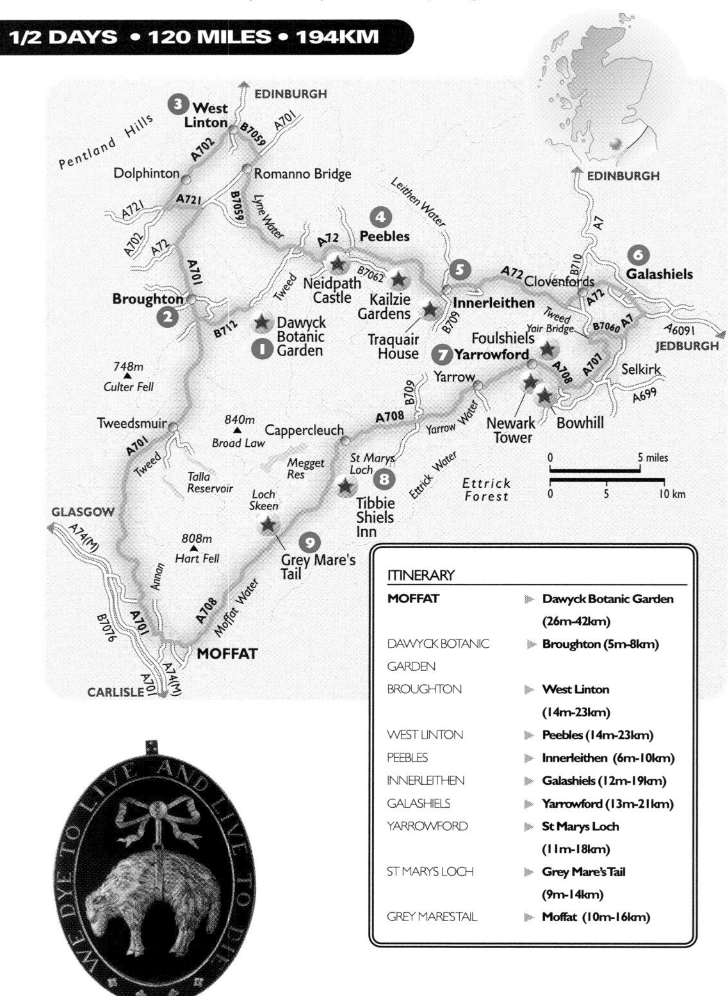


ITINERARY

| | |
|---|---|
| **MOFFAT** | ► **Dawyck Botanic Garden (26m-42km)** |
| DAWYCK BOTANIC GARDEN | ► **Broughton (5m-8km)** |
| BROUGHTON | ► **West Linton (14m-23km)** |
| WEST LINTON | ► **Peebles (14m-23km)** |
| PEEBLES | ► **Innerleithen (6m-10km)** |
| INNERLEITHEN | ► **Galashiels (12m-19km)** |
| GALASHIELS | ► **Yarrowford (13m-21km)** |
| YARROWFORD | ► **St Marys Loch (11m-18km)** |
| ST MARYS LOCH | ► **Grey Mare's Tail (9m-14km)** |
| GREY MARE'S TAIL | ► **Moffat (10m-16km)** |

[i] *Unit 1, Lady Knowe (seasonal)*

### BACK TO NATURE

Scotland has a number of spa towns and Moffat has always been one of the most popular. The water is rather sulphurous – one writer compared it to a 'slightly putrescent egg'! Nevertheless, it has attracted many sufferers afflicted with lung infections, dyspepsia, rheumatism and other disorders. The waters flow from the local greywacke rock, a type of limestone. The wells are signposted from the village, and are worth visiting.

▶ *Leave by the **A701** and turn right at the **B712** to Dawyck Botanic Garden.*

## 1 Dawyck Botanic Garden, Scottish Borders

This outstation of the Royal Botanic Garden in Edinburgh was developed from the gardens laid out around Dawyck House during the last 300 years. Some of the conifers stand 130 feet (40m) high. Daffodils are the main attraction in the spring, while autumn colour is provided by magnificent beeches and maples. Many unusual rhododendrons and narcissi can be found here. Plants are on sale in the conservatory shop.

▶ *Return along the **B712** and turn right at the **A701**. This leads to Broughton.*

## 2 Broughton, Scottish Borders

The John Buchan Centre is dedicated to the life and work of the novelist whose best-known novels were *The 39 Steps* and *Greenmantle*. Apart from spy stories, he also wrote biographies of historical figures such as Sir Walter Scott and Oliver Cromwell. He later became Lord Tweedsmuir and was Governor-General of Canada until his death in 1940. Nearby Broughton Gallery is housed in a building designed by Sir Basil Spence to resemble a 17th-century fortified tower, and sells paintings and crafts by living artists.

▶ *Continue on the **A701** and turn right at the **A72**. Turn left at the **A721** and right at the **A702**. Follow this to West Linton.*

## 3 West Linton, Scottish Borders

West Linton was once busy with cattle drovers bringing their beasts over the Pentland Hills on their way to buyers in England, but today it is a peaceful little place, pleasant for exploring the narrow streets.

The village was famous for its stonemasons, who became the chief gravestone carvers in the area. Gifford's Stone, a bas-relief on a wall in the main street, shows the stonemason James Gifford and his family. Opposite it is another of his works, the Lady Gifford Well, which was carved in 1666.

▶ *Leave by the **B7059**. Turn right at the **A701** and left at the **B7059**. Turn left at the **A72** for Peebles.*

Strolling in the tranquil and restful Dawyck Botanic Garden

The parish church in Peebles overlooks the River Tweed

### RECOMMENDED WALKS

There is great scope for walking in this area and many parts of the Southern Upland Way provide well-marked paths that are straightforward to follow. For those who can organise transport at the end of the walks, the Way offers pleasant outings on the eastern shore of St Marys Loch, from the loch to Traquair and from Traquair to Galashiels (via cairns known as the Three Brethren).

Peebles is the start of the Tweed Walk, where a choice of circular walks of different lengths allows walkers to pass Neidpath Castle and follow the river upstream, visiting various points of interest; contact the Tourist Information Centre for further details.

**4 Peebles,** Scottish Borders
This is certainly one of the Scottish Borders' most impressive towns, with an attractive position beside the River Tweed and a fine array of buildings along both sides of the main street. It developed under the protection of a royal castle and its modern prosperity came from tweed and knitwear. The Chambers Institute in High Street was given to Peebles by the publisher William Chambers, who was born here. It dates from the 16th century and houses the Tweeddale Museum and Gallery, featuring local history, contemporary art exhibitions and the 'Secret Room', with its 62-foot (19m) long plastercast of a frieze from the Parthenon in Athens. Plasterwork is also the theme of the Cornice Museum of Ornamental Plasterwork along Innerleithen Road. It re-creates a plasterer's workshop of around 1900, and visitors can get kitted out in apron and wellington boots to try their hand at the craft. At the top of High Street, the 15th-century mercat cross stands in the middle of the road.

One of the town's oldest buildings is the Old Cross Kirk, built in the 13th century on the order of King Alexander III after the discovery of a 'magnificent and venerable' cross.

Neidpath Castle stands to the west of Peebles. This substantial five-storeyed building was built in the 14th century by the Hayes family and sits on a steep rocky crag overlooking the River Tweed. South of the town are Kailzie Gardens and its art gallery.

*i* *Ladyknowes*

View along Peebles' busy broad main street

The dining room at Traquair House

*Continue on the **A72** for 6 miles (10km) to Innerleithen.*

**5 Innerleithen,** Scottish Borders

The town's wells, which were associated with St Ronan, became very popular in the 19th century, helped enormously by Sir Walter Scott's novel *St Ronan's Well.* The poet James Hogg also played a role in publicising the village as he helped organise the St Ronan's Games from 1827 to 1835. The wells can still be visited and are found by following Hall Street and St Ronan's Terrace. This is the oldest spa in Scotland and the present pump-room was built in 1826. The NTS has taken Robert Smail's Printing Works in the High Street under its care. This fascinating little print shop was started in 1840, when the original press was water-powered. Visitors can try typesetting by hand, and see the machines in action.

The history of Traquair, just over a mile (2km) south, goes back to Roman times when it was a town of similar importance to Peebles. Today it is best known for nearby Traquair House, the country's oldest and most interesting continuously inhabited house. Attractions include an 18th-century working brewery which produces three rich dark ales – sample them in the brewery shop, a maze, craft workshops and extensive grounds, but the most famous feature of the house are the wrought iron 'Bear Gates' at the end of the driveway. These were closed in the 18th century by the 5th Earl, who promised they would not be reopened until another Stuart king was on the British throne.

*Continue on the **A72** for 12 miles (19km) to Galashiels.*

### 6 **Galashiels,** Scottish Borders

Galashiels gained early importance when it was a hunting seat for the Scottish kings. But its real growth came when woollen mills diverted Gala Water to power their machinery. This is now a busy town and one of the main centres of the Borders' textile industry. The story of the mills is told in the Lochcarron Cashmere Wool of Scotland Visitor Centre; tours round these mills show the entire process of tartan manufacture.

The town's most historic building is Old Gala House, which was founded around 1583; it has a fine painted ceiling of 1635. The mercat cross, which marks the centre of the old town, stands near Gala House and was erected in 1695. As all the public business of the medieval town was conducted here, this is one of the places involved in the town's Braw Lads Gathering, the annual festival during which the boundaries of the town are ridden round on horseback.

The local war memorial is in the form of a statue of a mounted Border 'reiver'. Although these men have become romanticised figures of legend, they were basically cattle thieves and their activities gave rise to the word 'blackmail' for payment as an 'insurance' that livestock would be safe from theft.

**SPECIAL TO...**

Many of the towns have a justly famous reputation for producing high-quality knitted goods and many of the mills have their own shops where bargains can be found. Although it might be thought that the word 'tweed' (meaning the cloth) comes from the river of the same name, that is not so. The word is said to have originated in 1832 from a one-time misreading in London of the word 'tweel', which was the name given locally to one of the types of cloth.

Spools of wool ready for the loom at the Lochcarron Cashmere Wool of Scotland Visitor Centre

*i* ***3 St John Street (seasonal)***

▶ *Leave by the **A7** (to Selkirk). Turn right at the **B7060**, then left at the **A707** at Yair Bridge. Continue on this road which becomes the **A708** near Selkirk. Follow Ettrick Water and then Yarrow Water on the **A708** to Yarrowford, a distance of 13 miles (21km).*

### 7 **Yarrowford,** Scottish Borders

The scattered village of Yarrowford lies by Yarrow Water, about which William Wordsworth wrote no fewer than three poems! Downstream of the village lie three buildings that are of interest: Newark Tower, Foulshiels and Bowhill.

The name Newark Tower signifies that it is the 'new work' which was erected to replace an unsuitable 'auld work'. It was constructed some time before 1423 as a royal hunting lodge in what was known as Ettrick Forest. The term 'forest' in this case does not necessarily imply that the whole area was wooded, but that special laws governed its

The aptly named Grey Mare's Tail waterfall

use as a playground for the king and his entourage. However, the forest was inhabited not only by wild animals; it made a splendid hiding place for thieves, until the king decided to chase them as well! In the 16th century, James V replaced 10,000 deer with an equal number of sheep, greatly increasing the importance of sheep farming and the woollen industry in the area. In conjunction with this step, many trees were felled – thus destroying the oak, birch and hazel forest that had prospered here since the end of the Ice Age.

Foulshiels, now a ruin, was the birthplace of Scots explorer Mungo Park who travelled in West Africa between 1795 and 1796 in search of the source of the River Niger. His exploits were described in his book *Travels in the Interior of Africa*, but his second trip into these uncharted lands led to his death.

Bowhill House and Country Park features a very large country mansion built in the early 19th century. It has an outstanding collection of French furniture as well as a large collection of paintings by Old Masters including Van Dyck, Canaletto and Gainsborough.

▶ *Continue on the **A708** to the southern end of St Marys Loch.*

### FOR HISTORY BUFFS

Sir Walter Scott, writer of so many 'romantic' stories of Scotland, is connected wth many places in this district. He often visited the village of Clovenfords and a statue of him stands there; he lived at the house of Ashiestiel (further down the Tweed from Innerleithen) from 1804 to 1812; and he had his last meeting with James Hogg at the Gordon Arms (east of St Marys Loch) in 1830.

## 8 St Marys Loch, Scottish Borders

This is one of the largest lochs in southern Scotland and it is a popular place with walkers, boating enthusiasts and anglers. At the southern end of the loch stands a monument to the local poet James Hogg. He was a good friend of Sir Walter Scott and the two of them, along with other literary figures, spent convivial evenings in the nearby Tibbie Shiels Inn.

▶ *Continue on the **A708** for 9 miles (14km) to the car park at the Grey Mare's Tail waterfall.*

## 9 Grey Mare's Tail, Dumfries and Galloway

Just a short distance from the roadside, the Tail Burn tumbles 200 feet (60m) over the waterfall known as the Grey Mare's Tail. A path runs up the eastern bank of the burn offering different views of the waterfall and the opportunity to explore Loch Skene. Leaflets warn about the dangers of leaving the path. The burn joins attractive Moffat Water, whose valley the road follows towards Moffat. The valley is a magnificent textbook example of a glacial valley, with its U-shape formed as the glacier smoothed the mountainsides.

▶ *Continue on the **A708** for 10 miles (16km) in order to return to Moffat.*

### SCENIC ROUTES

Much of this tour goes through beautiful countryside as it winds its way through the hills of the Southern Uplands. Perhaps the nicest stretches are north of Moffat (look out for the large depression called the Devil's Beef Tub, where Border cattle-rustlers once hid their ill-gotten gains, between the Tweedsmuir and the Lowther hills), and through the valleys of the Yarrow Water and the Moffat Water.

# Walter Scott Country

Much of the countryside explored in this tour was the inspiration behind Sir Walter Scott's *Waverley* novels: the ruined abbeys of Melrose, Dryburgh and Jedburgh; the Eildon Hills. It is only fitting, therefore, that this tour should end with a visit to Scott's home.

**1/2 DAYS • 116 MILES • 187KM**

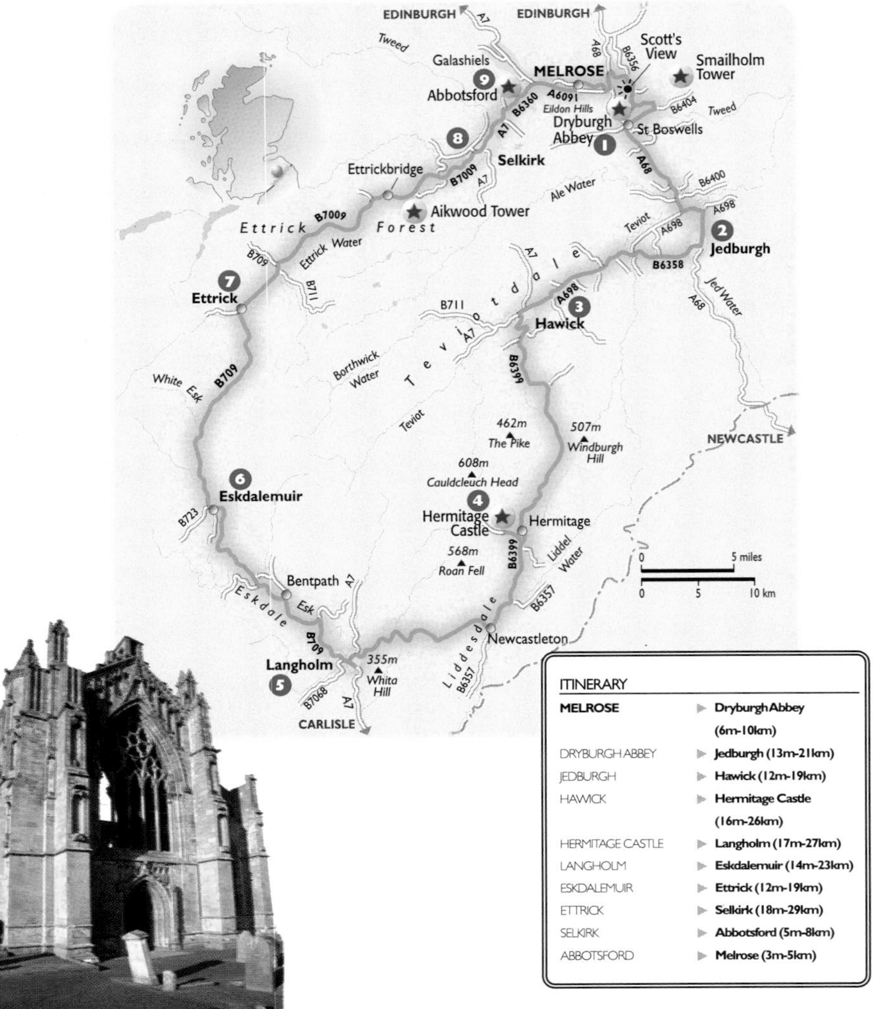


ITINERARY

| | |
|---|---|
| **MELROSE** | ▶ **Dryburgh Abbey (6m-10km)** |
| DRYBURGH ABBEY | ▶ **Jedburgh (13m-21km)** |
| JEDBURGH | ▶ **Hawick (12m-19km)** |
| HAWICK | ▶ **Hermitage Castle (16m-26km)** |
| HERMITAGE CASTLE | ▶ **Langholm (17m-27km)** |
| LANGHOLM | ▶ **Eskdalemuir (14m-23km)** |
| ESKDALEMUIR | ▶ **Ettrick (12m-19km)** |
| ETTRICK | ▶ **Selkirk (18m-29km)** |
| SELKIRK | ▶ **Abbotsford (5m-8km)** |
| ABBOTSFORD | ▶ **Melrose (3m-5km)** |

The heart of Robert the Bruce is buried within the imposing ruins of Melrose Abbey

### FOR HISTORY BUFFS

A strategically important Roman camp was established near the small village of Newstead, just to the east of Melrose. This accommodated about 1,000 soldiers and lay on the important road of Dere Street that ran from the North Tyne, over the Cheviot Hills and then on to Inveresk (near Edinburgh). The fort was given the name *Trimontium,* possibly because of the three Eildon Hills near by, and was much needed to subdue the tribe known as the *Selgovae* who lived to the west. Other Roman remains associated with the fort can be seen on the Eildon's North Hill; this hilltop position had previously been occupied by the *Selgovae*. The *Votadini* tribe, who lived to the east, did not cause problems so there were fewer Roman fortifications to the east of Newstead. The Trimontium Exhibition in the centre of Melrose relates the way of life in Roman Scotland as well as giving information on current excavations.

[i] *Abbey House (seasonal)*

*Leave Melrose by the **B6361** and turn left at the **A68**. Cross the River Tweed, then turn first right and first left. Head towards Dryburgh following the **B6356**. Turn right after passing Scott's View and continue to Dryburgh Abbey.*

### SCENIC ROUTES

As the B6356 makes its way to Dryburgh, there is a wonderful view of the River Tweed and the Eildon Hills at a spot known as Scott's View. Sir Walter Scott passed this way on many occasions and always halted here to enjoy the view, describing it as the 'grandest and most extensive panorama in the Borderland'. When he died his funeral cortège made its way past here to his final resting place at Dryburgh Abbey and his horses, without being commanded to, stopped quite naturally at the viewpoint.

## 1 Dryburgh Abbey,
Scottish Borders

Much of the abbey's substantial ruins date from the 12th and 13th centuries and they occupy a wonderfully peaceful position on a horseshoe bend of the River Tweed. Founded in 1150, the abbey suffered at the hands of the English raiders but nevertheless remains the most complete of the Border abbeys. The grave of Sir Walter Scott can be found in the north transept. A short woodland walk leads to a massive 19th-century statue of the Scottish patriot Sir William Wallace.

To the northwest of the abbey (and reached via the B6404) stands the very attractive Smailholm Tower. This was erected in the 16th century as a defensive structure, which explains why the few windows it has are very small. There is a marvellous panoramic view from it and ships approaching Berwick once used it as a landmark as it was so conspicuous. During medieval times this area was often attacked by English forces and tall towers were needed to spy on the movements of the enemy and to warn others of the approach of an attacking force. This is why the parapet wall has a watchman's seat and a recess for a lantern, in accordance with an Act of Council in 1587 which stated that castle owners must 'keep watch nyght and day, and burn baillis (bales) according to the accoustomat ordour observit as sic tymes upoun the borderis'. At one time it was owned by Sir Walter Scott's grandfather and Scott used to visit here as a boy; he later featured the tower in *Marmion*.

> *Return to the* ***B6356*** *and continue following that road. Turn right at the* ***B6404*** *and enter St Boswells. Turn left at the* ***A68*** *and follow it to Jedburgh.*

**2 Jedburgh,** Scottish Borders
The town's location close to the border meant that it was forever being attacked by the English, and its castle was often under siege by the ancient enemy. The locals, fed up with all this harassment, managed to persuade the Scottish parliament to pull the castle down in 1409, thus relieving them of the task of having to fight the invaders to defend it! The present building occupying the site is still called the 'castle' but it was built in the 19th century as a gaol and is now used as a museum.

The other major building in the town is Jedburgh Abbey, founded as a priory in 1138. After various attacks by the English, the building was destroyed by them between 1545 and 1546. However, the abbey walls still soar skywards and the tower stands as it did when rebuilt in 1504 to 1508. Mary, Queen of Scots visited the town in 1566 and stayed in the Spread Eagle Hotel in High Street, which is claimed to be the oldest continually occupied hotel in the country. A fire here forced Mary to leave and she stayed at what is now the Mary, Queen of Scots' House, a fine 16th-century fortified house.

*i* *Murray's Green*

Jedburgh Abbey was founded in the 12th century and colonised by monks from Beauvais in France

### BACK TO NATURE

Just north of Jedburgh, Harestanes Countryside Visitor Centre offers walks, a wildlife garden with a pond, and traditional craft demonstrations. Melrose's Priorwood Garden, which is run by the NTS, specialises in flowers for drying. A variety of plants are grown and dried here and advice on this craft is always available. The orchard has a wide variety of apple trees, arranged to illustrate the history of the fruit. Nearby Harmony Garden has herbaceous and mixed borders, vegetable and fruit areas and lovely views. The monks of Melrose Abbey established their orchards at Gattonside, just over the Tweed from the abbey.

Priorwood Garden, where a large variety of plants are grown especially for drying

SPECIAL TO...

Many of the Border towns have Common Ridings, an annual event when horse riders follow the town's boundaries in an enactment of the ancient tradition of checking the integrity of the boundary. Many of the celebrations have both pagan and Christian elements in them. The principal participant in the Common Riding has a variety of different names: in Jedburgh it is the Callant, in Selkirk the Souter, in Galashiels the Braw Lad, in Hawick the Coronet, and in Kelso the Laddie.

Visitors who are interested should consult the local tourist information centre to find out if there is a riding taking place near them.

FOR CHILDREN

Pony trekking is popular in the Borders as many good tracks cross the undulating countryside. There are riding facilities at places such as Hawick, Jedburgh and Selkirk.

As a wet-weather alternative, there are swimmimg pools at Hawick, Jedburgh and Selkirk.

At the Jedforest Deer and Farm Park there are many rare breeds to be seen, as well as the herds of deer. There are daily displays of birds of prey.

FOR HISTORY BUFFS

Drumlanrig's Tower started its life as a 16th-century tower house and it featured in many battles. Thereafter it served as a house, a hotel and now a visitor centre featuring displays on its turbulent past.

*Leave by the **B6358**, then join the **A698** to Hawick.*

**3 Hawick,** Scottish Borders

Hawick is the largest and busiest of the Border towns. Its numerous woollen mills have brought it much prosperity since frame knitting was introduced here and commercialised in 1771. When mechanisation came to the industry, production changed from hose to fine underwear, which as the advertisements of the day put it, 'enjoyed the patronage of many of the crowned heads of Europe!' Peter Scott & Co offer mill tours, and at nearby Trowmill tours of Wrights' weaving flat are available.

Many of the mills stand by the River Teviot, which provided their original source of power. The river also flows past Wilton Lodge Park, where a museum and art gallery includes displays on Border history, the knitwear industry and the natural history of the area.

*i* *Drumlanrig's Tower (seasonal)*

*Leave by the **B6399**. Just after Hermitage, turn right at the unclassified road signposted to Hermitage Castle.*

**4 Hermitage Castle,** Scottish Borders

This must be one of the grimmest-looking castles in Scotland, with its very small windows and the high arch that joins the east and west towers together. It's also sited on an isolated expanse of moorland, well away from any settlement.

In 1566, when she was holding court at Jedburgh, Mary, Queen of Scots heard that her lover Bothwell was lying wounded in the castle. She rode the 20 miles (32km) at a furious speed, stayed for a couple of hours then returned, an exertion that cost her a 10-day fever.

*Return to the **B6399** and turn right. Turn right at the **B6357** and enter Newcastleton. Within the village, turn right at the minor road to Langholm and turn left when you join the **A7**, 17 miles (27km).*

**5 Langholm,** Dumfries and Galloway

This small town sits at the confluence of the Esk, Ewes and

Sandstone monument to James Hogg, the Ettrick Shepherd

Wauchope Waters. There is a fine view of it from the summit of Whita Hill (to the east), on top of which there is a monument to Sir John Malcolm. Close to the start of the path to the monument, there is a rather interesting (or bizarre, depending on your taste) monument dedicated to the modern Scots poet Christopher Murray Grieve, who wrote under the pen-name Hugh McDiarmid.

Another of Langholm's sons was the great engineer Thomas Telford, whose famous designs include the Caledonian Canal, the Menai Straits Bridge and St Katharine's Docks in London. Many roads and bridges in Scotland are also his. Telford started his working life as a stonemason, and an archway, an early example of his own handiwork, can be seen beside the town hall. A memorial to him is sited at Bentpath, on the road to Eskdalemuir.

*Leave by the **B709** and follow it to Eskdalemuir.*

### 6 **Eskdalemuir,** Dumfries and Galloway

There is a settlement at Eskdalemuir (at the junction of the Langholm and Lockerbie roads), but the name is more commonly applied to the tract of moorland near the upper reaches of the White Esk. To be correct, it used to be a great moorland, but the land is now given over to huge conifer plantations.

The Romans built an important road here, some 24 feet (7m) wide, and this eventually led to *Trimontium*, near Melrose. The most intriguing group of modern incomers were Tibetan Buddhist monks who left their country in 1959 and settled here in Johnstone House. The community that they founded flourished and they later built one of Scotland's most remarkable buildings, the Samye Ling Temple, a colourful four-storey structure. This is the largest Buddhist temple in western Europe and numerous examples of Tibetan art can be seen inside.

The meteorological station at Eskdalemuir is sited further along the road. This was originally founded in 1908 to continue the terrestrial magnetism measurements formerly made at Kew (in southeast London). To broaden the scope

The Old Manse at Ettrick

of scientific research in this area, a seismological station has been established near by.

▶ *Continue on the **B709** to Ettrick.*

**7 Ettrick,** Scottish Borders

The collection of houses and farms at Ettrick is found where the B709 meets Ettrick Water at Ramseycleuch. The poet James Hogg was born here and a tall sandstone memorial at his birthplace can be found on the roadside by following Ettrick Water upstream. Hogg is one of the Borders' most famous characters and was affectionately known as the Ettrick Shepherd. His poetry was first published in 1794 and he went on to write countless poems, articles and books. Ettrick's church is further upstream and this is where Hogg is buried. Beside his headstone is one inscribed 'Here lyeth William Laidlaw the far-famed Will o'Phaup who for feats of frolic, agility and strength had no equal in his day'. This gentleman was Hogg's grandfather and he was the last man in Ettrick to speak to the fairies. There is a James Hogg Exhibition at Aikwood Tower, further along on the B7009. The tower also hosts art exhibitions, and is set in lovely medieval-style gardens.

▶ *Continue on the **B709**. Turn right at the **B7009** to enter Selkirk.*

**8 Selkirk,** Scottish Borders

The town occupies a hilly site where a Tironensian abbey was founded around 1113. The abbey was eventually moved to Roxburgh and then to Kelso, so Selkirk never developed as a religious centre like the other Border towns which had their splendid abbeys. As the town grew it became famous for its shoemaking, to the extent that its burgesses were given the name 'souters' (Scots for 'shoemakers'). This trade died out and Selkirk's modern prosperity is based on the woollen mills beside Ettrick Water.

The triangular marketplace is dominated by a statue of Sir Walter Scott. Behind is his Courtroom, with displays on Scott, James Hogg and Mungo Park, an audio-visual presentation and Scott's bench and chair from his time as Sheriff of Selkirkshire.

Sir Walter Scott's romantic creation, Abbotsford

The local museum in Halliwell's House is to the west of the marketplace and is reached through a narrow lane. The museum has an excellent display of local material including the reconstructed interior of an old ironmonger's shop.

To the east of the marketplace, and past the statue of the explorer Mungo Park, is the Flodden Memorial, dedicated to the local men who perished at the Battle of Flodden in 1513. The statue is of a man called Fletcher, reputedly the only Selkirk man out of 80 to return from the battle, carrying a captured English standard.

*i* ***Halliwell's House (seasonal)***

▶ *Leave by the **A7** towards Galashiels. Turn right at the **B6360** to reach Abbotsford.*

**9 Abbotsford,** Scottish Borders

Sir Walter Scott bought the site on which he built Abbotsford in

Abbotsford interior

1811. The house took a long time to complete as he kept adding bits on, eventually ending up with a great variety of styles. Basically, it is of Scots baronial style but he included a 16th-century door from Edinburgh's Tolbooth, a copy of a porch at Linlithgow Palace and even medieval gargoyles. He was, apparently, no less a romantic in his architectural taste than he was in his writings. The house also contains wonderful memorabilia, such as a gun belonging to Rob Roy, and a cup which Bonnie Prince Charlie carried around with him.

Scott was a lawyer and served as Sheriff in Selkirk. He assiduously collected and wrote down the oral tradition of the old Border tales that had been handed down through the generations, thus ensuring that many of them were preserved. He also began to write his own material and started to make a reputation for himself as a poet and then as a novelist. His best-known works include *Kenilworth*, *Redgauntlet* and *Ivanhoe*. Unfortunately, the financial collapse of a publisher landed him with huge personal debts of about £114,000 which he tried to work off; sadly his exertions led to his untimely death in 1832.

▶ *Continue on the **B6360** and turn right at the **A6091** for 3 miles (5km) for Melrose.*

The beautiful walled garden at Abbotsford

# The Border Country

Few cities match Edinburgh's city centre: Princes Street and its gardens; Edinburgh Castle; the Royal Mile, with its medieval 'lands', or blocks of flats; the Palace of Holyroodhouse, and the elegant Georgian architecture of New Town. The best view of all the city's treasures is from Arthur's Seat, a volcanic hill 823 feet (251m) above sea level.

**2 DAYS • 148 MILES • 239KM**

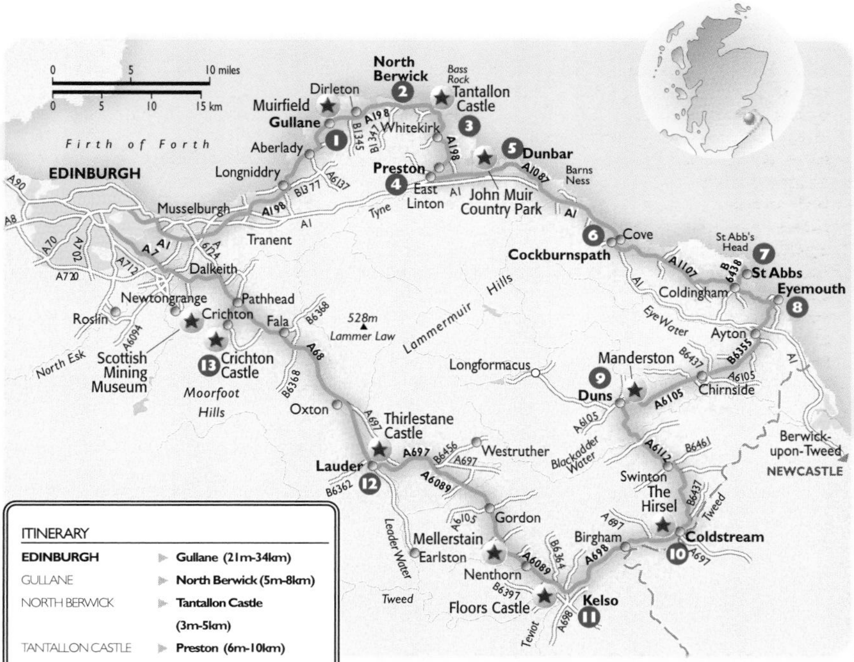

ITINERARY

| | |
|---|---|
| **EDINBURGH** | ▶ **Gullane (21m-34km)** |
| GULLANE | ▶ **North Berwick (5m-8km)** |
| NORTH BERWICK | ▶ **Tantallon Castle (3m-5km)** |
| TANTALLON CASTLE | ▶ **Preston (6m-10km)** |
| PRESTON | ▶ **Dunbar (6m-10km)** |
| DUNBAR | ▶ **Cockburnspath (8m-13km)** |
| COCKBURNSPATH | ▶ **St Abbs (12m-19km)** |
| ST ABBS | ▶ **Eyemouth (5m-8km)** |
| EYEMOUTH | ▶ **Duns (14m-23km)** |
| DUNS | ▶ **Coldstream (12m-19km)** |
| COLDSTREAM | ▶ **Kelso (9m-14km)** |
| KELSO | ▶ **Lauder (18m-29km)** |
| LAUDER | ▶ **Crichton Castle (26m-42km)** |
| CRICHTON CASTLE | ▶ **Edinburgh (13m-21km)** |

TOUR
7

FOR HISTORY BUFFS

Rosslyn Chapel, to the south of Edinburgh, is one of the most ornamented churches in the country. It dates from the mid-15th century and has all kinds of embellishments carved out of the stone. Its most famous carving is the Prentice Pillar, carved by an apprentice when his master was away. So beautiful was it that when the master saw it he killed the lad in a jealous rage, or so the story goes. Latterly the chapel has gained notoriety by being featured in the much-hyped novel and film, *The Da Vinci Code.*

A few miles away stands the Scottish Mining Museum at the Lady Victoria Colliery, built between 1890 and 1894, in Newtongrange, the centre of an important coal-mining area.

*i 3 Princes Street*

*Leave by the **A1** and turn left at the **A198** to reach Gullane.*

**1 Gullane,** East Lothian

Gullane is renowned as a golfing centre, with a number of courses including a championship course at nearby Muirfield.

Further east, the centre of the old village of Dirleton, claimed to be the most beautiful village in Scotland, is dominated by the grand Dirleton Castle, which dates back to the 13th century. Perched on top of a rocky platform, it has massive towers and was defended by a moat at least 50 feet (15m) wide.

*Continue on the **A198** for 5 miles (8km) to North Berwick.*

**2 North Berwick,** East Lothian

This seaside golf resort is dominated by the nearby 613-foot (187m) North Berwick Law, which offers fine views over the town and the coast.

By the harbour, the Scottish Seabird Centre is an award-winning wildlife centre and one of Scotland's five star attractions. Its vantage point overlooking the sea and the islands of the Forth make it the ideal place to see and find out about the wide variety of wildlife that inhabits the area. Depending on the time of visit, you may see whales, dolphins and grey seals, as well as a number of seabirds, ranging from puffins to guillemots.

Princes Street at sunset

*i Quality Street*

*Continue on the **A198** and turn left at a signposted minor road to Tantallon Castle, 3 miles (5km).*

**3 Tantallon Castle,** East Lothian

This grim-looking 14th-century castle stands in a spectacular clifftop position, with three sides protected by the sea and the fourth by thick walls. Two great sieges took place here: the first ended by negotiation (the attackers ran out of gunpowder!) and in the second, General Monk attacked it for 12 days in 1651, damaging the towers. This is the best place on the mainland to view the Bass Rock. The island has huge numbers of gannets breeding there and the colony is so important that the birds' scientific name *Sula bassana* comes from the island.

Whale jaw crowning the top of Berwick Law

▶ *Return to the **A198** and continue southwards. Turn right at the **B1407** to enter Preston.*

**4 Preston,** East Lothian
On the outskirts of the village stands the charming 18th-century water-driven Preston Mill. Originally a meal mill, the unusual design of its kiln has similarities with an English oast house. The buildings are constructed of orange sandstone rubble and roofed with traditional east coast pantiles. A short walk leads to the Phantassie Doocot, a dovecot which once housed some 500 pigeons.

▶ *Leave by the **B1047** and turn left on to the **B1377**. Turn left at the **A1**, then left at the **A1087** to Dunbar.*

**5 Dunbar,** East Lothian
This popular seaside resort is now a rather peaceful place, a far cry from the turbulent times when its castle was of some importance. The castle was eventually sacked by Cromwell in 1650 and its walls torn down, the stones being used to improve the harbour. The remains sit forlornly by the harbour entrance. The attractive harbour is home to a busy fishing fleet and to the local lifeboat station. John Muir, the conservationist, was born in Dunbar in the mid-19th century.

[i] *143 High Street*

▶ *Continue on the **A1087** and turn left at the **A1** to Cockburnspath.*

**6 Cockburnspath,** Scottish Borders
The position of this village, which is so close to the border, has meant a turbulent and rather troubled history. This was an important stopping point for horse-drawn coaches (a mode of travel which peaked in the 19th century) and the layout of the village and its marketplace owes much to this time. The parish church is worth a look; it has a fine tower in the middle of the west gable and an unusual sundial on the southwest corner.

The mercat cross is the finishing point of the Southern Upland Way, the long-distance footpath that starts at Portpatrick, over on the west coast. By following the Southern Upland Way from its terminus, you will find yourself by a group of houses at Cove, below which is the picturesque Cove Harbour. The harbour is reached by going through a tunnel cut into the cliff; this was made in the 18th century and was connected to cellars probably used for curing and barrelling fish, and possibly by smugglers.

Preston's Phantassie Doocot once housed over 500 pigeons but is now home to considerably fewer

The picturesque little harbour at St Abbs

### BACK TO NATURE

The cliffs at St Abbs Head are home to countless kittiwakes, guillemots, razorbills and other seabirds. A marked path starts from just before St Abbs village and leads past the bird cliffs, allowing a very good view of the colonies – but stick to the path!

▶ *Continue on the **A1** and turn left at the **A1107**. At Coldingham, turn left at the **B6438** and follow this to St Abbs.*

**7 St Abbs,** Scottish Borders

This neat little fishing village is now a resort, often busy with divers who come to explore the local bays.

Nearby Coldingham has an ancient priory. Founded in 1098 by King Edgar, the 13th-century priory church was built on a site that had a religious house way back in the 7th century. Life could hardly have been peaceful for those who stayed here during the frequent outbreaks of hostilities, as the monks were subject to the English king and the priors to the Scots king!

▶ *Return along the **B6438** to Coldingham and turn left at the **A1107**. Turn left at the **B6355** for Eyemouth.*

**8 Eyemouth,** Scottish Borders

This busy fishing port has regular fish markets which are worth visiting. This is home to a large fleet and the local people have been connected with fishing for a very long time. The town's saddest day came on 14 October, 1881 when a sudden gale blew up and 129 local fishermen were drowned, some of them in full sight of their families on shore. The local museum tells the story.

*i* *Auld Kirk, Manse Road (seasonal)*

▶ *Return along the **B6355**, then follow the **A6105** to Duns.*

**9 Duns,** Scottish Borders

This long-established village, with its well-built stone houses, makes a useful stopping point for touring this part of the Borders. Duns was the home town of the world motor-racing champion Jim Clark, who died in a race in Germany in 1968; a small museum has mementoes of his short but fascinating life. A short drive away from Duns is the Manderston mansion, with formally laid-out gardens and a marble dairy, both of which are worth a tour.

▶ *Leave on the **A6112** for 12 miles (19km) to reach Coldstream.*

Tapestry from Eyemouth museum, showing the 1881 fishing tragedy

## 10 **Coldstream,** Scottish Borders

Coldstream stands on the banks of the River Tweed, which at this point marks the border with England. The river is crossed by a magnificent seven-arch bridge and on the Scottish side a toll house was the east coast equivalent of Gretna Green, a place where marriages could take place with the minimum of delay. Like many Border towns, Coldstream has a wealth of well-built houses. The Market Square is a little off this street and is the location of the Coldstream Museum, telling the story of the town and the Coldstream Guards regiment.

Outside Coldstream stands the Hirsel Homestead Museum comprising a museum, craft centre and walks in the estate.

*i* *Town Hall, High Street (seasonal)*

► *Leave by the **A697** and turn left at the **A698** to reach Kelso.*

## 11 **Kelso,** Scottish Borders

Kelso has one of the most attractive town centres in the Borders, with a huge open square. The town stands at the confluence of the rivers Teviot and Tweed and from the fine bridge which crosses the Tweed there is a good view of Floors Castle, a huge mansion built by William Adam between 1721 and 1725, offering glittering excesses of fine French furniture, porcelain and paintings. Kelso Abbey was once the Borders' greatest abbey but only the west end of it stands today. It was founded here in 1128 but its position on the 'invasion route' meant that it suffered frequent attacks. North of Kelso, Mellerstain House is one of Scotland's finest Robert Adam mansions.

*i* *Town House, The Square*

► *Leave by the **A6089**. Turn left at the junction with the **A697** and left at the **B6362**. Follow this to Lauder.*

The surviving ruin of Kelso Abbey, showing fine Norman detail

## 12 **Lauder,** Scottish Borders

This attractive town has a wide main street in the middle of which stands the Tolbooth. This was originally built in 1318 and the ground floor was used as a gaol up to 1840. Lauder's parish church is an interesting structure in the form of a Greek cross with an octagonal steeple and four arms; it is dated 1673. Impressive Thirlestane Castle, close to the town, houses the Border Country Life Exhibitions.

The village of Earlston lies only a few miles south of Lauder. This was Ercildoune in medieval days and the home of Thomas the Rhymer, who lived during the 13th century. His ability to see into the future was considered to be a gift from the Queen of the Fairies with whom it was believed he stayed for a number of years.

► *Take the **A68** north to Pathhead, then turn left at the **B6367** to Crichton Castle.*

## 13 **Crichton Castle,** Midlothian

Crichton was at one time the home of the Earl of Bothwell, the ill-fated third husband of Mary, Queen of Scots. The ruins of this substantial structure stand on the edge of Middleton Moor and above the Tyne Water. It dates from the 14th century and one architectural curiosity is a Renaissance-influenced wall erected in the late 16th century. This is an arcade of seven bays topped by diamond-patterned stone-work and is unique in the country. Crichton's church is a fine building which was restored in 1896.

► *Return along the **B6367** to Pathhead. Turn left and follow the **A68** to Edinburgh.*

### FOR CHILDREN

There are a number of good beaches, notably at Gullane Bay. Indoor swimming pools are located in Kelso, Duns, Dunbar and Eyemouth and there is an outdoor one at North Berwick. Pony trekking is available at Earlston, Ford (near Pathhead) and Westruther (east of Lauder). You can get close to puffins, gannets, seals and dolphins at the Scottish Seabird Centre in North Berwick.

# CENTRAL SCOTLAND

Black Mount and the Rannoch Moors, seen from the River Bá

The great firths of the Clyde, the Forth and the Tay have narrowed the middle of Scotland to a thin neck of land only 30 miles (48km) wide. This is where the majority of the Scots live, in an area that is rich with history. Bronze-Age cemeteries, medieval castles, battlefields and architectural follies all have their statements to make about their builders' views of the world and how they lived – and died.

Much of the region's history has been bloody. Land- and sea-borne invaders attacked, plundered and wrought destruction. But many invaders stayed and left their mark, often introducing foreign influences that have added to the common heritage of the modern Scottish nation. The Celts, Vikings, French and the peoples of the countries washed by the Baltic and the North Sea have all contributed to the country's history, but it has been the English who, despite being the 'auld enemy', have in so many ways changed the country – and also radically influenced how the Scots see themselves today as a nation.

Central Scotland's modern prosperity was based on the Industrial Revolution and many would argue that this was where that important period of history began. One of the world's first major ironworks, the first significant use of efficient steam engines, the world's biggest shipbuilding industry – all of these were based right here.

Although the manufacturing industry has declined, the outstanding engineering marvels of Scotland are now today's tourist attractions in their own right. Eighteenth-century ironworks, 19th-century canals and the world's most famous railway bridge – spanning the Firth of Forth – are all showpieces of an industrial nation's genius for design. The region can also boast many architectural gems: the rich legacy of Victorian buildings in Glasgow, the grand country houses designed in Scots baronial style and the distinctive cottages of farmer and fisherman all display a very Scottish flavour. Glasgow itself has enjoyed regeneration in recent years, and now takes its rightful place as one of Europe's most lively and interesting cities. But it is the quality of life that matters more than bricks and mortar and one of the greatest attractions of the populated areas is their closeness to the hills and glens of the Highlands. The hills are never far away and even Glasgow, the country's industrial 'capital', has the Campsie Fells only a few miles from its centre.

**Tour 8**
Although this route is only a couple of hours' drive away from the industrial heartland of Scotland, it nevertheless encompasses some superb Highland scenery. The highly indented coastline, backed by 3,000-foot (900m) high hills, provides a backdrop to some fascinating places like the 5,000-year-old cairns at Kilmartin, medieval castles and the picturesque setting of Crinan Canal.

**Tour 9**
The Cowal Peninsula is made up of a group of narrow peninsulas, shaped like a grasping hand trying to get a hold on the northern shore of the island of Bute. The narrow, twisting roads of Cowal give ever-changing vistas over the sea lochs and the great estuary of the Firth of Clyde, the busy waterway that linked local communities before the arrival of the railway and the motor car.

**Tour 10**
The 'border' between the Highlands and the Lowlands is studded with lochs that were gouged out of the landscape by long-lost glaciers. Some of the country's best-known lochs are found here, and today's visitors follow in the footsteps of the 19th-century tourists, eager to sample the 'wild' scenery so vividly romanticised by Sir Walter Scott.

**Tour 11**
This historic corner of Scotland has an abundance of important buildings that armies fought over for centuries. Abbeys, grand palaces and austere castles were the prizes sought by the warring parties, and Stirling, the 'gateway to the Highlands', was the jewel in the crown that invaders tried to capture and that the Scots defended to the last. The battle sites excavated here testify to the lives sacrificed in the centuries of turmoil. But some places can often evade change and the small coastal town of Culross retains a rich legacy in its preserved buildings that time just passed by.

**Tour 12**
A rich agricultural area, Strathmore provides the background to this tour which skirts the southern limits of the Grampian Highlands. Prosperous farming communities, busy east-coast fishing ports and the industrial town of Dundee all add their interest. In many ways this area is one of Scotland's 'hidden gems', as it is often missed by visitors who are more intent on heading straight for the Highlands.

**Tour 13**
Although never a separate legal entity, Fife earned the title 'Kingdom of Fife' through the influence of its ancient abbey in Dunfermline and later its medieval university in St Andrews. Cut off from the rest of the country by the great firths of the Forth and the Tay, it has a character that is very different from the rest of Scotland. This is most evident in its traditional architecture, especially the small white stone buildings with their pantiled roofs that are such a common feature in the many picturesque fishing villages of the East Neuk.

The cantilevered Forth Rail Bridge at dusk

TOUR
8

# Argyll
## Coast & Castles

Oban is still a thriving fishing port and the gateway to the Inner Hebrides. From Oban the tour winds along the dramatic coastline and then goes inland to the heart of the Highlands and Glen Coe, site of Scotland's most infamous massacre.

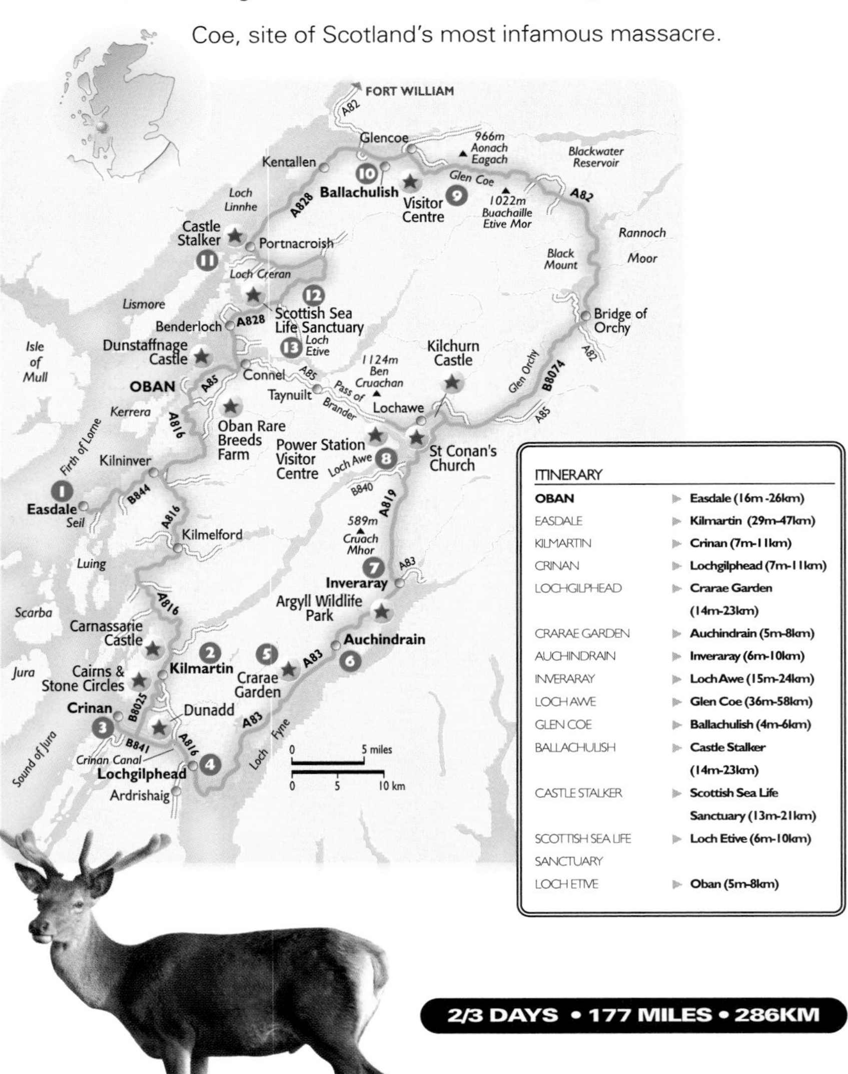


| ITINERARY | |
|---|---|
| **OBAN** | ▶ **Easdale (16m-26km)** |
| EASDALE | ▶ **Kilmartin (29m-47km)** |
| KILMARTIN | ▶ **Crinan (7m-11km)** |
| CRINAN | ▶ **Lochgilphead (7m-11km)** |
| LOCHGILPHEAD | ▶ **Crarae Garden (14m-23km)** |
| CRARAE GARDEN | ▶ **Auchindrain (5m-8km)** |
| AUCHINDRAIN | ▶ **Inveraray (6m-10km)** |
| INVERARAY | ▶ **Loch Awe (15m-24km)** |
| LOCH AWE | ▶ **Glen Coe (36m-58km)** |
| GLEN COE | ▶ **Ballachulish (4m-6km)** |
| BALLACHULISH | ▶ **Castle Stalker (14m-23km)** |
| CASTLE STALKER | ▶ **Scottish Sea Life Sanctuary (13m-21km)** |
| SCOTTISH SEA LIFE SANCTUARY | ▶ **Loch Etive (6m-10km)** |
| LOCH ETIVE | ▶ **Oban (5m-8km)** |

**2/3 DAYS • 177 MILES • 286KM**

## FOR CHILDREN

An animal-based attraction is the Oban Rare Breeds Farm Park with its collection of pigs, sheep and cattle.
The Argyll Wildlife Park near Inveraray boasts many animals including wildcats, badgers, wild boar and deer.

## BACK TO NATURE

Oban Bay can be seen from the town's harbour. Look for common seals, black guillemots and eiders. There is a nature trail at nearby Glen Nant 10 miles (16km) northeast via the B845, south of Taynuilt. Look for wood warblers, redstarts and roe deer in the woodlands

*i* *Argyll Square*

▶ *Head south on the* ***A816****, then turn right at the* ***B844*** *which leads to Easdale (16 miles/26km).*

**1 Easdale,** Argyll & Bute
The village of Easdale is situated on the island of Seil, and is connected to the mainland by the picturesque little humpbacked bridge known as the 'Bridge over the Atlantic'.

Quarriers' houses lining the harbour at Easdale

A centre of slate quarrying, its rows of quarriers' houses look much as they did in the 19th century, when a ferocious sea broke into and flooded the workings; the industry never recovered. A museum tells the story.

▶ *Return along the* ***B844*** *and turn right at the* ***A816*** *and follow this to Kilmartin.*

**2 Kilmartin,** Argyll & Bute
The area around the small village of Kilmartin has some of Scotland's most outstanding large cairns. West of the village is the massive Bronze-Age Glebe Cairn and southwest of the village are the three Nether Largie Cairns. The cairns were used as tombs from around 5,000 years ago, with bodies or cremated remains interred in stone-clad cells ('cists') within the cairns. A little further to the southwest lie the two Temple Wood Stone Circles.

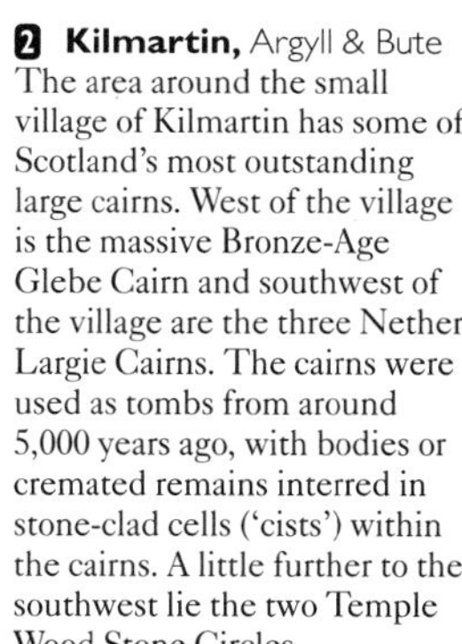

Kilmartin church's graveyard contains many celebrated sculptured gravestones, including the Poltalloch Stones, and others can be seen inside the church.

Kilmartin House contains an award-winning museum, with a superb audio-visual presentation.

The 16th-century fortified house known as Carnassarie Castle can be seen on a hill just before the village.

Stone circle at Temple Wood, near Kilmartin

*Continue on the **A816**, then turn on to the **B8025** to meet the Crinan Canal. Turn right at the **B841** to Crinan.*

FOR HISTORY BUFFS

Dunadd is a rocky promontory that rises above the River Add, south of Kilmartin. This was the capital of the ancient Scots kingdom of Dalriada and the coronation site of the first Scottish kings, and was occupied intermittently between the 6th and 9th centuries. Ramparts guard the summit where a flat rock has carvings of a foot and a boar.

Inveraray Castle, obviously modelled on the romantic French châteaux

**3 Crinan,** Argyll & Bute
The Crinan Canal was opened in 1801 so that boats could avoid the cruel seas around the Mull of Kintyre. This was a great boon to fishermen as the short-cut was only 8½ miles (14km) long compared to the sea route of 130 miles (200km). The advent of steamships dealt the canal a severe blow, but it is still in use today and is often busy with pleasure craft.

*Return along the **B841**, which follows the canal. Join the **A816** and follow it to Lochgilphead, 7 miles (11km).*

**4 Lochgilphead,** Argyll & Bute
The town developed as an administrative centre for the region and also because of the trade brought by the canal. A popular attraction today is a visit to the local Highbank Pottery.

*i* *Lochnell Street (seasonal)*

*Leave by the **A83** for 14 miles (23km) to Crarae Garden.*

**5 Crarae Garden,** Argyll & Bute
The garden was founded in 1912 in a steep-sided gorge and today has a rich collection of rhododendrons, magnolias, azaleas and many other trees and shrubs from around the world. The warmth of the Gulf Stream and an annual rainfall of 75 inches (190cm) help ensure that the garden delights visitors throughout the year, especially in early summer (for the rhododendrons) and in autumn.

*Continue on the **A83** for 5 miles (8km) to Auchindrain, just beyond the village of Furnace.*

**6 Auchindrain,** Argyll & Bute
Queen Victoria visited this little Highland township in 1875 and was impressed enough to record it in her diary. Today, the houses, barns, smiddy (traditional term for blacksmith) and other buildings have been preserved as an open air folk-life museum to show how people have lived here through the centuries.

*Continue on the **A83** for 6 miles (10km) to Inveraray.*

**7 Inveraray,** Argyll & Bute
This neat and well-planned village on Loch Fyne has been a royal burgh since 1648, but its 'modern' planning dates back to the middle of the 18th century, and the exteriors of the houses have hardly changed since then.

The large parish church, in the middle of the main road, dominates the centre. It was built at the turn of the 18th century with a central dividing wall so that services in Gaelic and English could be conducted simultaneously.

The fascinating Inveraray Jail Museum consists of the former courthouse (with actors in period costume) and two prisons. The older of the two was erected in 1820 as the Argyll County Prison and the newer one was built to 'modern' standards in 1849. The cells feature displays explaining the harshness of prison life and the appalling conditions that the prisoners had to endure. Near

'Let's be havin' yer' – Jail Museum at Inveraray

the gaol are the 'lands', rows of houses reminiscent of some old Edinburgh houses. Neil Munro, author of the Para Handy tales, was born close by.

Down at the pier, the *Arctic Penguin* is now a floating museum of maritime history, with exciting hands-on displays and on-board cinema. It has exhibits on Scottish pirates, the Highland Clearances and the Victorian era.

Inveraray Castle stands a short distance away from the village. The present building is mid-18th-century and replaces a castle built by Colin Campbell in about 1415. This is the home of the Dukes of Argyll, the chiefs of Clan Campbell, and it has many exhibits relating to the clan's history.

[i] *Front Street*

**SPECIAL TO...**

Fresh seafood is a speciality of the region. Crabs, prawns and lobsters should be available in many restaurants and Loch Fyne is famous for its herrings. Herrings were once given the alternative name of 'Glasgow Magistrates' as the quality of those sold in the city had to be approved by the magistrates. Indeed, the city used to give barrels of these delicious fish to people who rendered the city a great service!

*Leave by the* ***A819*** *and turn left at the* ***A85*** *for Loch Awe.*

**8 Loch Awe,** Argyll & Bute

Loch Awe is dominated by the massive Ben Cruachan, a mountain with a pump storage hydro-electric power station inside it. Visits into the heart of the mountain start from the visitor centre (west along the A85). At the head of the loch stands the imposing ruin of Kilchurn Castle, a Campbell stronghold built in the 15th and 17th centuries. It was abandoned in the 18th century and in 1879 a hurricane blew down the top of the tower that can be seen lying in the courtyard.

The intriguing St Conan's Church sits below the south-eastern slopes of Ben Cruachan. This was started in 1881 and added to over the next 50 years. It has elaborate carvings, including fragments from Iona Abbey, rich woodwork and a rare mixture of styles.

Winter sun on the hills around Kilchurn Castle on the banks of Loch Awe

**RECOMMENDED WALKS**

There are many walks in Argyll suitable for family outings, for example on the western shore of Loch Awe. The Crinan Canal towpath also provides pleasant walks, with lots to see when boats are passing through the locks.

*Return eastwards along the* ***A85****, then bear left at the* ***B8074*** *towards Bridge of Orchy. Turn left at the* ***A82*** *and follow it across Rannoch Moor to Glen Coe.*

**9 Glen Coe,** Highland

Glen Coe itself is regarded by many Scots as the country's finest glen and whatever the weather, the scenery is dramatic.

The visitor centre near the foot of the glen has displays on

The Three Sisters in Glen Coe, Scotland's most infamous glen

### SCENIC ROUTES

There can be few journeys in Scotland more exciting than that through Glen Coe. The route to it is over Rannoch Moor, a high peaty wasteland that was one of the last places to lose its ice at the close of the Ice Age. The final approach is heralded by Buachaille Etive Mor, one of Scotland's most imposing mountains.

### RECOMMENDED WALKS

Near Glen Coe, there are interesting stretches of the West Highland Way, such as the Devil's Staircase. The Lost Valley in Glen Coe is another good walk, but needs a bit of scrambling experience. Advice on walks in Glen Coe can be obtained from the NTS Visitor Centre.

the district and tells one of Scotland's most tragic stories – the Glencoe Massacre. In 1691 William III offered a pardon to the warring clans on condition that they took an oath of allegiance to the crown by 1 January, 1692. The local MacDonald chief reluctantly made his way to Fort William just before the deadline, only to be told that he should go to Inveraray. He did so, but arrived a day after the deadline. The regiment in Glen Coe, under the command of a Campbell, were billeted with the MacDonalds for 10 days. A message was sent to them, which had the King's private approval, and at a given signal, without warning, the Campbells rose up and slaughtered 38 of their hosts, supposedly because of the failure to take the oath. About 300 people escaped into the hills, but the atrocity was never forgotten. A restored cottage with a heather-thatched roof houses a museum of local history. It shows life in this area over the past three centuries, with exhibits ranging from domestic and agricultural history to the story of the Jacobites.

*i* *NTS Visitor Centre (seasonal)*

*Golden sunset silhouetting romantic Castle Stalker*

▶ *Continue on the **A82** past the village of Glencoe to Ballachulish.*

**10 Ballachulish,** Highland

This was once Scotland's main slate producer and in the 1880s, the quarries' peak of production, 600 men produced 16 million slates a year. This ended in 1955 but the massive quarries can still be seen.

Steps under the Ballachulish Bridge lead to a memorial to James Stewart who was hanged here in 1752 for the murder of Colin Campbell, a government official. He was undoubtedly a scapegoat convicted by a partisan court and Robert Louis Stevenson used this terrible miscarriage of justice in his novel *Kidnapped*.

*i* *Albert Road (seasonal)*

▶ *Continue on the **A82**, then follow the **A828** to the village of Portnacroish for Castle Stalker.*

**11 Castle Stalker,** Argyll & Bute

This romantically set rectangular keep (not open) is perched on a low rocky platform at the mouth

Feeding the seals at the Scottish Sea Life Sanctuary in Oban

of Loch Laich. It was built in the 13th century, and in 1689 it was exchanged for an eight-oared galley during a drunken spree, when the owner was clearly not in full control of his senses!

▶ *Continue on the **A828** for 13 miles (21km) to the Scottish Sea Life Sanctuary, near Barcardine.*

**12 Scottish Sea Life Sanctuary,** Argyll & Bute
Scotland's west coast is famous for its important fishing grounds so it is entirely appropriate to have the Scottish Sea Life Sanctuary here. Crabs, lobsters, rays and a huge shoal of herring are just some of the creatures on view. There are also seals and the sanctuary provides a refuge for abandoned seal pups. Make sure you are there for one of the feeding times.

▶ *Continue on the **A828** to Connel where the road crosses the mouth of Loch Etive, 6 miles (10km).*

**13 Loch Etive,** Argyll & Bute
Just under the Connel Bridge are the unusual Falls of Lora, a tidal waterfall where the direction of the falls depends on whether the tide is going in or out. To the east stands the village of Taynuilt. This was once one of Scotland's iron-smelting centres and the impressive Bonawe Furnace has been conserved to show something of what an 18th-century ironworks looked like; however, you will have to forget the peace and quiet of the countryside to imagine all the dust, dirt and smoke it must once have produced.

▶ *At Connel, join the **A85** and return to Oban.*

**BACK TO NATURE**

**One of the most notable sights in many parts of western Scotland, particularly Argyll, is the rhododendron, a plant introduced in the 18th and 19th centuries. Its ability to colonise poor ground, together with its dense foliage that inhibits light reaching smaller plants, often makes people regard it more as a weed than an exotic plant to be nurtured.**

Fishing boats, car ferries and yachts make Oban one of the busiest harbours in Scotland

# 'Doon the Watter'

The town of Paisley grew up around its abbey, founded in 1163, and is best known for its shawls featuring the distinctive teardrop-shaped Paisley pattern. From Paisley the tour explores the sea lochs and green-clad mountains of the Cowal Peninsula.

**2 DAYS • 132 MILES • 213KM**

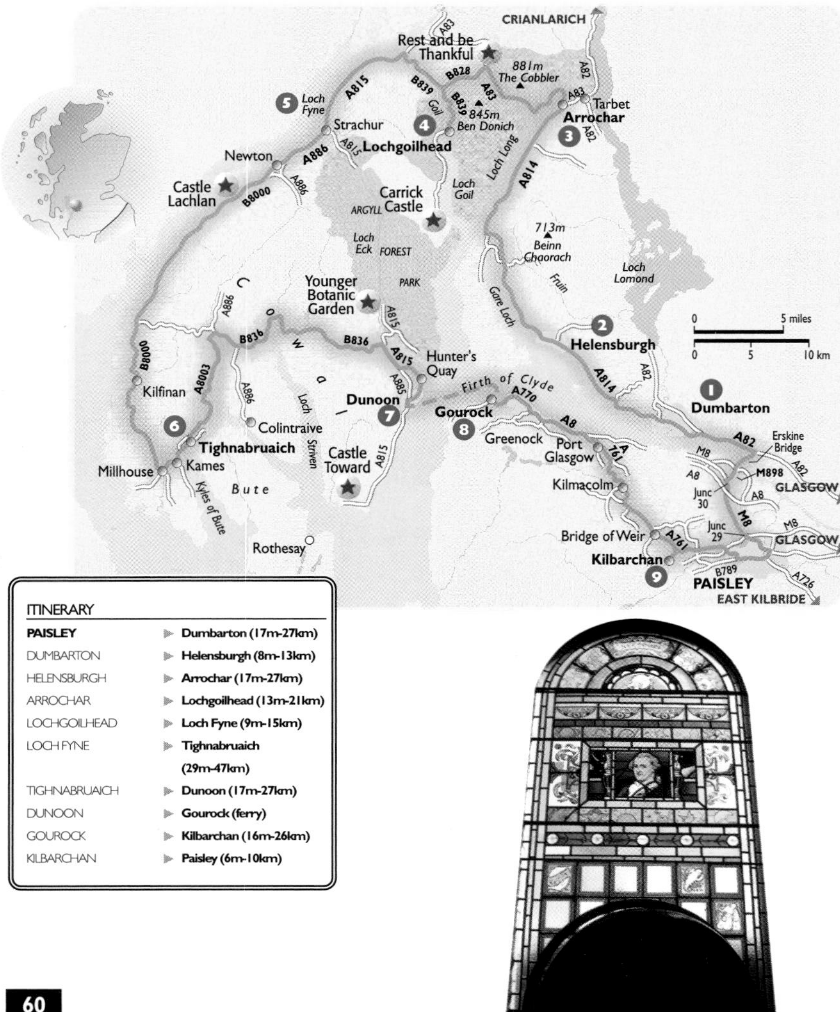


| ITINERARY | |
|---|---|
| **PAISLEY** | ▶ **Dumbarton (17m-27km)** |
| DUMBARTON | ▶ **Helensburgh (8m-13km)** |
| HELENSBURGH | ▶ **Arrochar (17m-27km)** |
| ARROCHAR | ▶ **Lochgoilhead (13m-21km)** |
| LOCHGOILHEAD | ▶ **Loch Fyne (9m-15km)** |
| LOCH FYNE | ▶ **Tighnabruaich (29m-47km)** |
| TIGHNABRUAICH | ▶ **Dunoon (17m-27km)** |
| DUNOON | ▶ **Gourock (ferry)** |
| GOUROCK | ▶ **Kilbarchan (16m-26km)** |
| KILBARCHAN | ▶ **Paisley (6m-10km)** |

The river port of Dumbarton, now more famous for its whisky distilling than for its shipbuilding

[i] *Glasgow International Airport, Paisley*

▶ *Leave Paisley on the* ***A726*** *(to Greenock and Erskine Bridge). Join the* ***M8*** *and head towards Greenock, then take the* ***M898/A898*** *to the Erskine Bridge over the River Clyde. Head west along the* ***A82*** *(towards Crianlarich) then bear left on to the* ***A814****.*

**1 Dumbarton,** West Dunbartonshire

A modern industrial town owing its historic importance to its prominent position on the northern shore of the River Clyde, Dumbarton was the capital of the ancient kingdom of Strathclyde and it has had a royal castle since medieval times. Dumbarton Castle stands on Dumbarton Rock overlooking the river and much of the present fortification dates from the 16th to 18th centuries. The hilltop behind the castle gives a superb view of the area.

Dumbarton is now an important whisky distilling centre but it used to have a flourishing shipbuilding industry. Although few ships are built on the Clyde these days, one important structure that remains is the Denny Tank, which has been preserved by the Scottish Maritime Museum. This was used for experiments: models of proposed ships were towed along the 330-foot (100m) tank in order to show how the full size ship might perform at sea.

[i] *Milton A82 northbound*

▶ *Leave Dumbarton by the* ***A814*** *and follow it along the coast for 8 miles (13km) to Helensburgh.*

Dumbarton Castle and the 18th-century Governor's Mansion above the River Clyde

Loch Fyne – one of Scotland's best known sea lochs

### 2 Helensburgh, Argyll & Bute

Helensburgh's grand architecture dates back to the late 18th century when it was built as a planned dormitory town for Glasgow, to which it was connected by regular sailings. The town's long promenade gives a pleasant walk and by the seafront is a tall granite obelisk commemorating Henry Bell, designer of the world's first sea-going steamship, *The Comet*.

The recent revival in interest in the work of the outstanding Scottish architect and designer Charles Rennie Mackintosh makes a trip to Hill House one of the town's main attractions. This mansion was built at the beginning of the 20th century for the publisher Walter Blackie and remains an outstanding example of modern Scottish domestic architecture. The exterior design and the household furnishings reflect Mackintosh's individual style.

John Logie Baird, pioneer of the television, came from Helensburgh and a memorial bust to him is in the town's Hermitage Park. After leaving Helensburgh, the route passes the huge complex of the Clyde Submarine Base.

[i] *Clock Tower, The Pier (seasonal)*

▶ *Continue along the **A814** for 17 miles (27km) to Arrochar.*

### 3 Arrochar, Argyll & Bute

The little village of Arrochar sits at the head of Loch Long and below the hills often referred to as the 'Arrochar Alps'. These rise steeply from the shore and provide wonderful walking and climbing, especially 2,891-foot (881m) Ben Arthur, which is usually known as The Cobbler.

Loch Long has been associated with seafarers for many centuries. The most notable naval exploit was in 1263 when the Viking King Haakon landed at Arrochar. He had his boats hauled 1½ miles (2km) over the strip of land to Tarbet and then sailed over Loch Lomond to attack inland settlements!

To the west of Arrochar, the A83 climbs steeply up Glen Croe to the well-named 'Rest and be Thankful', at 803 feet (245m). Below this can be seen the earlier military road which was built after the 1745 Jacobite uprising in order to 'pacify' (meaning 'subdue') the Highlands.

*i* *Main Street, Tarbert*

**RECOMMENDED WALKS**

Experienced walkers will head for the Arrochar Alps, but there are other walks of varying grades in the Argyll Forest Park, which lies in the area of lochs Long, Goil and Eck. Information can be obtained from tourist information centres.

The 20th-century Hill House in Helensburgh

▶ *Leave Arrochar on the **A83** to Campbeltown. Turn left at the 'Rest and be Thankful' on to the **B828**, then join the **B839** to reach Lochgoilhead.*

### 4 Lochgoilhead, Argyll & Bute

At the head of Loch Goil, this village is popular with visitors for its excellent walking and sailing.

Five miles (8km) down the western shore of the loch stands the ruin of Carrick Castle, destroyed by fire in 1685. The structure dates at least from the 15th century and was probably used by James IV when he came to this area, known as Cowal, to hunt wild boar.

▶ *Leave Lochgoilhead by the **B839** and follow this to the shore of Loch Fyne. Turn left on to the **A815** just before the shore.*

### 5 Loch Fyne, Argyll & Bute

This long sea loch is set among beautiful ranges of green-clad mountains. Apart from the little village of Strachur, where there is a blacksmithing museum and craft shop, the district's settlements are small and scattered and many of the houses are used as retirement homes.

South of Strachur stands Castle Lachlan, home of the chief of the MacLachlans. During the Clearances the local people were moved out of their homes and settled in the village of Newton, which the chief built between the castle and Strachur. This is now a sleepy hamlet, and many homes are used only at weekends. The 18th-century Clearances, when landowners moved thousands of people off the land to make way for more profitable sheep farming, led to depopulation of the area. However, the importance of sheep has diminished greatly and much of the poorer land has been given over to extensive conifer plantations.

**BACK TO NATURE**

The sea lochs around Cowal are home to many seabirds including gulls, cormorants and ducks. Keep a sharp look out for seals from the shore of Loch Fyne. Of all Cowal's lochs, Loch Striven is probably the quietest and least touched by agriculture.

▶ *Follow the **A815** to Strachur. Keep to the lochside by joining the **A886** and later bear right on to the **B8000** to Kilfinan. Follow this to Tighnabruaich.*

### 6 Tighnabruaich, Argyll & Bute

Both Tighnabruaich and neighbouring Kames grew during the heyday of steamship navigation on the Clyde. This is a popular sailing centre and many yachts can be seen in the narrow waterways around the northern coast of Bute. Just north of Tighnabruaich is one of Scotland's most famous viewpoints – across the narrow strait known as the Kyles of Bute.

**FOR CHILDREN**

Cowal is an area for outdoor activities with sailing at Tighnabruaich and pony-trekking at Lochgoilhead and Inellan (south of Dunoon). Alternatively, Helensburgh Pier Family Amusement Park has rides for all ages.

▶ *Leave Tighnabruaich by the **A8003**. Turn right at the **A886** and then left at the **B836**. Turn right on the **A815** for Dunoon.*

### 7 Dunoon, Argyll & Bute

Dunoon has built up a reputation as one of the most popular stopping places for people sailing 'Doon the Watter', as the Glaswegians say, and its picturesque pierhead buildings have welcomed countless visitors. As befits a seaside resort, it has a long promenade and colourful Castle Gardens. Here you will find the excellent Castle House Museum, with furnished Victorian rooms and other exhibits.

Near the pier stands a statue of Robert Burns' 'Highland Mary', who was born in the town. This was Mary Campbell, who was betrothed to Burns but died. Burns tried hard to cover up their relationship, probably because it complicated his life with his future wife, Jean Armour.

The Cowal Bird Garden includes donkeys, goats, macaws, owls, a play area, a nature trail and a shop.

Dunoon is world famous for its Cowal Highland Gathering, which takes place on the last Friday and Saturday in August. The Gathering was started in the 1890s and today it attracts competitors from many countries as it hosts World Championship Highland dancing. Pipe bands from near and far compete and some 20,000 visitors have been known to throng the main street for the parade.

The Younger Botanic Garden is at Benmore, just 7 miles (11km) north of Dunoon on the A815. This outstanding garden is an outstation of

### FOR HISTORY BUFFS

Eight miles (13km) south of Dunoon stand the ruins of 15th-century Castle Toward. This was a stronghold of the Lamont clan, but in 1646 it was surrounded by a force of Campbells. Although the Lamonts accepted and signed a truce they were seized and taken to Dunoon where they were summarily executed and their bodies thrown into mass graves. This bloody act is commemorated by a memorial on Tom-a-Mhoid Road near Castle Hill.

### SPECIAL TO...

The development of steamships in the 19th century led to the 'discovery' of Cowal by visitors keen to go 'Doon the Watter' (the River Clyde) from Glasgow to the smoke-free countryside. Many wealthy Glasgow merchants built villas in the Cowal villages and decanted their families there during the summer months. Cruising on the Clyde is now an increasingly popular pastime and cruises from places such as Dunoon and Tighnabruaich are available. One ship to look out for around Cowal is the PS *Waverley*, the world's last sea-going paddle steamer. It is based in Glasgow and operates many summer cruises, calling at piers on both sides of the Firth of Clyde.

Younger Botanic Garden – woodland gardens on a grand scale

Edinburgh's Royal Botanic Garden; it has magnificent rhododendrons and an impressive avenue of tall redwoods that was planted here in 1863.

*i* *7 Alexandra Parade*

▶ *Take the Caledonian MacBrayne ferry from Dunoon to Gourock. Alternatively, take the Western Ferries' ferry from Hunter's Quay (just north of Dunoon) to a point a little southwest of Gourock; then head towards Gourock on the **A770**.*

**8 Gourock,** Inverclyde
Gourock is a pleasant coastal town with excellent views of the Clyde, notably from Lyle Hill above the southeastern side of Gourock Bay. On top of the hill is a monument to Free French sailors who sailed from here and died during World War II's Battle of the Atlantic.

To the east of Gourock are the industrial towns of Greenock and Port Glasgow. Greenock was a shipbuilding centre and once an important embarkation point for emigrants leaving Scotland for new lives in North America or Australasia. The Custom House Museum explores the Customs and Excise service, including a display on one of its former employees, Robert Burns. The town's most famous son was the engineer James Watt, whose invention of the condensing steam engine, the first efficient use of steam power, paved the way for the Industrial Revolution. The McLean Museum has a display on James Watt among its collections.

Port Glasgow gained its present name in 1688 when it became the city's port as ships could not progress further upstream (its previous name had been Newark). The city's 16th-century castle still stands by the shore, although it is rather overshadowed these days by the many industrial buildings all around it.

*i* *7a Clyde Square, Greenock*

▶ *Leave Gourock by the coastal road (the **A770** which joins the **A8** at Greenock) and bear right on to the **A761** to Bridge of Weir, via Kilmacolm. After Bridge of Weir, continue on the **A761** for 1½ miles (2.5km) after the local railway station, then turn sharp right at a signposted minor road to Kilbarchan.*

**9 Kilbarchan,** Renfrewshire
In the 18th century the village of Kilbarchan was an important centre where wool, linen and cotton were hand woven. A weaver's cottage of 1723 has been preserved by the NTS at The Cross. This continued to be used for weaving until 1940 and it has a 200-year-old loom on which demonstrations of weaving are now given.

Hand-woven tartans are still made today at Kilbarchan

▶ *Rejoin the **A761** (to Paisley, via Linwood), then turn left on to the **A737** to return to Paisley.*

**SCENIC ROUTES**

**The nicest part of this tour is on the A8003, when the narrows of the Kyles of Bute are seen. If you are lucky you may see a ship negotiating the passage past the Burnt Islands. The true narrows are opposite Colintraive, whose name means 'straight of swimming', dating from the times when cattle drovers used to swim their beasts across here.**

TOUR
**10**

# Rob Roy Country

This tour includes Loch Lomond and the Trossachs, Scotland's first national park, and Loch Tay – but starts in Glasgow, one of Britain's most exciting cities. It is certainly worth spending a few days in Glasgow: its museums and galleries are among Britain's finest and the city is well endowed with green spaces.

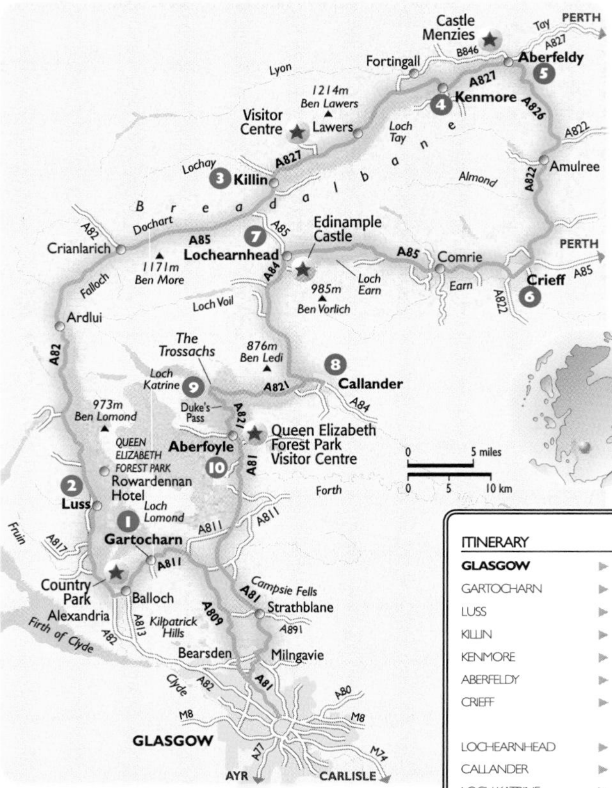

**ITINERARY**

| | |
|---|---|
| **GLASGOW** | ▶ **Gartocharn (20m-32km)** |
| GARTOCHARN | ▶ **Luss (12m-19km)** |
| LUSS | ▶ **Killin (39m-63km)** |
| KILLIN | ▶ **Kenmore (17m-27km)** |
| KENMORE | ▶ **Aberfeldy (6m-10km)** |
| ABERFELDY | ▶ **Crieff (23m-37km)** |
| CRIEFF | ▶ **Lochearnhead (19m-31km)** |
| LOCHEARNHEAD | ▶ **Callander (14m-23km)** |
| CALLANDER | ▶ **Loch Katrine (10m-16km)** |
| LOCH KATRINE | ▶ **Aberfoyle (7m-11km)** |
| ABERFOYLE | ▶ **Glasgow (29m-47km)** |

**2/3 DAYS • 196 MILES • 316KM**

*11 George Square, Glasgow*

*Leave by the* ***A81****, then the* ***A809*** *and turn left at the* ***A811*** *to reach Gartocharn.*

**1 Gartocharn,** West Dunbartonshire

This small village gives a good introduction to Scotland's most-loved loch, Loch Lomond. Although Gartocharn doesn't actually sit on the lochside, there is a superb view of it from the hill behind, Duncryne. For little effort this is a vantage point that gives views towards the loch, 3,194-foot (974m) Ben Lomond on the east shore and the Luss Hills, which rise from the western shore.

The area around the loch was one of the last places to lose its glaciers at the end of the Ice Age and the smooth, U-shaped glacial valleys in the Luss Hills are obvious features of this type of landscape. The careful observer will notice a change between this glacially eroded highland landscape and the smoothly sculpted hillocks around Gartocharn's farmland. This change in scenery marks the geological divide between the Highlands and Lowlands. Further along the road, at Balloch, is the National Park Gateway Centre at Loch Lomond Shores.

*Drymen Library, The Square, Drymen (seasonal)*

*Continue on the* ***A811*** *and turn right at the* ***A82****. Follow this northwards, turning right at an unclassified road sign-posted to Luss, a distance of 12 miles (19km).*

**2 Luss,** Argyll & Bute

The delightful little lochside village of Luss has many exceptionally picturesque cottages. The National Park Centre is located here, and the renowned Thistle Bagpipe Works are close by. Further north, a ferry operates from Inverbeg across the loch to Rowardennan.

Contestant giving his best at the World Pipe Band Championships in Glasgow

Majestic Loch Lomond as seen from Duncryne Hill

Kenmore church and boats on Loch Tay

### RECOMMENDED WALKS

Hillwalkers will find plenty of good hills near a number of villages. Crainlarich has two interesting pairs of hills in Beinn a' Chroin and Beinn Tulaichean, and Ben More and Stob Binnein. Killin has Ben Lawers and the group of hills called the Tarmachans. Lower hills further south include Ben Venue, Ben Ledi and Ben An. The forests, especially around Aberfoyle, offer many walks, though views of the hills and lochs may be restricted at times by the trees. The Queen Elizabeth Forest Park Visitor Centre at Aberfoyle is run by Forest Enterprises, and many marked paths start from here. Other walks include parts of the West Highland Way (which follows the eastern shore of Loch Lomond), to the Bracklinn Falls (near Callander) and to the Falls of Moness (near Aberfeldy).

▶ *Rejoin and continue on the* ***A82****, then turn right on to the* ***A85*** *at Crianlarich. Turn left at the* ***A827*** *to Killin (39 miles/63km).*

### BACK TO NATURE

The rich flora on Ben Lawers attracts many botanists, both amateur and professional, to this remarkable mountain. The hill is rich in lime and other minerals which provide the nutrients needed by the Arctic/Alpine species that grow here. Cliff edges, which are out of reach of sheep and deer, support such plants as roseroot, angelica and wood cranesbill, while shady crevices host oak fern and wood anemone. Birds are not too common on the higher slopes but look out for buzzards and kestrels, with occasional sightings of golden eagles and peregrines. Mountain hares can be seen on the high ground.

### 3 Killin, Stirling

Killin attracts hill walkers for the many fine hills in the district, the best known of which is Ben Lawers, at 3,984 feet (1,214m). The NTS has established a visitor centre on the western flank of the mountain.

The River Dochart flows past the village before debouching into Loch Tay. Before reaching the village it tumbles over the wide Falls of Dochart, which are quite fearsome when the river is in spate. Overlooking the falls is the fascinating Breadalbane Folklore Centre.

### SCENIC ROUTES

Much of the route is through fine scenery, with perhaps the best parts being along the shores of lochs Lomond and Tay for views of the lochs and their mountains.
Another fine stretch is through the pretty Sma'Glen (between Aberfeldy and Crieff) where the River Almond winds its way through the hills.

[i] *Breadalbane Folklore Centre (seasonal)*

▶ *Continue on the* ***A827*** *for 17 miles (27km) to Kenmore.*

### 4 Kenmore, Perth & Kinross

On the shores of Loch Tay, Kenmore has been developed as a small resort and watersports centre. Beside the village is

SPECIAL TO...

Every visitor to Scotland wants to see Highland cattle, those fierce-looking, shaggy beasts with long curved horns. In reality, these lovely creatures turn out to be very docile and more interested in eating than worrying about hordes of people. They can be seen in a number of localities, but keep a special look-out for them north of Loch Lomond and at the western end of Loch Tay.

the ornamental gateway to Taymouth Castle (private). Part of its park has been developed as a golf course. To the north lies the quiet settlement of Fortingall, reputedly the birthplace of Pontius Pilate. A yew tree in the churchyard is said to be over 3,000 years old.

*Continue on the **A827** for 6 miles (10km) to Aberfeldy.*

**5 Aberfeldy,** Perth & Kinross
This pleasant touring centre stands beside the splendidly ornate bridge which General George Wade built in 1733 at this important crossing of the River Tay. Wade was responsible for some 250 miles (400km) of military roads in the Highlands between 1726 and 1735, as part of the government's attempt to gain control over the region. This network included 40 stone bridges, of which this is the best known, and at the time it was the only bridge over the Tay. The Black Watch Memorial, which stands quite close to the bridge, was erected in 1887. The regiment was enrolled into the British Army in 1739 and took its name from the men's dark tartan, chosen to differentiate them from the Guardsmen or Red Soldiers.

Aberfeldy lies in a belt of good agricultural land and the water mill is one enduring reminder of how the local grain was processed. This was originally built in 1825 and has been restored to allow it to produce stoneground oatmeal. To the northwest of the village, at Weem, stands Castle Menzies, home of the chief of Clan Menzies. The present castle, constructed to a Z-shaped design, was built in the 1570s, and has been restored by the Clan Society.

*i The Square*

*Leave by the **A826**. Turn right at the **A822**, then right at the **A85** and follow this into Crieff.*

**6 Crieff,** Perth & Kinross
Crieff is a traditional Highland resort and one that offers much to the visitor wanting a base to explore the countryside. The visitor centre has its own pottery offering factory tours, and the local Glenturret Distillery, founded in 1775, has a visitor centre and tours round the premises.

West of Crieff, on the A85, is Comrie, a pretty village surrounded by wooded crags.

*i High Street*

*Continue on the **A85** for 19 miles (31km) to Lochearnhead.*

**7 Lochearnhead,** Stirling
Lochearnhead, at the western end of Loch Earn, was developed when the railway was built through Glen Ogle. The line's route can be followed through the glen – look out for the massive boulders that have tumbled down the hillside and must have threatened the trains that chugged up the steep incline. Near the village, where the Burn of Ample meets the loch, stands Edinample Castle, which was built in 1630.

Crieff's local Glenturret Distillery

▶ *Leave by the* ***A84*** *and follow it for 14 miles (23km) to Callander.*

**FOR HISTORY BUFFS**

**The peaceful little settlement of Balquhidder, by Loch Voil, was where Rob Roy died. He is buried in the local churchyard.**

**8 Callander,** Stirling

This is one of Central Scotland's busiest little resorts as it is a favourite stopping place for many visitors.

The town stands by the banks of the River Teith and has many good walks near by. Serious walkers head for Ben Ledi, which dominates the local scenery at 2,882 feet (879m), or the rather higher Ben Vorlich, at 3,231 feet (985m), which stands between Callander town and Loch Earn.

Much of the town was laid out in the 18th century as a planned village with its centre at Ancaster Square, which now houses the Rob Roy and Trossachs Visitor Centre. Rob Roy MacGregor (1671–1734) was a most intriguing character and the hero of Sir Walter Scott's novel *Rob Roy*. The story of Rob Roy's life is intertwined with legend and Scott's artistic licence. However, he did represent the last flings of Gaeldom against the encroaching 'civilization' of the Highlands by English and lowland Scottish 'culture' as well as naked economic and political might. At the end of the 17th century the king, William of Orange, was determined to subdue the Highlanders and even took the step of proscribing the name MacGregor. Rob Roy then used his mother's clan name of Campbell and allied himself with his kinsman, the Duke of Argyll, in feuds with the Duke of Montrose. When Montrose chased him out of his home, he turned his hand from cattle-

The summit of Ben Ledi, viewed from Duke's Pass

dealing to reiving (cattle-raiding), earning a reputation as the Scots' equivalent of Robin Hood, stealing from the rich landowners and giving the money to destitute Highlanders.

*i* *Rob Roy and Trossachs Visitor Centre, Ancaster Square (seasonal)*

► *Return along the **A84** and then turn left at the **A821**. After passing the Trossachs Hotel, follow the signs (right) to Loch Katrine.*

**9 Loch Katrine,** Stirling
The loch lies in the heart of the area known as the Trossachs, though the name is properly given to the little pass between lochs Achray and Katrine. Its fame as a beauty spot stemmed from Sir Walter Scott's description of it in the poem *The Lady of the Lake*; Dorothy Wordsworth and others also described its charms. The road between the loch and Aberfoyle is known as the Duke's Pass, as it was built in the 19th century by the Duke of Montrose to cater for the ever-increasing number of visitors, drawn here after reading Scott's work.

The loch is one of the main sources of Glasgow's water and the 1855 scheme to pipe this very pure water the 35 miles (56km) to the city was a massive feat of civil engineering. Today, visitors can cruise on the *Sir Walter Scott* across the waters of the loch and sail under the slopes of Ben Venue.

► *Return to the **A821** and turn right. Follow the **A821** to Aberfoyle, 7 miles (11km).*

**10 Aberfoyle,** Stirling
Aberfoyle is a tourist centre by the River Forth hemmed in by a huge conifer plantation, much of it within the Queen Elizabeth Forest Park. The 'Clachan at Aberfoyle' was one of the settings used by Scott in *Rob Roy* (a clachan is a hamlet). The village's Scottish Wool Centre features many varieties of sheep bred in Scotland.

*i* *Trossachs Discovery Centre, Main Street (seasonal)*



Local attraction to be sampled at Aberfoyle

A steamer trip on the *Sir Walter Scott* provides a splendid view of Loch Katrine

► *Continue on the **A821** and the **A81**. Follow this back to Glasgow, 29 miles (47km).*

**FOR HISTORY BUFFS**

To the east of Aberfoyle lies the Lake of Menteith, one of only a handful of 'lakes' in Scotland. On one of the lake's islands, Inchmahome, stands the Priory of Inchmahome, founded in 1238. Mary, Queen of Scots was sent to the island at the age of five, prior to sailing to France in 1547. The island can be reached by ferry from the Port of Menteith.

# Abbeys, Battlefields & Castles

This tour covers many of the historic sights which make up Scotland's bloody history. Strategically positioned on the eastern route into the Highlands, Stirling saw two great battles during the Wars of Independence – in 1297 at Stirling Bridge and in 1314 at Bannockburn.

**1/2 DAYS • 91 MILES • 148KM**

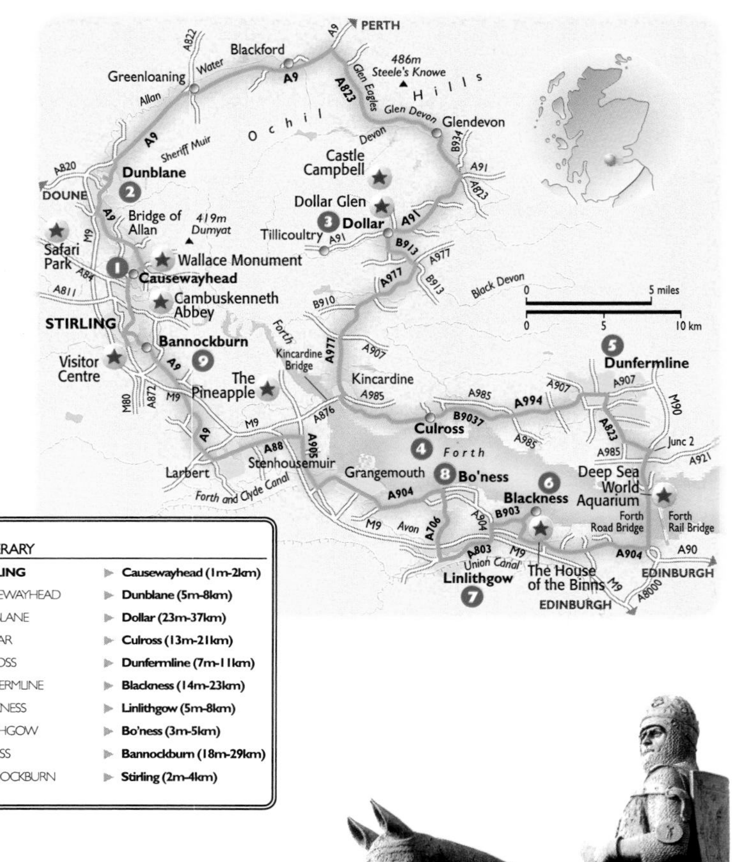


ITINERARY

| | |
|---|---|
| **STIRLING** | ▶ **Causewayhead (1m-2km)** |
| CAUSEWAYHEAD | ▶ **Dunblane (5m-8km)** |
| DUNBLANE | ▶ **Dollar (23m-37km)** |
| DOLLAR | ▶ **Culross (13m-21km)** |
| CULROSS | ▶ **Dunfermline (7m-11km)** |
| DUNFERMLINE | ▶ **Blackness (14m-23km)** |
| BLACKNESS | ▶ **Linlithgow (5m-8km)** |
| LINLITHGOW | ▶ **Bo'ness (3m-5km)** |
| BO'NESS | ▶ **Bannockburn (18m-29km)** |
| BANNOCKBURN | ▶ **Stirling (2m-4km)** |

Panoramic view of the ramparts of Stirling Castle and the Church of the Holy Rude

*i* *41 Dumbarton Road; Castle Esplanade; M9/M80 Junction 9 Pirnhall Motorway Service Area (seasonal)*

> **FOR CHILDREN**
>
> The Blair Drummond Safari and Leisure Park is to be found to the northwest of Stirling, on the flat agricultural land of the Carse of Stirling. The most fascinating part of the park is the drive round the main enclosure, where you can observe wild animals such as lions, zebra and deer roaming around at very close quarters; don't be surprised if you find there are monkeys clambering all over your car!

*Leave by the* ***A9*** *and follow it for 1 mile (2km) to Causewayhead.*

### 1 Causewayhead, Stirling

This small village is dominated by the Abbey Craig, upon which is perched the 220-foot (67m) high Wallace Monument, erected in tribute to Sir William Wallace, victor of the Battle of Stirling Bridge. The top of the monument gives an outstanding view of the district. Close to the village in a meander of the Forth stands the ruined Cambuskenneth Abbey, founded around 1147.

*Continue on the* ***A9****. Just before Dunblane, turn right at a roundabout at the end of the* ***M9*** *and follow the* ***B8033****. Take a signposted road on the left into the village, 5 miles (8km).*

### 2 Dunblane, Stirling

The cathedral, which is situated near Allan Water, was founded around 1150 and its presence raises the status of what is essentially just a village to that of a small city. The story of the cathedral and Dunblane is told in an interesting little museum that stands opposite the cathedral. To the west lies the quiet village of Doune. Its main attraction today is the fine medieval castle.

*i* *Stirling Road (seasonal)*

Costume pageant at the Queen Mary Gardens, Stirling Castle

Bird's-eye view of the impressive stronghold of Castle Campbell, Dollar

> **SCENIC ROUTES**
>
> The journey through Glen Eagles and Glen Devon is the most scenic part of the tour, with the road making its way through the heart of the Ochils. Two misconceptions about Glen Eagles should be explained: firstly, the name means 'churches' and not 'eagles' and secondly, the golfing hotel of Gleneagles is not here but near Auchterarder.

▶ *Return to the **B8033** and turn left. Join the **A9** and head towards Perth. Turn right at the **A823**, then right at the **A91** in order to enter Dollar.*

**3 Dollar,** Clackmannanshire

This neat little town lies in a sheltered position at the foot of the Ochil Hills and one of its chief attractions is the wooded Dollar Glen, through which a path runs to Castle Campbell. This stands on a promontory overlooking the confluence of two streams, intriguingly named the Burn of Sorrow and the Burn of Care. Until 1490 it was called Castle Glume, hence it is sometimes referred to as the 'castle of gloom'.

Dollar is one of the Hillfoot towns, small mill towns which gained prosperity through the woollen industry. A mill trail links these communities and guides visitors through the district. The Mill Trail Visitor Centre at Alva is the focal point of this trail and it has displays explaining the history of the local woollen industry.

*[i] Mill Trail Visitor Centre, Alva*

▶ *Leave by the **B913** and turn right at the **A977**. Turn right at the **A876**, heading towards Kincardine Bridge, turn left just before and follow an unclassified road along the coast to Culross.*

**4 Culross,** Fife

Culross, frozen in time, is possibly Scotland's most remarkable town. During the 16th and 17th centuries, it prospered by trading in coal and salt with ports across the North Sea, but when this failed, the town declined. Fortunately it never really changed during the industrial development of the succeeding centuries, so although it is quite small it preserves many of the features that have been lost in other ancient towns. The NTS has played a major part in conserving this unique place, especially through its 'Little Houses Scheme', and today numerous buildings can be visited, whisking you back through the centuries. Cobbled streets and white-painted buildings with pantile roofs help to produce an air that is so very different from any other Scottish town and the virtual completeness of the medieval character of Culross has attracted many television and film companies to locations here.

The town's main building, the Palace, was never in fact a royal mansion at all, but the home of the local laird, George Bruce, and was originally built between 1597 and 1611. The title deeds describe it as 'the Palace of Great Lodging in the Sand Haven of Culross'. Among the other fascinating buildings here, visitors should look out for the Town House, the Study, the House of the Evil Eye and the abbey.

▶ *Continue on the unclassified road, then turn right at the **B9037**. Join the **A994**, which leads to Dunfermline (7 miles/11km).*

**5 Dunfermline,** Fife
Dunfermline was built around a substantial Benedictine abbey which was constructed in the 12th century. Apart from the abbey church, there are ruins of the monastery's domestic buildings and the palace, which was often used as the abbey's guest house. The abbey church was a favoured place with the Scottish kings and it superseded Iona as their place of burial.

The great warrior King Robert the Bruce was buried here, but it was only in 1818 that this fact was known for certain. During some restoration work, a skeleton, dressed in what may have been royal robes, was discovered and it was noticed that the breast bone had been sawn in order to remove one of the organs. This would have been in accordance with Bruce's deathbed wish in 1329 that upon his death his heart be removed and taken to the Holy Land as his way of making up for not taking part in the Crusades. His heart was buried in Melrose Abbey. Abbot House was the administrative centre of the abbey and it now has a new lease of life as a museum depicting its use over the centuries. Opposite the door of the abbey church is the entrance to the extensive and pleasant Pittencrieff Park. Within the grounds is Pittencrieff House, built in the 17th century. There is a small museum of local history with an art gallery and a costume exhibition here.

The great fortress of Blackness Castle looking out over the North Sea

**SPECIAL TO...**

There can be few bridges in the world so distinctive in appearance as the Forth Rail Bridge, which can be seen from many places on this route. This was the world's first major structure to be made entirely of steel and it took eight years, from 1883 to 1890, to erect. It is over 1½ miles (2.5km) long and from mid-winter to mid-summer it expands by 3 feet!

Just by the edge of the park stands the cottage where Andrew Carnegie was born in 1835. In 1848 his family emigrated to the US where he made his massive fortune in the steel industry. He then began to give much of his wealth away, buying Pittencrieff Park for the town and establishing trusts that endowed libraries and other public enterprises. The cottage is now the location of the Andrew Carnegie Birthplace Museum.

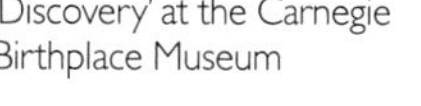

Detail of the plaque 'Discovery' at the Carnegie Birthplace Museum

[i] *13–15 Maygate (seasonal)*

▶ *Leave by the **A823** and the **A823M**, then join the **M90** to cross the Forth Road Bridge (toll). Turn right on to the **A904**, then right along the **B903** to Blackness (14 miles/23 km).*

**6 Blackness,** West Lothian
The little village of Blackness, once an important seaport, is dominated by the great fortress of Blackness Castle. This was built to protect the port which was the harbour for the great royal palace at Linlithgow. Construction of the castle started as a fairly small affair in the 15th century, but with later technical improvements in artillery it became necessary to strengthen it to withstand massive sea-borne attacks. After the Union with England in 1707, it was one of the four castles in Scotland allowed to be left fortified.

▶ *Return until the **A904** is met. Turn left on to the **A904** and then follow the **A803** to Linlithgow.*

**7 Linlithgow,** West Lothian
The history of the town is intimately interwoven with that of the palace, the birthplace of Mary, Queen of Scots, and one of the country's most important historical buildings. There was some form of royal residence here in the 14th century, but the present palace was not started until the early 16th century. It was certainly a substantial and well-defended building, occupying an attractive site overlooking Linlithgow Loch. Everything seems to have been constructed to a grand scale, especially the enormous fireplaces and the ornate fountain that stands in the quadrangle in the heart of the building.

Linlithgow has a number of other fine buildings and monuments sited near the palace or on the main street and these include the Church of St Michael, the Burgh Halls, the House of the Binns and the Cross Well. The history of the town is told in The Linlithgow Story.

The Union Canal, which joined the Forth and Clyde Canal to the heart of Edinburgh, runs along the town's outskirts. This was originally built to bring coal from Lanarkshire into the capital. Work on the canal started in 1818 and it opened in 1822, finally closing in 1965. Today there is a canal museum at the Manse Road Basin and cruises are available.

[i] *Burgh Halls, The Cross (seasonal)*

▶ *Leave by the **A706** to Bo'ness.*

**8 Bo'ness,** Falkirk
This long-established industrial town was once the third most important seaport in Scotland until the building of the Forth and Clyde Canal and the establishment of the major port at Grangemouth put it into decline. Bo'ness's past has included such diverse enterprises as potteries, salt pans, iron foundries and coal mines and it is most appropriate that the town's visitor facilities have taken advantage of this rich industrial legacy. It is possible to walk through the tunnels of the Birkhill Clay Mine, accessible via the the Bo'ness and Kinneil Railway, which operates steam trains on its 3½-mile (6km) track along the foreshore.

Interior of the House of the Binns, Linlithgow, the historic home of the Dalyell family

[i] *Car Park, Seaview Place*

▶ *Leave by the **A904** and turn right at the **A905**. Turn left at the **A88** and right at the **A9**. Continue on this road towards Stirling and turn left at the **A872** to reach the NTS Visitor Centre at Bannockburn.*

One of the old trains on Bo'ness's steam railway

### FOR HISTORY BUFFS

In Dunmore Park, southeast of Stirling on the A905, is a curious garden retreat called the Dunmore Pineapple, complete with a pineapple-shaped roof. It was originally part of an extensive walled garden at Dunmore Park and was built in 1761 by the Earl of Dunmore on his return from holding the governorship of Jamaica. It has been restored by the NTS and can be rented as a holiday home.

**9 Bannockburn,** Stirling
The Battle of Bannockburn in 1314 was one of the most important events in the fight for Scottish independence. At the time, an English force held Stirling Castle and was being besieged by Robert the Bruce's brother. The English army, led by their king, came north to relieve the castle and a pitched battle took place here. The Scots army, led by Bruce, eventually routed the enemy after they took fright at seeing a 'new' army (in reality, the Scots camp followers) come over the Gillies Hill. The story of the battle and the history of that period is explained in the NTS's Heritage Centre and the impressive memorial to the battle is in the form of a bronze equestrian statue of Bruce erected where his command post is thought to have been positioned.

[i] *NTS Visitor Centre*

► *Return along the **A872** and turn left at the **B8051** to Stirling.*

### BACK TO NATURE

As Scotland's ice caps receded at the end of the last Ice Age, the reduction of the great weight of ice made the land rise slowly. This happened gradually and the sea level slowly fell to its present position. Areas such as the low-lying 'carselands' around remained undrained until the agricultural improvements of the late 18th century. The Blairdrummond Moss remained untouched until 1767 when the layers of peat were stripped off; extensive draining, ploughing and liming have now led to the establishment of a rich stretch of agricultural land.

A dramatic view of the Forth Rail Bridge

TOUR
12

# Raspberry Fields Forever

**1/2 DAYS • 120 MILES • 192KM** The land circling the Sidlaw Hills is an area often overlooked by tourists, yet it has much to offer in terms of pretty coastal villages and green, gentle countryside. The renowned 'Fair City' of Perth is the chief town of this important farming region, and is located in a most attractive setting beside the River Tay.

ITINERARY

| | |
|---|---|
| **PERTH** | ▶ **Dunkeld (15m-24km)** |
| DUNKELD | ▶ **Blairgowrie (11m-18km)** |
| BLAIRGOWRIE | ▶ **Meigle (8m-13km)** |
| MEIGLE | ▶ **Glamis (7m-11km)** |
| GLAMIS | ▶ **Brechin (17m-27km)** |
| BRECHIN | ▶ **House of Dun (5m-8km)** |
| HOUSE OF DUN | ▶ **Montrose (4m-6km)** |
| MONTROSE | ▶ **Arbroath (13m-21km)** |
| ARBROATH | ▶ **Carnoustie (7m-11km)** |
| CARNOUSTIE | ▶ **Dundee (11m-18km)** |
| DUNDEE | ▶ **Perth (22m-35km)** |

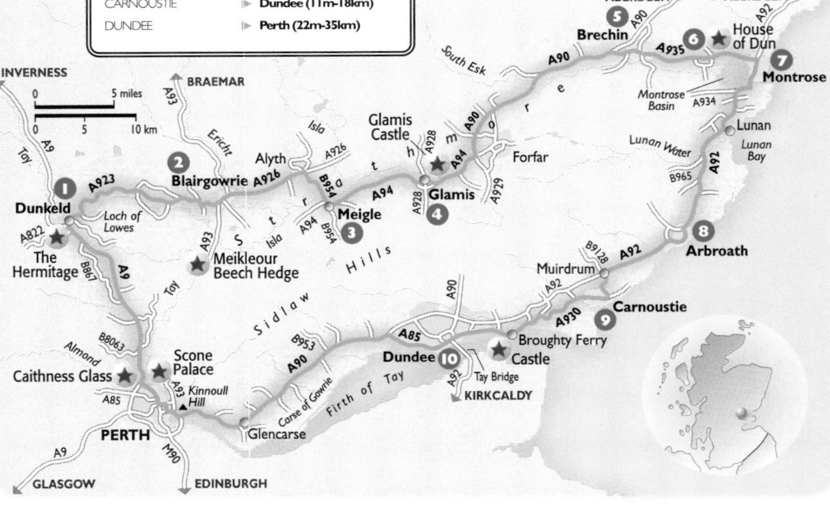

[i] *Lower City Mills, West Mill Street, Perth; Caithness Glass Car Park, Inveralmond, by the A9*

► *Leave by the **A912** and join the **A9** (to Inverness). Turn right at the **A923** and follow this into Dunkeld (15 miles/24km).*

**1 Dunkeld,** Perth & Kinross
The history of Dunkeld goes back to Pictish times but the town's importance in Scottish history is as Kenneth MacAlpin's ecclesiastical capital in the 9th century. This eventually led to the construction, in the early 14th century, of the cathedral which stands by the banks of the River Tay. Although much of it is roofless, the choir was restored and within it is the tomb of Alexander Stewart, the notorious 'Wolf of Badenoch'.

In the centre of Dunkeld stands a very ornate fountain and between this and the cathedral are the Little Houses, which were built in the late 17th century. Look out for the NTS's The Ell Shop on whose wall is an original ell measure, a little over a metre long, which was used for measuring cloth. Beside it The Duchess Anne, formerly a school, is the venue for the cathedral art exhibition each summer.

[i] *The Cross*

**FOR HISTORY BUFFS**

Perth became important when Scotland's first king, Kenneth MacAlpin, took the legendary Stone of Destiny to Scone Palace which lies just to the north of the town. Legend has it that this was the biblical Jacob's pillow and it became the 'throne' upon which Scottish kings were crowned. In 1296, Edward I (the 'Hammer of the Scots') removed this symbol of Scottish nationhood to London's Westminster Abbey, but on Christmas Eve in 1950 the stone was taken by a small group of Scots. It 'disappeared' until 1952, when the stone was recovered at Arbroath Abbey (whether or not it was the original stone remains unresolved), and in 1997 it was finally returned to the Scots.

**RECOMMENDED WALKS**

Kinnoull Hill, about a mile (1.5km) from the centre of Perth, offers an outstanding view over the surrounding countryside. The Hermitage near Dunkeld is the site of a woodland walk in the care of the NTS. Two interesting follies and a waterfall make a stroll here a pleasant outing.

**BACK TO NATURE**

The Loch of the Lowes lies to the east of Dunkeld and there are plenty of hides from which it is possible to see many birds, including ospreys and Slavonian grebes in the summer. In winter, look out for greylag geese, pochards and goldeneyes.

► *Continue on the **A923** and follow it for 11 miles (18km) to Blairgowrie.*

Detail from the window above the altar in Dunkeld Cathedral

The wonderfully ornate Glamis Castle, childhood home of the late Queen Mother

**SPECIAL TO...**

Much of the area, especially near Blairgowrie, is famous for its raspberries. Look out for 'pick your own' signs where you can sample this delicious fruit.

**2 Blairgowrie,** Perth & Kinross

Blairgowrie is well situated as a touring centre, lying at the junction of five roads. The district's most remarkable feature is just 5 miles (8km) to the south on the A93: the magnificent Meikleour Beech Hedge. This was originally planted in 1746 and is now some 110 feet (33m) high and 2,000 feet (600m) long. It is trimmed back once every 10 years.

*i* *26 Wellmeadow*

▶ *Leave by the* ***A926*** *then turn right at the* ***B954*** *to Meigle.*

**3 Meigle,** Perth & Kinross

For such a small village, the local museum has a remarkable collection of carved stones. More than 30 significant stones have been found in the area and these portray ancient symbols such as Pictish beasts, a Persian god and a horseman. The dates vary, but most of them are from the 8th to 10th centuries.

To add further interest to the local history, the village may have had connections with King Arthur – his consort, Queen Guinevere, is believed to be buried here (a claim also made by Glastonbury).

▶ *Leave by the* ***A94*** *to approach Glamis, then take a minor road on the left to reach the village and the castle.*

**4 Glamis,** Angus

Glamis Castle, the childhood home of the late Queen Mother, and birthplace of the late Princess Margaret, is an excellent example of a large medieval tower house that has, over the centuries, been transformed into a palace. The long straight driveway leads directly up to its rather small entrance, an approach that seems to emphasise the symmetrical structure of the castle.

In comparison to the castle and its grand style of living, the village of Glamis houses the Angus Folk Museum. This occupies a row of 18th-century cottages and consists of rooms furnished as in bygone days. There are, for example, a kitchen, laundry, schoolhouse and a forge, all with appropriate equipment.

▶ *Continue on the* ***A94****, then turn left on to the* ***A90****. Bear right at the* ***A935*** *to enter Brechin (17 miles/27km).*

**5 Brechin,** Angus

The pleasant town of Brechin, with its many red sandstone buildings, lies in the heart of the rich agricultural area of Strathmore. Its most interesting feature is the tall, slim Round Tower, one of only two in Scotland. It dates from the 11th century and stands beside the remains of the 13th-century cathedral.

*Brechin Castle (seasonal)*

*Continue on the **A935** and follow it for 5 miles (8km) to the House of Dun. (The driveway is to the left.)*

**6 House of Dun,** Angus
This 18th-century house was designed by William Adam, father of the Adam brothers who designed so many important buildings in Scotland. Restored by the NTS, it now reflects how it would have looked over 250 years ago, with its public rooms featuring a wealth of exceptionally ornate baroque plasterwork.

*Continue on the **A935**, then turn right at the **A92** for Montrose.*

**7 Montrose,** Angus
Montrose's wide main street lends an air of spaciousness to this seaside town. Its history, going back to the 10th century, owes much to the Montrose Basin, which gave the town a uniquely strategic position on the east coast. It has been an important port for a long time and its economy enjoyed a boost from the North Sea oil industry. Of more interest to most visitors is the town's beach, which is backed by sand dunes.

*Bridge Street (seasonal)*

*Continue on the **A92** and follow it to Arbroath.*

FOR CHILDREN

The seaside resorts have good beaches but one 'remoter' stretch of sand can be found at the village of Lunan. The car park at Lunan Bay's superb beach is reached by turning seawards just as the village is entered.

**8 Arbroath,** Angus
Arbroath is a busy seaside town which attracts many visitors each summer. It also has an active fishing industry and this is the home of the delicious 'Arbroath smokie', a line-caught haddock that is smoke-cured using oak chips. The town's place in Scottish history was assured by the Declaration of Arbroath, a document drawn up in 1320 to state the independence of Scotland after the Battle of Bannockburn in 1314. The declaration was drawn up in the abbey, originally a priory founded in the 12th century.

*Market Place*

*Continue on the **A92**, then turn left at the **A930** to enter Carnoustie.*

**9 Carnoustie,** Angus
Carnoustie's fame as a resort is based on its extensive beach and the golf courses which lie on the sandy links. The championship courses have hosted the British and Scottish Open events.

*1B High Street (seasonal)*

*Continue on the **A930** to Dundee.*

**10 Dundee,** Dundee City
The old saying that the industrial town of Dundee is famous for jute, jam and journalism is less correct these days as the town's prosperity is now based on a much broader spectrum of industries, the jute mills having been converted into luxury flats. Its coastal site has meant that the sea has always been of importance and many wooden ships for the whaling industry were built here. These ships had to withstand cruel polar conditions and this expertise was used in 1901 to build Captain Scott's ship *Discovery*, now berthed alongside the Discovery Point Visitor Centre. In the nearby Victoria Dock is the frigate *Unicorn*, built in 1825. The city's history is told in the McManus Galleries, which hold the local art collection. The galleries also house a natural history collection that includes the skeleton of a whale. The city's connections with the whaling industry are displayed in the 15th-century Broughty Castle Museum, appropriately sited by the Firth of Tay.

*21 Castle Street*

*Leave by the **A85**, then turn left along the **A90** for the return to Perth.*

SCENIC ROUTES

Hills are never very far away from much of this route and the views of the Sidlaw Hills and the foothills of the Grampian Mountains are good. On the drive to Dunkeld, it is interesting to note that the road is approaching a distinctive line of hills. These mark the geological boundary called the Highland Boundary Fault and indicate the 'real' start of the Scottish Highlands.

Scott's ship *Discovery*, berthed at Discovery Point

TOUR
13

# The Kingdom of Fife

**1/2 DAYS • 97 MILES • 156KM** Surrounded by the firths of Forth and Tay, the most important town in the Kingdom of Fife is undoubtedly St Andrews. Famous primarily for being the golfing capital of the world and home to the Royal & Ancient Golf Club, St Andrews is also the location of Britain's third oldest university after Oxford and Cambridge, founded in 1410. The rest of the region is dominated by pretty fishing villages and much land is given over to agriculture.

| ITINERARY | |
|---|---|
| **ST ANDREWS** | ► **Crail (10m-16km)** |
| CRAIL | ► **Anstruther (4m-6km)** |
| ANSTRUTHER | ► **Pittenweem (1m-2km)** |
| PITTENWEEM | ► **St Monans (2m-3km)** |
| ST MONANS | ► **Elie (3m-5km)** |
| ELIE | ► **Falkland (21m-34km)** |
| FALKLAND | ► **Scotlandwell (12m-19km)** |
| SCOTLANDWELL | ► **Kinross (8m-13km)** |
| KINROSS | ► **Abernethy (13m-21km)** |
| ABERNETHY | ► **Cupar (13m-21km)** |
| CUPAR | ► **St Andrews (10m-16km)** |

*i* *70 Market Street*

**1 Crail,** Fife
Crail's small harbour is a delightful place set at the bottom of a steep lane. The Museum and Heritage Centre tells the story of the village. Another attraction is the working pottery, occupying restored medieval buildings.

*i* *Crail Museum and Heritage Centre (seasonal)*

*Follow the **A917** for 4 miles (6km) to Anstruther.*

**2 Anstruther,** Fife
The Scottish Fisheries Museum on the seafront tells the story of the fishing industry in this part of the country. In the harbour is one of the museum's great attractions, the fishing boat *The Reaper*. To the north is Scotland's Secret Bunker, where visitors can explore the 100-foot (30m) deep labyrinth created during the Cold War to house government and military bosses in the event of nuclear war.

*i* *Scottish Fisheries Museum, Harbourhead (seasonal)*

*Continue on the **A917** for 1 mile (1.5km) to Pittenweem.*

Crow-stepped and pantiled houses cluster round Crail harbour, once the haunt of smugglers

**3 Pittenweem,** Fife
There is always lots to see in Pittenweem, the busiest fishing port along this coast, when the fishing fleet are coming in with their catches. Herring used to be the major catch here, but nowadays the fishermen concentrate on whitefish.

The religious buildings date back many centuries: the parish church's tower was built in the 16th century and there are remains of a 12th-century priory where witches were 'done to death'.

Nearby St Fillan's Cave is reputed to be the 7th-century sanctuary of St Fillan. It is responsible for the name of the town, since Pittenweem in the ancient Pictish language means 'the Place of the Cave'.

Laid-up fishing boat being painted

To the north of Pittenweem stands Kellie Castle, dating from 1360, which has very pleasant sheltered gardens.

*Continue on the **A917** for 2 miles (3km) to St Monans.*

**4 St Monans,** Fife
St Monans (or St Monance) is a pleasant fishing town, with houses clustered around the local harbour and its kirk standing almost in the sea.

One rather unusual feature of the town is that it has fewer licensed premises than neighbouring villages, the result of the town being 'dry' between 1900 and 1947. The 18th-century windmill tower is all that remains of a more extensive industrial complex.

*Continue on the **A917** for 3 miles (5km) to Elie.*

The sands stretch away into the distance along this section of the Fife coastal walk between Elie and St Monans

**RECOMMENDED WALKS**

The path from St Monans to Elie offers an interesting route past St Monans' church and the ruins of two castles, and ends at Elie Ness where there is a fine view of the village. Inland, the walk to the top of East Lomond gives good views over the countryside.

**5 Elie,** Fife

This appealing resort offers fine sandy beaches and bathing, golf courses and shelter to the yachts that lie in the harbour. The sea has not always been kind to Elie and the houses along the bay have high walls to protect them. There are many fine 17th-century houses in South Street.

▶ *Continue on the* ***A917*** *to Upper Largo, then join the* ***A915*** *to Windygates. Join the* ***A911*** *and head towards Glenrothes. Turn right at a roundabout at the junction with the* ***A92*** *and head northwards. Turn left when the* ***A912*** *is met and follow this to Falkland.*

**6 Falkland,** Fife

The village of Falkland is dominated by the very grand palace, which was originally erected by the Stuarts as a royal hunting seat. It dates from the 16th century and stands on a site that had been fortified from the 13th century. The buildings on the southern side of the main courtyard are in French Renaissance style, and are arguably the best of their kind in Britain. They are in a fine state of preservation and have some excellent furnishings; the painted wooden ceilings are particularly good. Within the grounds is a Royal Tennis Court, built for James V in 1539, before rackets were invented.

The village itself has numerous fascinating small houses, many of them dating back to the 17th and 18th centuries.

▶ *Continue on the* ***A912*** *and turn left at the* ***A91*** *and left again at the* ***B919****. Turn left at the* ***A911*** *and follow it to Scotlandwell.*

**SCENIC ROUTE**

The Fife Coastal Tourist Route has been devised and signposted by the Scottish Tourist Board (look for the brown signs). It guides visitors along a scenic journey through pretty ports, historic towns and rolling farmland between the Kincardine and Tay road bridges, taking in views of the Isle of May, the Bass Rock and distant Edinburgh.

**7 Scotlandwell,** Perth & Kinross

The village is named after the well to which pilgrims travelled during medieval times. Roman soldiers are said to have drunk from it in AD 84. However, the present stone cistern dates back only to the 19th century.

▶ *Leave by the* ***B920*** *and turn right at the* ***B9097****. On meeting the* ***B996****, turn right and follow it to Kinross.*

**8 Kinross,** Perth & Kinross

Kinross, the county town of the former Kinross-shire, stands by the shores of Loch Leven, the largest loch in the Scottish lowlands. Of the two largest islands in the loch, St Serf's Island has the remains of a 9th-century priory.

Castle Island is rather nearer the town and can be reached by a local ferry. On it stands Loch Leven Castle, best known as the prison from which Mary, Queen of Scots made her escape in 1568. The castle dates from the 14th century and the building and its garden used to occupy the whole of the island until in the early 19th century the loch's level was lowered, increasing the size of the island. The castle, a five-storey keep, was occupied for about 250 years but was roofless by the end of the 17th century. Kinross town is dominated by imposing Kinross House.

*i* *Kinross Service Area, Junc 6, M90*

▶ *Continue on the* ***B996*** *and join the* ***A922****. After Milnathort, follow the* ***B996*** *then the* ***A91****. Turn left at the* ***A912*** *and right at the* ***A913*** *to Abernethy.*

Loch Leven Castle, prison to Mary, Queen of Scots

### 9 Abernethy, Perth & Kinross

One of the main features of this quiet little village is the 11th-century round tower, very similar to Brechin's. Abernethy may have been an important centre in Pictish times and several symbol stones have been found in the vicinity; one of them is set against the wall of the tower.

▶ *Continue on the* ***A913*** *and follow it for 13 miles (21km) to Cupar.*

### 10 Cupar, Fife

It is rather surprising that this little town, and not St Andrews, was the county town of Fife, but this was due to its central position and because it was the seat of the Thanes of Fife.

Cupar must surely have a place in the history of drama as it was here in 1535 that the first public performance of the satire *Ane satire of the Thrie Estaits* took place. This scorned the church, the nobility and the burgesses of the towns. The play has certainly stood the test of time and it is still performed on the Scottish stage.

To the south of Cupar stands the Hill of Tarvit, a mansion house under the ownership of the NTS. The present building was constructed at the beginning of the 20th century to house a fine collection of antique furniture, much of it French. In contrast to all the finery, the restored Edwardian laundry holds a special fascination for most visitors.

To the west of it is Scotstarvit Tower, a well-preserved five-storey tower house built in the 17th century.

▶ *Leave by the* ***A91*** *and follow it back to St Andrews.*

#### FOR CHILDREN

The Scottish Deer Centre at Rankeilour Park includes trailer rides around the park and close encounters with many species of deer. This is also the home of Raptor World, which offers three flying demonstrations a day, Bird of Prey Experience days and handling sessions which bring visitors close to a variety of owls, hawks and falcons. The park also has indoor and outdoor playgrounds.

# THE NORTHEAST

The Cairngorm Mountains, Britain's highest land mass, dominate the northeast of Scotland in many ways. The great glaciers that flowed down from these granite hills during the Ice Age cut their way through the rock, leaving behind a series of river valleys that radiate out from the mountains and flow down to the sea.

In days gone by, it was easier to travel by sea than land and this encouraged coastal settlements to prosper wherever there was a sheltered harbour and the opportunity to trade with other ports, notably those in countries across the North Sea. Today, this coastline boasts some of Britain's most important fishing harbours. But while the fishing industry is long established, it is the North Sea oil developments that have transformed the Aberdeen area and made that city Scotland's 'oil capital'.

The northeast lies in the hills' rain shadow, making this region much drier than the west coast and helping to produce some of Scotland's most profitable farming land. Agriculture continues to be an important industry and much of the region's population lives in scattered towns and villages set among good agricultural land.

The often turbulent times of the Middle Ages saw the establishment of a class of rich farmers, warriors and traders who built keeps, castles and fortified houses. In time, many of these were destroyed while others were extended and embellished and some later transformed into great country houses. Today, we are left with a rich legacy of castles, large and small, reflecting the changing fortunes of family, clan and nation.

The wide variety of landscapes is reflected in the wildlife found in the region. The hills and the high forests are home to deer and birds of prey while the coast, with its sandstone cliffs providing ledges for nesting birds, has countless millions of seabirds.

Walkers, birdwatchers, families seeking tranquil beaches and visitors simply touring around will all find lots to do in this corner of Scotland. To many foreign visitors, Scotland is famous as the home of whisky, and in the northeast a number of internationally famous distilleries are linked together by the 'Malt Whisky Trail', which allows people to learn the secrets of the whisky-making process and inevitably to enjoy a 'wee dram' at the end of a distillery tour.

Traditional Scotsware is sold at MacNaughton's shop at Pitlochry

Farming exhibits from the Falconer Museum, Forres

**Tour 14**

Inverness's strategic position at the meeting point of so many land and sea routes has meant that the town and its surrounding district have seen the comings and goings of many different people. Picts, Vikings and warring Scots clans have all left their mark, but the most significant historical event, the Battle of Culloden in 1746, has left its mark all over Scotland; in order to understand the history of the Highlands, the battlefields should be visited. This tour encompasses a wide variety of scenery, from the glorious sandy beaches of the Moray Firth to the pine forests that lie below the Cairngorms, a combination which attracts tourists throughout the year.

**Tour 15**

The seaside towns and villages of Moray have much to offer the visitor: picturesque harbours, sandy beaches and a wealth of traditional buildings that give the district its own particular charm. Inland, the districts by the peaty waters of the River Spey are home to many of Scotland's most celebrated whisky distilleries.

**Tour 16**

The coastal part of this route visits a variety of harbours, from the small picture-postcard ones like charming Crovie to the big, bustling Peterhead. Each has its own fascination and each reflects the ways in which the sea has been so important to the people of this area. Behind this, the rich countryside, with its landscape of rolling hills, has prosperous farming towns and villages. The long history of settlement in this part of the country is marked by the existence of prehistoric stone circles.

**Tour 17**

The fact that this tour is the longest one in the region reflects the sheer scale of the Cairngorms. Motorists have to drive round the margins of the hills, but this does allow the visitor many different opportunities to explore the small glens that cut into the sides of these great mountains. There is a great deal of variety on the route; the traditional highland resort of Pitlochry, the more modern Aviemore and the small villages that lie to the east. Walkers will find plenty to keep them busy on this tour, as will followers of other outdoor pursuits.

**Tour 18**

The visitor to this part of the country might be forgiven for getting the impression there's a castle round every corner! But the district has more to offer than fine old buildings; there are peaceful villages, a rugged coastline and rich agricultural countryside to explore.

A splendid border at Crathes Castle Gardens

TOUR
**14**

# Land of Macbeth

**1/2 DAYS • 106 MILES • 169KM**

History and magnificent scenery are ever present on this tour. Just outside Inverness lies Culloden, where the defeat of Bonnie Prince Charlie ruined the last hope of a Stuart restoration to the British throne. Mysteries, too, abound on this tour, from brooding Cawdor Castle, of which Shakespeare's Macbeth was Thane, to the dark waters of Loch Ness, perhaps home to Britain's most famous monster.

ITINERARY

| | |
|---|---|
| **INVERNESS** | ▶ **Fort George (12m-19km)** |
| FORT GEORGE | ▶ **Cawdor Castle (8m-13km)** |
| CAWDOR CASTLE | ▶ **Nairn (5m-8km)** |
| NAIRN | ▶ **Brodie Castle (7m-11km)** |
| BRODIE CASTLE | ▶ **Forres (4m-6km)** |
| FORRES | ▶ **Findhorn (5m-8km)** |
| FINDHORN | ▶ **Grantown-on-Spey (27m-43km)** |
| GRANTOWN-ON-SPEY | ▶ **Carrbridge (10m-16km)** |
| CARRBRIDGE | ▶ **Culloden (23m-37km)** |
| CULLODEN | ▶ **Inverness (5m-8km)** |

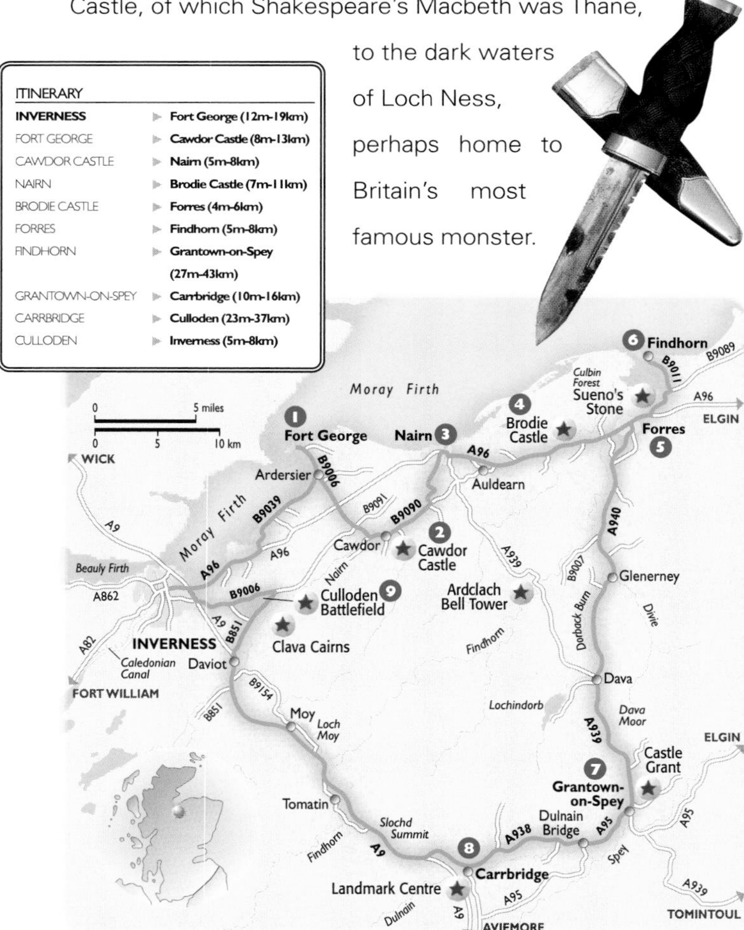

*i* *Castle Wynd*

**SPECIAL TO...**

While some visitors might have a few difficulties understanding the dialects of northeast Scotland, they should have no problem in Inverness. According to the experts, the 'purest' English is spoken here!

*Leave on the **A96**. Turn left at the **B9039** to reach Ardersier, then take the **B9006** to Fort George, a distance of 12 miles (19km).*

**1 Fort George,** Highland
This outstanding piece of military architecture, which is still used by the army, was originally built between 1748 and 1769, after the Battle of Culloden. It was guarded by 2,000 men and it has a series of walls, ramparts and ditches cleverly designed so that an attacking army would come under fire from several positions within the safety of the fort. It controls the seaward approach to Inverness as it is sited on a promontory that juts into the Moray Firth; this is rather fortunate for visitors as it allows good views across the firth to the Black Isle.

The fort is impressively huge, indeed the whole of Edinburgh Castle could fit into the parade ground! Since the fort has never seen military action, very few alterations have been made to its layout and a number of original buildings have been opened to visitors.

The B9006, which leads to the fort, was one of the military roads built by Caulfield in the 18th century when the government was trying to 'tame' this area. It follows the much older Via Regis (King's Road) which came from Aberdeen and crossed the Moray Firth to Chanonry Point at Fortrose.

*Return to Ardersier, then follow the **B9006** and the **B9090** to Cawdor Castle, 8 miles (13km).*

**2 Cawdor Castle,** Highland
The castle is dominated by the great 14th-century tower. Later additions had far less of a defensive role to play since they were built in less turbulent times. Still, the castle has many of the features that might be expected of a fortified house such as a drawbridge, a moat and a prison that was reached only by a trap door. The proprietors of Cawdor were called the Thanes of Cawdor, a title given by Shakespeare to Macbeth, but there is still much speculation about the real nature of this warrior king.

To the west stands 15th-century Kilravock Castle, a massive tower with walls some 7 feet (2m) thick. The tower has survived through the centuries, despite the laird backing the losing side at Culloden, and the victor, Cumberland, paying it a visit after the battle. Few castles in a similar position survived a visit by the 'Butcher'.

The Woodcock Room at Cawdor Castle

The golf course at Nairn

▶ *Continue on the **B9090** and follow it to Nairn.*

**3 Nairn,** Highland
This popular holiday resort, situated where the River Nairn meets the Moray Firth, has a fine beach, good golf course and activities for family holidays. Charlie Chaplin's favourite holiday resort for many years, it is a prosperous town, with large villas and hotels behind the main centre. Nearer the shore, the former fishermen's houses are tightly packed together in Fishertown, where there is a small museum.

To the east, the village of Auldearn was the site of a major battle in 1645 when the Royalist army defeated a force of Covenanters. The battleground can be seen from the top of a 12th-century motte, upon which now sits a 17th-century doocot (dovecot) which has 546 nest holes for pigeons.

*i 62 King Street (seasonal)*

▶ *Leave by the **A96** and turn left at the entrance to Brodie Castle.*

FOR HISTORY BUFFS

Highland Ardclach Bell Tower, southeast of Nairn, off the A939, was built in 1655 when the local laird, a Covenanter, was continually being harassed by Royalists. The tower served both as a prison and a watchtower and its bell was used to summon people to the local church.

BACK TO NATURE

Culbin Forest is a large conifer plantation between Nairn and Findhorn, planted in order to stabilise the area of shifting sand. The dunes increased in size during the 17th century and inundated the village of Culbin and its surrounding rich farmland. The forest is now home to varied wildlife, like badgers and capercaillie. Woodland plants include coralroot and twayblade orchids.

**4 Brodie Castle,** Moray
Originally, the castle had a Z-plan design, based on a rectangular block with square projecting towers at two opposite corners. This structure, dated 1567, was later added to and has seen many alterations over the centuries. Inside the castle is a good collection of 17th-, 18th- and 19th-century paintings, porcelain and French furniture.

At the eastern entrance to the castle stands the Pictish Rodney's Stone, decorated with a Pictish beast and fish monsters.

▶ *Regain the **A96** and continue on it to Forres.*

**5 Forres,** Moray
Forres' street pattern gives clues to the town's antiquity, with a main street wide enough to accommodate a market place and narrow 'wynds' (lanes) linking the medieval streets. High Street is dominated by the Town House of 1838, built on the site of the old Tolbooth, and the market cross which was erected in 1844. The Falconer Museum in Tolbooth Street has displays

of local history, natural history and geology.

The town's main antiquity lies just to the east of Forres, as the B9011 leaves the A96. This is Sueno's Stone, a huge cross-slab monument, over 20 feet (6m) high, carved out of a block of sandstone. It may date back to the 9th century and celebrate a victory by the men of Moray over Vikings based in Orkney.

*i* *116 High Street (seasonal)*

▶ *Continue on the **A96** then turn left at the **B9011** and follow this to Findhorn.*

**6 Findhorn,** Moray
This is the third village on this site to be called Findhorn. The first was destroyed by the sea and the second was inundated by shifting sand. The people rebuilt the village near the sea and it was once a prominent port, but its harbour is now given over to pleasure craft. The beaches here are extensive, with huge stretches of sand and dunes along the coast on either side of the estuary.

▶ *Return along the **B9011** and **A96** to Forres. Head south on the **A940** and join the **A939** for Grantown-on-Spey, 27 miles (43km).*

**7 Grantown-on-Spey,** Highland
This prosperous village, with its sturdy granite buildings along the main street, is a good touring centre for the district. It began as a planned village and from the start gained a reputation as a place to which Victorian doctors would send patients who were in need of a change of air. Today it is noted for its salmon-fishing, and walkers; anglers and families frequent the village during the summer, while in winter it accommodates skiers, Aviemore being only a short drive away.

Grantown Museum and Heritage Trust, opened in early 1999, illustrates the story of Grantown with exciting displays.

*i* *54 High Street (seasonal)*

▶ *Leave on the **A95** towards Aviemore, and at Dulnain Bridge turn on to the **A938** to Carrbridge.*

SPECIAL TO...

The thistle may be the symbol of Scotland, but heather is equally significant – in landscape, song and the hearts of homesick Highlanders. Visit the Speyside Heather Centre to find out all there is to know.

FOR CHILDREN

As well as its long sandy beaches, Findhorn is a centre for all kinds of water sports. Another popular attraction is the Landmark Highland Heritage and Adventure Park at Carrbridge (see page 92).

As well as its many treasures, Brodie Castle also has extensive grounds and a playground

**RECOMMENDED WALKS**

Grantown-on-Spey has many opportunities for walking, either through forests and woodlands or up some of the nearby hills; the Tourist Information Centre should be able to supply some details of suitable walks.

Culbin Forest has many marked walks that lead from the edge of the forest to the seashore, where there are long stretches of sandy beach.

**8 Carrbridge,** Highland

The old bridge at Carrbridge was built in 1717 after two men drowned at the traditional fording place. The bridge has since lost many of its stones and is precariously balanced over the river making it one of the most photogenic bridges in the country.

The village is a popular touring centre, all the more so because of the nearby Landmark Forest Heritage and Adventure Park, an entertaining park which features Clydesdale Horse demonstrations, a steam-powered sawmill, a 70-foot (21m) fire tower, a 3-D show on 'The Great Wood of Caledon', a runaway raft ride and a forest skills area. It is set in a pine forest and has many walks, including a tree-top trail 20 feet (6m) above the ground.

► *Continue on the **A938** and join the **A9**, heading towards Inverness. Just after Daviot, turn right on the **B851**. Turn left at the **B9006** and follow it to the NTS Visitor Centre at Culloden Moor.*

**9 Culloden,** Highland

Many bloody battles have been fought on Scottish soil, but of all the country's battlefields, Culloden is the saddest. Here, in 1746, the last great battle fought on British soil ended forever the Jacobite hopes of regaining the British crown. It was not a battle of Scots against English, nor was it a battle between different parts of Scotland, but it was the final battle of a long civil war. In its bloody aftermath, the face of the Highlands was changed forever. After the government's victory, the might of the British army was used to subjugate Scotland and to destroy many aspects of the Highlanders' way of life.

The battlefield has been laid out to show how the government troops, led by the Duke of Cumberland, faced the army of Charles Edward Stuart (the 'Bonnie Prince Charlie' of song and legend). Displays in the visitor centre describe the course of that dreadful battle, and the equally violent events which followed. Various small memorials on the battlefield indicate where particular clans were buried where they fell, but the principal monument is the Memorial Cairn, erected in 1881. The battle was fought on open moorland and Old Leanach Cottage, which was standing at the time of the battle, still remains. Its reconstructed interior illustrates how Scots people lived at the time of the battle in the mid-18th century.

A little to the east of Culloden, a minor road passes Clava Cairns, some of the most important cairns in the country. The three cairns may have been erected in the Late Stone Age or Early Bronze Age. The two outer ones are called 'passage graves' as a small passageway led through the cairn to a central chamber where bodies or cremated remains were deposited. These cairns have been topped with a massive flat slab and their perimeters were (and still are) marked by a ring of standing stones. Many of these perimeter stones have 'cup marks', small round indentations of unknown origin.

[i] *Daviot Wood, on the A9 by Inverness (seasonal)*

► *Continue along the **B9006** to the **A9**. Join the **A9** and return to Inverness, 5 miles (8km).*

The much-photographed pack-horse bridge at Carrbridge

# The Malt Whisky Trail

**1/2 DAYS • 89 MILES • 144KM** A tour for all members of the family, taking in as it does the wide, sandy beaches of Moray and the famed Speyside whisky distilleries of Strathisla, Glenfiddich and Glen Grant. The town of Elgin is the starting point for this tour; its many fine buildings, cathedral and ruined castle make it an ideal base which merits further exploration. It's still possible to wander down narrow 'wynds' that link the streets.

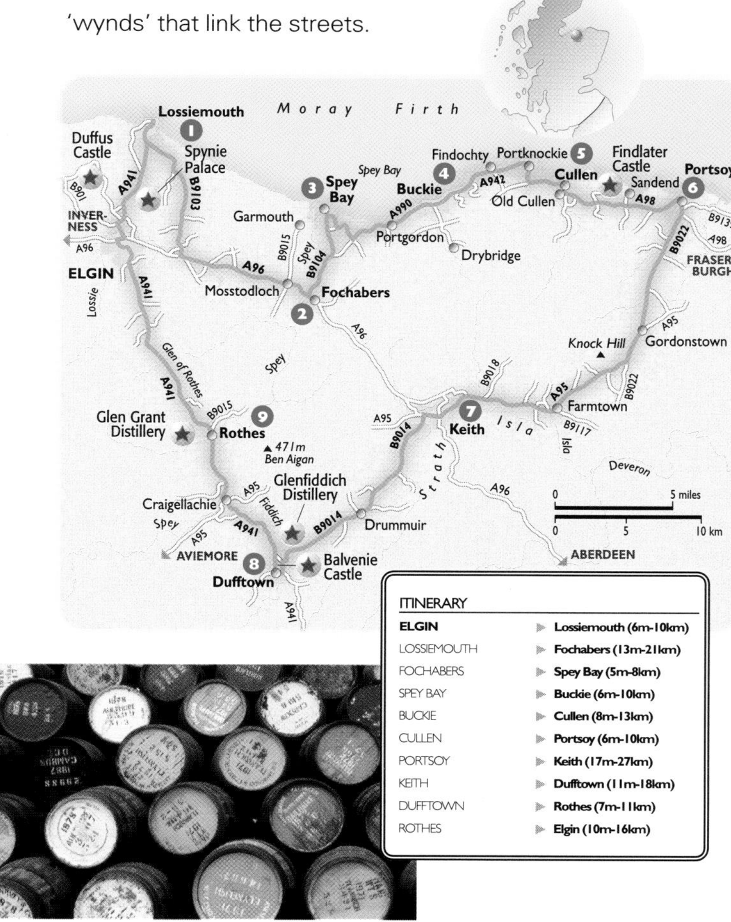


ITINERARY

| | |
|---|---|
| **ELGIN** | ▶ **Lossiemouth (6m-10km)** |
| LOSSIEMOUTH | ▶ **Fochabers (13m-21km)** |
| FOCHABERS | ▶ **Spey Bay (5m-8km)** |
| SPEY BAY | ▶ **Buckie (6m-10km)** |
| BUCKIE | ▶ **Cullen (8m-13km)** |
| CULLEN | ▶ **Portsoy (6m-10km)** |
| PORTSOY | ▶ **Keith (17m-27km)** |
| KEITH | ▶ **Dufftown (11m-18km)** |
| DUFFTOWN | ▶ **Rothes (7m-11km)** |
| ROTHES | ▶ **Elgin (10m-16km)** |

Braco's Banking House in Elgin High Street

[i] *17 High Street*

FOR HISTORY BUFFS

All around this area there are reminders of the trail of destruction that was left by the notorious Wolf of Badenoch, the outlawed son of Robert II, who terrorised the district in the late 14th century. Elgin's cathedral ruin is a notable example.

▶ *Leave Elgin on the* ***A941*** *and follow it north to Lossiemouth.*

**1 Lossiemouth,** Moray
This was developed as a port for landlocked Elgin after its original port of Spynie was cut off from the sea by shifting sand. It later became important during the 19th-century herring boom but today the catches are mainly shellfish and whitefish.

Lossiemouth is now a popular seaside resort, with extensive sandy beaches, a marina and a championship golf course. The Lossiemouth Fisheries and Community Museum features many aspects of local life and also has a display dedicated to Ramsay MacDonald, Britain's first Labour Prime Minister, who was born locally.

Just inland stand the ruins of the 15th-century Palace of Spynie, once the seat of the Bishops of Moray.

Duffus Castle is to the southwest of Lossiemouth in an area of flat, fertile farmland, lying only a few feet above sea level. This was a swamp when the original motte-and-bailey castle was built. A massive tower was added around 1300. Unfortunately the gravel foundations could not support the extra weight and part of the building's walls gave way and slid downhill.

FOR CHILDREN

The coast has many good beaches, which makes this area popular with families. Lossiemouth has two beaches; the east one is suitable for surfing while the west one offers safe bathing. Buckie, Elgin and Keith have swimming pools and pony-trekking is available at Lossiemouth, Drybridge and Garmouth.

► *Return along the **A941** and turn left at the **B9103**. Turn left at the **A96** and continue to Fochabers.*

**2 Fochabers,** Moray

Fochabers was originally situated within the grounds of Gordon Castle (not open) but was demolished at the end of the 18th century to make way for an extension to the castle. When it was being re-established in its present position, the streets were laid out in a grid pattern, and a number of fine Georgian houses remain, especially along the main street. The village's position beside the River Spey led to its growing importance as a river-crossing point, though no bridge crossed the river here until 1804 when the ferry was superseded by Fochabers Old Bridge. The river's east bank offers good walks and there are paths leading southward from the village to the very unusual 'earth pillars'. These were formed by erosion of the huge quantities of sand and pebble deposits that were laid down here by the Spey.

The factory of Baxters of Speyside is where the well-known tinned soups and other foodstuffs are made, and tours round the premises are available. The original Baxters' grocery shop, where the family's soups were first sold in Spey Street, has been reconstructed in the visitor centre and there is also a Victorian kitchen, showing how family meals were prepared during the 19th century.

The Fochabers Folk Museum in High Street has displays outlining the local history, as well as a costume collection and a display of horse-drawn vehicles.

► *Return along the **A96**, then turn right at the **B9104** to Spey Bay, 5 miles (8km).*

**3 Spey Bay,** Moray

The River Spey is Scotland's second longest river, with a length of 98 miles (158km), and it drains a large area of high ground, including part of the Cairngorms. Huge quantities of ice and water flowed down the river during the Ice Age, accounting for its great width and the massive deposits of sand and gravel. At Spey Bay, where the river meets the sea, the huge volume of peaty water stains the sea for quite a distance offshore. Longshore drift has encouraged a huge shingle spit to form at the river's mouth and salmon fishers have traditionally netted fish from this point. The Tugnet Ice-House, built in 1830 to store the ice that was used for packing salmon, stands near by. This is Scotland's largest ice-house and it has been restored to take on its new role as a museum that tells the story of the salmon fishery. The Moray Firth Wildlife Centre is also here, and features Moray Firth dolphins among its displays.

The bay is the northern terminus for the Speyside Way, the long-distance footpath that follows part of the river.

**BACK TO NATURE**

The coastline is home to many feeding birds when the tide is out. Spey Bay can be particularly good for birdwatchers, with terns, waders, oystercatchers and curlews to be sighted; and keep a look-out for seals a little offshore. Cruises to see dolphins in the Moray Firth leave from Inverness.

► *Return along the **B9104** and turn left at an unclassified road to Portgordon. Follow the roads to Portgordon, then join the **A990** and follow it to Buckie.*

Household goods on display at the Folk Museum in Fochabers

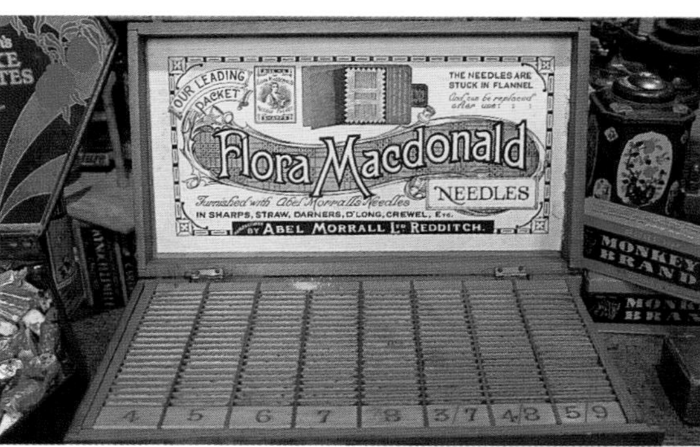

RECOMMENDED WALKS

The Speyside Way offers an opportunity to discover much about the district, and information on the various stages of the Way is available from local tourist information centres. There are also many good coastal walks offering fine views of the coastline. One interesting walk starts at Sandend (which is between Portsoy and Cullen) and follows the clifftop path to Findlater Castle; a return route past an old dovecot allows a circular walk to be made.

**4 Buckie,** Moray

Buckie stretches for about 3 miles (5km) along the coast and has developed through the amalgamation of smaller fishing communities. Its main harbour is very busy and the area behind it still has many traditional fishermen's houses dating back to the 19th century. The town's rich fishing tradition features strongly in the displays in The Buckie Drifter, the town's Maritime Heritage Centre.

The neighbouring village of Portgordon was once a centre for salmon-fishing and near the harbour stands a restored ice-house that was built in 1834.

▶ *Leave by the **A942** via Findochty and Portknockie. Turn left at the **A98** and follow this to Cullen.*

**5 Cullen,** Moray

The most obvious feature of this pleasant seaside village is the tall and graceful railway viaduct that slices Cullen in two. Trains no longer run on the line but its route is now part of a coastal path. Below the arches, the seaward part of the village has a little harbour with fishermen's houses and a fine stretch of beach. The golf course is jammed in between the shore and the former sea cliffs and on the course's seaward side stand the Three Kings, three tall sea stacks that have managed to withstand the onslaught of the pounding seas. The square has many interesting buildings round it, notably the old Town Hall. The very ornate mercat (market) cross was not originally in the square, but came from Old Cullen, which shared the same fate as the original Fochabers, and was demolished because the local laird felt the village was too close to his house. Cullen Auld Kirk, which is still in Old Cullen, dates from

Stone buildings above Portsoy harbour, the venue for the annual Scottish Traditional Small Boats Festival

the 16th century and contains some fine stone carvings.

At the western end of Cullen Bay is the curious Bow Fiddle Rock, an island with a natural arch that is probably best seen from the small village of Portknockie, which can be reached via a clifftop path.

To the east of the village stand the ruins of 15th-century Findlater Castle. This was owned by the Ogilvies but abandoned around 1600 in preference to the more comfortable Cullen House.

To the south, Deskford Church has rich carving.

*Continue on the **A98** to Portsoy.*

**6 Portsoy,** Aberdeenshire

Portsoy's sheltered harbour was once considered to be one of the safest in this part of Scotland, an attribute that did much to hasten the port's growth.

The village's great claim to fame, however, was its fine vein of pink and green serpentine stone, in great demand for its beauty. Some of it was used in the Palace of Versailles. This tradition still lives on and the harbourside Portsoy Marble Workshop has good examples of crafts made locally from Portsoy Marble, as well as pottery made on the premises.

*Leave by the **A98** and turn right at the **B9022**. Join the **A95** and follow it to Keith.*

**7 Keith,** Moray

Keith's role as an important centre for the rich neighbouring farmland reaches its high point each year during the long-established Agricultural Show.

The town lies in the broad valley of Strath Isla, hence the name of the local Strathisla Distillery. This is the gateway to the celebrated 'Malt Whisky Trail', a route connecting a number of distilleries that welcome visitors to their premises. Strathisla is the Highlands' oldest working distillery: production started in

Cullen harbour, with its famous railway viaduct

Speyside coopers still practising the old craft

1786, though illicit brewing and distilling may have taken place on the site as far back as the 13th century. Malt whisky tastings are a highlight of the tour, but as there are eight distilleries on the trail, make sure you have a teetotaller in the party to do the driving!

### SPECIAL TO...

The proximity of so many distilleries makes sampling the local whiskies a popular pastime for many visitors. The local tourist information centres can give details. The whisky is matured in oak barrels and at Craigellachie the Speyside Cooperage produces the barrels using time-honoured skills; there is a visitor centre where you can see the work in progress. The richness of the local fishing grounds means that much delicious fresh seafood should be available locally, and in Cullen the local delicacy is 'Cullen Skink', a soup based on smoked haddock.

► *Leave on the **A96** (to Inverness), then turn left at the **B9014** which continues into Dufftown.*

### 8 Dufftown, Moray

The centre of the village is dominated by the battlemented Clock Tower that was built in 1839. The clock on the tower came from Banff and played a part in the hanging of the unlucky James MacPherson. This poor fellow was a popular figure who had been robbing the rich and giving the proceeds to the poor, and a petition was raised to obtain a pardon for him. This was successful, but while the pardon was on its way, the local sheriff put the town's clock forward by an hour, making sure that the prisoner was duly dispatched before the reprieve arrived! Dufftown is the home of the Glenfiddich Distillery, which is on the Malt Whisky Trail. Production started here in 1887 and, unusually, the whisky is bottled on the site. At weekends, the Whisky Train departs from the town's railway station to run through several miles of picturesque scenery.

The substantial ruins of Balvenie Castle, ancient stronghold of the Comyns, lie close to the village. This was a massive building surrounding a central courtyard with a curtain wall 7 feet (2m) thick.

[i] *Clock Tower, The Square (seasonal)*

► *Leave by the **A941** and follow it for 7 miles (11km) to Rothes.*

### 9 Rothes, Moray

On the journey from Dufftown to Rothes the A941 crosses the River Spey near the village of Craigellachie. Just upstream from this crossing stands a graceful iron bridge, built by Thomas Telford between 1812 and 1815 to withstand floods when the river was swollen with spring meltwater from the mountains. Its great test came in 1829 when it survived a rise in water level of 15½ feet (4.5m). This is the country's oldest surviving iron bridge.

Founded in 1766 as a crofting township (a croft may be best described as a Scottish smallholding), Rothes developed into an important centre for distilling as no fewer than five distilleries were working here at one time. The Glen Grant Distillery, which is on the Malt Whisky Trail, was started in 1840 by two brothers and their whisky was one of the first to be bottled as a 'single malt'.

► *Continue on the **A941** for 10 miles (16km) to return to Elgin.*

### SCENIC ROUTES

The coastal part of this route is particularly pleasant as there are views of the cliffs, beaches and small settlements with their little harbours. Inland, the route goes through more good arable farming land, though south of Keith sheep farming becomes more important.

# The Fishing Trail

Much of Scotland's wealth has depended on the sea, and this tour takes in the major ports of Fraserburgh and Peterhead as well as the picturesque harbours of Crovie and Rosehearty. The tour starts at the town of Banff, whose history as a trading centre has left it with a legacy of fine buildings, including the 18th-century Adam-built Duff House.

| ITINERARY | |
|---|---|
| **BANFF** | ▶ **Macduff (1m-2km)** |
| MACDUFF | ▶ **Crovie (9m-14km)** |
| CROVIE | ▶ **Rosehearty (13m-21km)** |
| ROSEHEARTY | ▶ **Fraserburgh (4m-6km)** |
| FRASERBURGH | ▶ **Peterhead (18m-29km)** |
| PETERHEAD | ▶ **Cruden Bay (9m-14km)** |
| CRUDEN BAY | ▶ **Ellon (11m-18km)** |
| ELLON | ▶ **Pitmedden Garden (5m-8km)** |
| PITMEDDEN GARDEN | ▶ **Oldmeldrum (6m-10km)** |
| OLDMELDRUM | ▶ **Inverurie (5m-8km)** |
| INVERURIE | ▶ **Huntly (23m-37km)** |
| HUNTLY | ▶ **Banff (21m-34km)** |

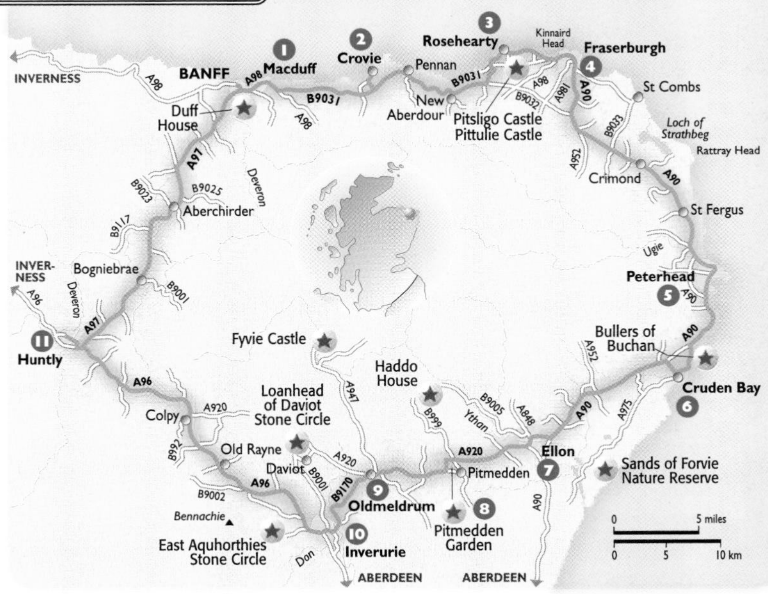


**2 DAYS • 125 MILES • 201KM**

*i* *Collie Lodge (seasonal)*

### RECOMMENDED WALKS

From Duff House, you can walk along a woodland path that leads beside the bank of the River Deveron and across the river's gorge via the Bridge of Alvah. From there, paths and country roads head towards Macduff and back to Banff.

▶ *Leave by the **A98** and follow it for a mile (2km) to Macduff.*

A decaying sea arch looms up from the shore at Tarlair, near Macduff

**1 Macduff,** Aberdeenshire
This is a busy fishing port and many of the townspeople are connected with some aspect of the industry. There is a weekday fishmarket and boats are still built and repaired in the local boatyard.

Doune church has a clock tower of which only three of the four sides have faces. The blank face looks towards neighbouring Banff and was deliberately left like that in response to the hanging of James MacPherson when his last-minute reprieve was on its way. The local people felt so enraged at this miscarriage of justice that they wanted to ensure the people of Banff would never know the correct time again.

### SCENIC ROUTES

On the journey round the coast, there are spectacular views of the cliffs, beaches and sand dune systems. Perhaps the best sections are between Macduff and Fraserburgh and between Peterhead and Cruden Bay.

▶ *Leave by the **A98** and turn left at the **B9031**. Turn left at the signposted minor road to Crovie.*

**2 Crovie,** Aberdeenshire
Crovie is one of the gems of the northeast, a tiny village of about 40 houses. Most of their gable ends face the shore to provide some form of protection from the furious sea that laps so close to them. There is no road beside the houses so the villagers use wheelbarrows to carry heavy objects along the sea wall from the car park to their homes.

### BACK TO NATURE

South of the charming little village of Pennan, used as the location for the film *Local Hero*, the Tore of Troup runs inland for about 8 miles (13km). This deep wooded ravine is very sheltered and is home to badgers, mink, foxes and deer; buzzards may also be seen.

▶ *Return to the **B9031** and turn left. Follow this road to Rosehearty, 13 miles (21km).*

**3 Rosehearty,** Aberdeenshire
Like so many little ports on this coast, Rosehearty's boom time was during the 19th century, when over 130 boats set out to fish for herring from here. Unfortunately, such heady days are long gone and many of the local fishermen work out of Fraserburgh.

Just outside the village lie the ruins of Pitsligo Castle,

Fraserburgh, one of Scotland's busiest ports

a courtyard castle which developed from a 15th-century keep. The building consisted of only three rooms – a kitchen, a dining room and a communal bedroom with 24 beds in it! To its east is Pittulie Castle, which dates from the 16th century but was abandoned in the 19th century.

### FOR CHILDREN

The Northfield Farm Museum, southwest of New Aberdour, features an aviary, llamas, farm machinery and a reconstructed smiddy.
Good beaches suitable for family outings are not as common as in other parts of this region, but St Combs and Cruden Bay are well worth visiting.

▶ *Continue on the **B9031** and turn left at the **A98** on the outskirts of Fraserburgh.*

### 4 Fraserburgh,
Aberdeenshire

This is one of the busiest fishing ports in the northeast, dealing in whiting, cod, sole, mackerel and herring. The fish-market is open most days of the week and there is usually something interesting to watch.

The town is built on the promontory of Kinnaird Head (which captured the attention of the Egyptian geographer Ptolemy in the 2nd century AD), and a castle was built here at the end of the 16th century, later converted into a lighthouse. This is now Scotland's Lighthouse Museum, with exhibits from around the country. Close to the castle stands the Wine Tower; this rather odd building, which has trap doors instead of an internal staircase, was erected in the 16th century but the use to which it was put is a mystery. Saltoun Square, in the centre of the town, has the old mercat cross and the Town House, which was built in 1855.

*i* *Saltoun Square (seasonal)*

▶ *Take the **A90** south to Peterhead (18 miles/29km).*

### 5 Peterhead,
Aberdeenshire

This was once Scotland's most important whaling centre until it gave way to the herring industry in 1818. Now Europe's busiest whitefish port and the EU's largest fishing port, it also sees a lot of commercial activity connected with supplying the North Sea oil rigs. The Peterhead lifeboat station is open to visitors. The history of the whaling and fishing industries is told in the Arbuthnot Museum and Art Gallery.

### SPECIAL TO...

This part of Scotland has important outcrops of granite, and many towns and villages on this tour have been built using this distinctive stone. Perhaps the most attractive is Peterhead's, which has large red crystals, quite different from Aberdeen's medium-grained blue-grey rock, or the light grey from Kemnay. Granite is formed when hot molten rock, called magma, cools while still beneath the earth's surface. The colour of the resulting rock depends on the minerals present and the size of the crystals on how slowly the rock cools (the slower the heat loss, the bigger the crystals).

▶ *Continue on the **A90**, then turn left at the **A975** to enter Cruden Bay.*

## 6 Cruden Bay,
Aberdeenshire

This popular summer resort has a long sandy beach and a fine golf course. Visitors may also like to know that the nearby ruins of 17th-century Slains Castle are said to have inspired the novel *Dracula*. The author, Bram Stoker, used to holiday at Cruden Bay and he began writing his famous gothic tale here in 1895.

A little further up the coast, the sea has carved deep clefts into the tall cliffs, the most spectacular feature being the Bullers of Buchan, a natural arch and a blow hole.

▶ *Leave by the minor road that leads to the **A90**. Turn left at this junction, and follow the **A90** to a right turn at the signposted road to Ellon.*

## 7 Ellon, Aberdeenshire

Ellon was the ancient 'capital' of Buchan, from the time of the Picts up to the defeat of the Norman Comyns, who held the land during the Middle Ages. The village gained importance as a crossing point over the River Ythan and its castle had a strategically important role to play in defending the district. Apart from the ruins of the old castle, the other historical remains are the Moot Hill Monument where there was a motte-and-bailey fort to defend the bridge.

Haddo House, to the northwest of the village, is an imposing mansion built by William Adam in 1732, though much of the interior was redecorated around 1880. The house, which is owned by the NTS, has extensive parklands with walks and an adventure playground.

### BACK TO NATURE

**The Sands of Forvie National Nature Reserve is a vast dune system that has in the past overwhelmed settlements. It is also home to many birds including arctic terns, Sandwich terns, eider ducks and shelducks. Sea ducks are particularly numerous in the winter, along with divers and grebes.**

Shiny copper drums at the Glengarrioch Distillery

▶ *Leave by the **A920** and follow it to Pitmedden House (a little to the northwest of Pitmedden).*

## 8 Pitmedden Garden,
Aberdeenshire

The gardens at Pitmedden were laid out in the 17th century and the formal garden is made up of elaborate geometric designs filled with brilliantly coloured flowers. The Museum of Farming Life, in the grounds of the estate, has many exhibits of tools and farm machinery from the past. The graveyard in Udny Green, just south of Pitmedden, contains a rather bizarre little building – a circular mort house, built in 1832 to thwart body snatchers. Coffins were placed in here on a turntable, then removed for burial after a maximum stay of three months, the idea being that they would be quite unsuitable for digging up and sale by then.

▶ *Continue on the **A920** and join the **A947** to Oldmeldrum.*

## 9 Oldmeldrum,
Aberdeenshire

The village retains its medieval street pattern, with the large Town Hall dominating the market square. Tucked away on the outskirts of the village is the Glengarrioch Distillery (not open), on a site said to have had a distillery in 1797. The distilling process consumes a great deal of energy and one rather novel feature of this distillery is that its waste heat is used to grow tomatoes in glasshouses.

To the west of the village lies the little settlement of Daviot, just beyond which is the celebrated Loanhead of Daviot stone circle. This imposing circle was constructed about 5,000 years ago and perhaps used in viewing the passage of the moon or in various local rites and customs. The most important part of the circle was the huge recumbent boulder which was put into position so that its uppermost face was horizontal. Ten upright boulders were then placed in a circle to complete the structure. The circle was later used for burials and cremations.

**RECOMMENDED WALKS**

The hill of Bennachie, standing to the west of Inverurie, gives outstanding views over the surrounding countryside. The remains of an ancient hillfort can be seen near the summit. One popular starting point for the ascent is from the car park on the northeastern side of the hill and on the way there, look out for the Maiden Stone, a 9th-century carved stone that stands by the roadside.

*Leave on the **A920** and bear left at the **B9170** to Inverurie.*

**10 Inverurie,** Aberdeenshire

This busy little town is the main shopping and administrative centre for the surrounding district. Its wide main street is dominated by the Town Hall, which was built in Grecian style in 1863.

West of the town, minor roads lead to East Aquhorthies stone circle which has a massive recumbent stone and a circle of smaller uprights.

Further north, Archaeolink Prehistory Park is an all-weather attraction illustrating ancient times, including a working Iron-Age farm, landscaped walkways, dramatic film presentations and interactive displays.

**FOR HISTORY BUFFS**

Fyvie Castle, northwest of Oldmeldrum, has undergone many changes from its original 13th-century structure but is known as the 'crowning glory of Scots baronial architecture'. The finest feature is the 13-foot (4m) wide stone staircase.

*i 18 High Street*

*Leave by the **A96** to Huntly.*

**11 Huntly,** Aberdeenshire

The long straight main road of this neat little town passes under the arch of the Gordon Schools and heads towards the impressive ruins of Huntly Castle, one of the finest castles in this part of the country. A 12th-century Norman motte can still be seen. Construction of the palace was started beside it in the mid-15th century. The most important decorative features are the carved entrance doorway and the fireplaces. Remarkably, for a roofless building of this age, some of the plasterwork still survives – complete with original graffiti!

Huntly Castle's carved entrance with its heraldic adornments

The castle also had its own prison, a dreadful place formed out of a pit cut deep into the foundations.

*i 9A The Square (seasonal)*

*Return eastwards to and continue along the **A96**, then turn left after a short distance at the **A97** to return to Banff.*

The Brandsbutt Stone near Inverurie, which bears ancient Pictish symbols

# Around the Cairngorms

The rugged granite mountains and forested glens of the Cairngorms National Park are the major features of this tour. Outside of the park, but an ideal highland base, Pitlochry nestles below the hills on the eastern bank of the River Tummel.

**2/3 DAYS • 204 MILES • 327KM**

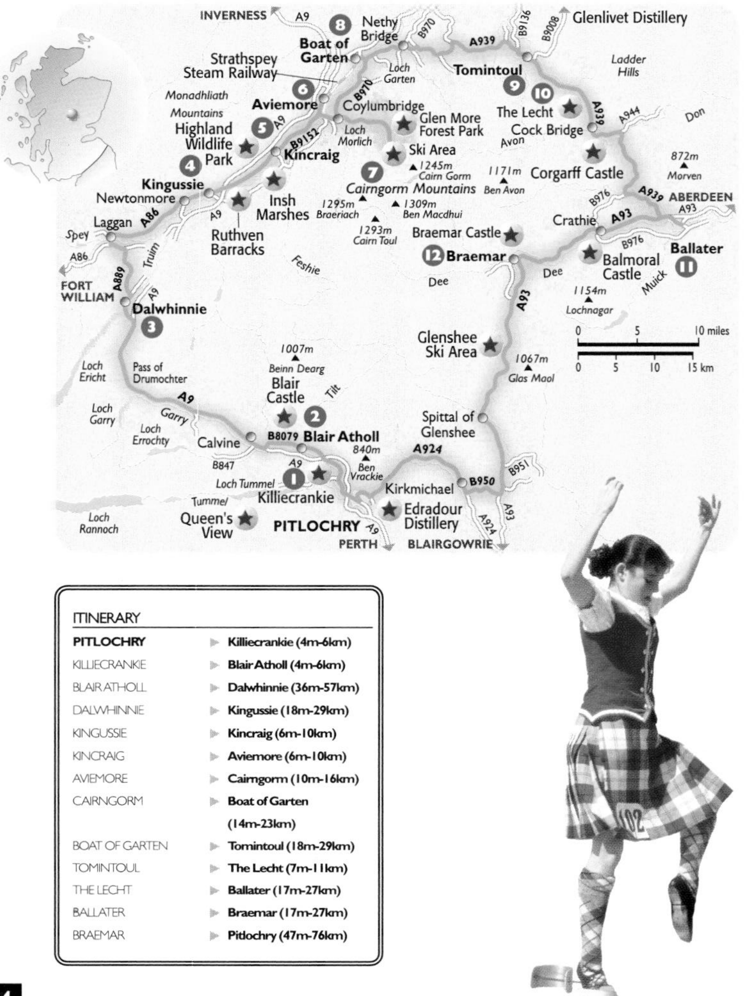


| ITINERARY | |
|---|---|
| **PITLOCHRY** | ▶ **Killiecrankie (4m-6km)** |
| KILLIECRANKIE | ▶ **Blair Atholl (4m-6km)** |
| BLAIR ATHOLL | ▶ **Dalwhinnie (36m-57km)** |
| DALWHINNIE | ▶ **Kingussie (18m-29km)** |
| KINGUSSIE | ▶ **Kincraig (6m-10km)** |
| KINCRAIG | ▶ **Aviemore (6m-10km)** |
| AVIEMORE | ▶ **Cairngorm (10m-16km)** |
| CAIRNGORM | ▶ **Boat of Garten (14m-23km)** |
| BOAT OF GARTEN | ▶ **Tomintoul (18m-29km)** |
| TOMINTOUL | ▶ **The Lecht (7m-11km)** |
| THE LECHT | ▶ **Ballater (17m-27km)** |
| BALLATER | ▶ **Braemar (17m-27km)** |
| BRAEMAR | ▶ **Pitlochry (47m-76km)** |

Hammer-throwing at the Pitlochry Highland Games

### SCENIC ROUTES

The whole of this route offers memorable scenery, but perhaps the most attractive parts are near Blair Atholl, the views of Cairn Gorm and the journey from Donside to Deeside. One very well-known viewpoint just off the route is the Queen's View, which is at the eastern end of Loch Tummel.

*i* *22 Atholl Road*

*Leave Pitlochry by the **A924**, then the **B8019** for about 1½ miles (2km) before turning on to the **B8079** to the National Trust for Scotland Visitor Centre at Killiecrankie.*

### 1 Killiecrankie, Perth & Kinross

The wooded gorge of Killiecrankie is a strategic Highland pass. A decisive battle was fought near here in 1689 when a Jacobite army defeated a government force. In the aftermath of the battle, one of the government soldiers, Donald MacBean, escaped from his pursuers by jumping 18 feet (6m) across the River Garry at a point now known as the 'Soldier's Leap'.

### FOR HISTORY BUFFS

The two ends of Glen Tilt are met during this tour – at Blair Atholl and at Braemar. This was an historically important route across the Highlands but is now the preserve of walkers. In 1861 Queen Victoria passed through it in her carriage, travelling 69 miles (111km) in one day! Earlier, in the 1840s, the Duke of Atholl attempted to close this right of way; the story is celebrated in *The Ballad of Glen Tilt.*

*i* *NTS Visitor Centre (seasonal)*

*Continue along the **B8079** for 4 miles (6km) to Blair Atholl.*

### 2 Blair Atholl, Perth & Kinross

This little village, situated where the Tilt and Garry rivers meet, is dominated by Blair Castle, home of the Dukes of Atholl. The oldest part dates back to 1269 but much of the present structure is relatively 'modern'. At the end of the 18th century the castle was completely renovated; parapets and towers were removed and it was turned into a Georgian mansion. The picturesque towers and crow-stepped gables were later additions when the Scots baronial style came into fashion. The castle has extensive grounds with many fine walks. The Duke of Atholl is the only man in Britain who is permitted to have a private army, a right granted him by Queen Victoria.

*Leave on the **B8079**, then turn right at the **A9** and head towards Inverness. Bear left at the **A889** and follow to Dalwhinnie.*

### 3 Dalwhinnie, Highland

At an altitude of 1,188 feet (362m), this is the highest village in the Highlands and was an important stopping place in the days when the main highway passed through here. It has a small distillery which is open to the public.

*Continue on the **A889** and turn right at the **A86** to Kingussie.*

Britain's only private army on display at Blair Atholl

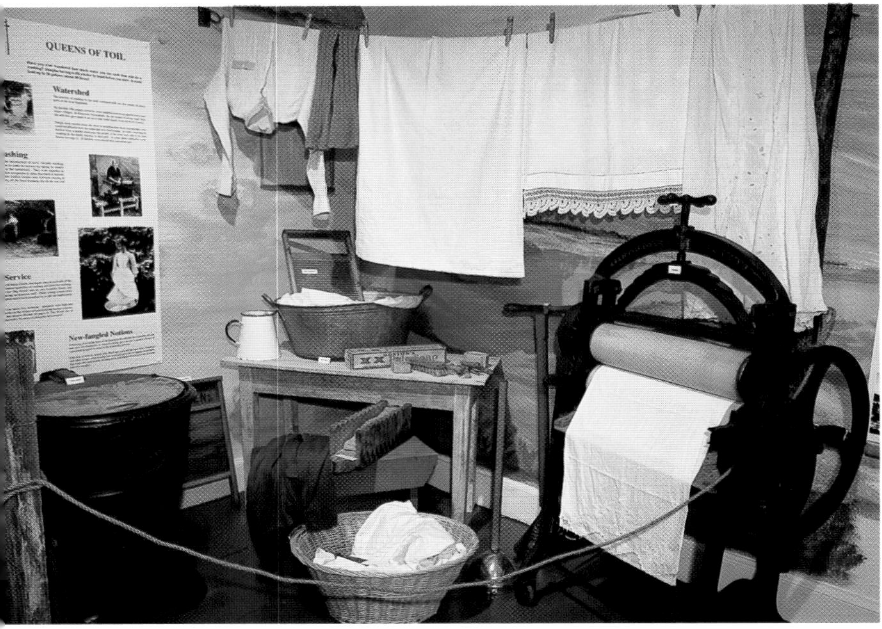

**4 Kingussie,** Highland

The main attraction here is the Highland Folk Museum and the most fascinating exhibit is the 'black house', built in the manner of the drystone houses that were common on the island of Lewis. Other exhibits focus on Highland agriculture, the life of the tinkers (travelling people) and the furniture used in Highland houses over the last 300 years.

SPECIAL TO...

There are numerous whisky distilleries in the area which offer guided tours round the premises and the chance to sample their particular malt. Shinty (which is similar to hockey) is very popular in the Kingussie/Newtonmore area and an opportunity to see a game should not be missed. For presents, have a look at jewellery incorporating 'cairngorms', the smoky semi-precious stones that are found in the area.

Across the River Spey stand the gaunt ruins of Ruthven Barracks, which were built in 1719 but destroyed by the Jacobite army in 1746 to prevent their use by the Hanoverians.

*i* *Ralia, on the A9 near Newtonmore (seasonal)*

▶ *Leave by the* ***B9152*** *and follow it for 6 miles (10km) to Kincraig.*

Highland Folk Museum: washing day exhibit

**5 Kincraig,** Highland

The Highland Wildlife Park at Kincraig is home to a collection of animals that once roamed here freely. Reindeer, wild horses, brown bears, wolves, lynx and even bison were at one time native to this part of Scotland. Now they can only be seen from the safety of a car when driving through the park.

The village stands by Loch Insh, which has a water sports centre, while further up the Spey the river widens at Insh

Highland cattle at Kincraig Highland Wildlife Park. The black variety are rarer than the red

Marshes. This is Scotland's largest inland marsh with a reserve administered by the RSPB (Royal Society for the Protection of Birds). It is particularly good for waders and wildfowl.

FOR CHILDREN

The wildlife park at Kincraig and the reindeer herd at Cairngorm are worth seeing. There are lots of outdoor activities, both land- and water-based, available in the area near Aviemore and the indoor facilities in the town offer useful wet-weather alternatives.

*Continue along the* ***B9152*** *for 6 miles (10km) to Aviemore.*

**6 Aviemore,** Highland
Until the 1960s Aviemore was just another small Highland village, but the huge leisure complex that was then established has transformed it into the busiest tourist centre in the Highlands. The new buildings sit uneasily in the Highland landscape, but they offer many indoor facilities that are not found elsewhere in the area, hence its popularity, especially with winter visitors who come flocking here to ski in the Cairngorms.

Aviemore has a station on the Perth to Inverness railway line and it is also at the southern end of the Strathspey Steam Railway.

*i* *Grampian Road*

*Take the Cairngorm road out of Aviemore. Follow it through Coylumbridge, past Loch Morlich and up the mountain road to the Coire Cas ski slopes at Cairngorm.*

Strathspey Steam Railway locomotive at Boat of Garten

**7 Cairngorm,** Highland
The Cairngorm Mountains are formed from a massive dissected plateau of granite with an altitude of around 4,000 feet (1,220m). The funicular railway at Coire Cas operates throughout the year and climbs to a restaurant near the summit of Cairn Gorm, but it should be remembered that even though it is calm and sunny at the chair-lift car park, it can be very windy and bitterly cold near the summit. The Cairngorm plateau is covered with frost-shattered boulders which give little shelter to man or beast,

The Cairngorms: view to Loch Morlich and Aviemore

but it does support a herd of reindeer which were introduced here in 1952.

The Rothiemurchus estate and the Glen More Forest Park lie between Aviemore and the Cairngorms and there are many attractive low-level walks through the stands of Scots pine. More walks thread around Loch Morlich, which is a popular water-sports centre.

► *Return to Coylumbridge and turn right at the **B970**. Follow this towards Boat of Garten and turn left at a signposted unclassified road close to the village.*

**8 Boat of Garten,** Highland
The name derives from a chain-operated ferry across the Spey that was replaced in 1899 by a substantial bridge. This is the northern terminal of the Strathspey Steam Railway, one of the finest tourist attractions in the area, particularly for those nostalgic for the days of steam! With some of the best views of any preserved steam railway in Britain, the Strathspey Steam Railway line runs along a scenic route to Aviemore.

East of the village stands Abernethy Forest, part of the old Caledonian Forest, where there are many splendid Scots pines. Beside Loch Garten, which lies within the forest, is an osprey breeding site and many birdwatchers come here each year to witness the progress of the current pair. The ospreys were hunted out of the Highlands altogether at the end of the 19th century, but in the 1950s one nest was discovered in the district. Nowadays, the RSPB maintains a close guard on the nest, but visitors are able to watch the birds from a covered hide. Those who spend some time in the district may be fortunate enough to see an osprey fishing in one of the lochs.

BACK TO NATURE

**The ospreys at Loch Garten RSPB reserve are the most obvious example of how wild animals are being encouraged to re-populate their old haunts. This is assisted by the careful management of the remains of the old Caledonian Forest in the area to the north of Cairngorm. Visitors should also look for Scottish crossbills and crested tits in the pine forest, and golden-eye ducks and Slavonian grebes on the lochs.**

Early morning mist rising above Loch Morlich

► *Return along the unclassified road to the **B970** and then turn left, and follow this road to Nethy Bridge. Turn right after crossing the River Nethy and follow an unclassified road to the **A939**. Turn right at this junction to reach Tomintoul.*

**9 Tomintoul,** Moray
This is another of the Highlands' highest villages and its position means that its weather can be rather unpredictable, with snow not unknown in June!

It has a broad main street and a large central square with the local museum. Although there are only a few shops, one which will be of interest to many visitors is the well-stocked Whisky Castle, which has a vast array of whiskies from many parts of Scotland.

To the north stands the Glenlivet Distillery, which is famous throughout the whisky-drinking world; it has a visitor centre and offers tours.

*i* *The Square (seasonal)*

► *Continue on the **A939** to the skiing area at The Lecht.*

**10 The Lecht,** Moray
Just beyond The Lecht stands the imposing Corgarff Castle. The loop-holed curtain wall surrounding it was added after the 1745 uprising in order that the government might use the castle to police this strong Jacobite centre.

Winter visitors should take care if snow is forecast as the Tomintoul to Cock Bridge section of the A939 is often blocked in the winter.

▶ *Continue on the* ***A939*** *then turn left at the* ***A93*** *for Ballater.*

**11 Ballater,** Aberdeenshire
Deeside became fashionable after Queen Victoria built a summer retreat at nearby Balmoral Castle, still a favourite holiday home of the royal family. The popularity of 'Royal Deeside' was further increased when the railway line, now closed, was built, but it only ventured as far as Ballater because the Queen did not wish her peace and quiet to be disturbed! A small exhibition about the local railway line is in the tourist information centre.

The town is a good centre from which to explore Deeside, and its solidly built granite houses make it a pleasant place to stroll around. Balmoral Castle was built in 1855 with local granite and is an impressive example of the Scots baronial style. It is the Scottish home of the British royal family and the grounds are open to the public during part of the summer.

*i* *Old Royal Station, Station Square*

▶ *Return along the* ***A93*** *and continue to Braemar.*

**12 Braemar,** Aberdeenshire
The village is situated in an important position at the junction of three glens and there have been fortifications here from at least 1390 when Kindrochit Castle (now a ruin) was built in what is now the centre of the village. Outside the village, Braemar Castle is a good example of a Hanoverian fort which was used to police the Highlands.

The Jacobite uprising of 1715 began here and the Invercauld Arms Hotel stands on the site where the standard was raised at the start of the campaign to put a Stuart back on the British throne.

Braemar can be busy at times, but never more so than in September when crowds flock to the local Highland games, the Braemar Gathering. The royal family are regular visitors and among the most popular events are the bagpipe-playing competitions and the tossing of the caber. Sport is not new to the village – in the 11th century King Malcolm Canmore, who needed a messenger, held a race here to find the fastest man.

**RECOMMENDED WALKS**

There are popular walks of all standards throughout this tour and most tourist information centres have small booklets outlining good walks in their localities. Interesting starting points include Pitlochry, Killiecrankie, the Rothiemurchus and Glen More area, and the upper reaches of the Dee beyond Braemar.

▶ *Continue on the* ***A93*** *past the Glenshee skiing area at Cairnwell and turn right at the* ***B950****. Turn right again when the road meets the* ***A924*** *and follow this road back to Pitlochry.*

Balmoral Castle, reputedly the Queen's favourite residence

TOUR
18

# The Castle Trail

Aberdeen, the 'Granite City', is the gateway to Royal Deeside and to the great spread of historic houses known as the Castles of Mar. Aberdeen itself is a fascinating city which has gained a reputation for its flowers, while Old Aberdeen has many buildings dating back to medieval times.

**2 DAYS • 143 MILES • 230KM**

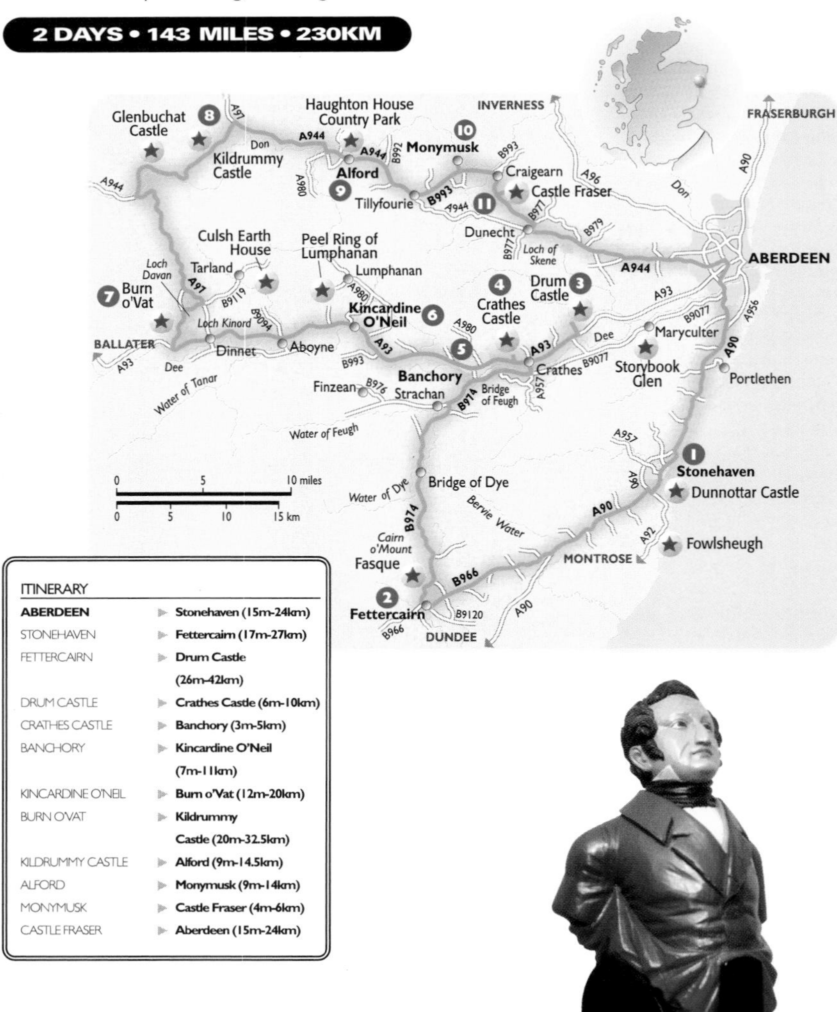


**ITINERARY**

| | |
|---|---|
| **ABERDEEN** | ▶ **Stonehaven (15m-24km)** |
| STONEHAVEN | ▶ **Fettercairn (17m-27km)** |
| FETTERCAIRN | ▶ **Drum Castle (26m-42km)** |
| DRUM CASTLE | ▶ **Crathes Castle (6m-10km)** |
| CRATHES CASTLE | ▶ **Banchory (3m-5km)** |
| BANCHORY | ▶ **Kincardine O'Neil (7m-11km)** |
| KINCARDINE O'NEIL | ▶ **Burn o'Vat (12m-20km)** |
| BURN O'VAT | ▶ **Kildrummy Castle (20m-32.5km)** |
| KILDRUMMY CASTLE | ▶ **Alford (9m-14.5km)** |
| ALFORD | ▶ **Monymusk (9m-14km)** |
| MONYMUSK | ▶ **Castle Fraser (4m-6km)** |
| CASTLE FRASER | ▶ **Aberdeen (15m-24km)** |

*i* *Provost Ross's House, Shiprow*

**SPECIAL TO...**

When in Aberdeen, look out for Aberdeen butteries in the bakers' shops. These are made from a butter-rich dough and are similar to French croissants.

▶ *Leave by the* ***A90*** *and turn left at the minor road that leads to Stonehaven, 15 miles (24km).*

Exhibit at the Aberdeen Maritime Museum

**1 Stonehaven,** Aberdeenshire
As well as being a port with a long-established harbour, Stonehaven also has the beaches and other facilities that attract many visitors. The oldest part of the town has a 16th-century Tolbooth which is now used as a museum, with special emphasis on local history and the fishing industry. Above the town, the war memorial stands on a hilltop which offers fine views of the coast and the countryside.

The Scots are well renowned for their celebrations at Hogmanay and Stonehaven celebrates the close of the old year with its Fireball Festival. The 'ceremony' may stem from ancient pagan rites, and as the Town House bells strike midnight, the participants march up High Street twirling burning balls of rags and twigs round their heads.

To the south of the town is Dunnottar Castle, a 14th-century building on a site fortified since the 5th century. The castle stands on a dramatically positioned headland and from 1651 to 1652 it was able to withstand eight months of siege by Cromwell's army before having to surrender. It was also the place where Scotland's royal regalia was hidden from Cromwell.

Dramatic Dunnottar Castle overlooking the sea

*i* *66 Allardice Street (seasonal)*

**BACK TO NATURE**

At Fowlsheugh, about 3 miles (5km) to the south of Stonehaven, the RSPB manages the largest seabird colony on the British mainland, with no fewer than 80,000 breeding pairs of birds raising their young on the steep cliffs that rise out of the sea. Guillemots, razorbills, kittiwakes and fulmars are among the birds to be seen here.

*Take the **A90** south. After 7 miles (11km) turn right at the **B966** to Fettercairn.*

## 2 Fettercairn,
Aberdeenshire

The older houses in this little village are built from a red sandstone, much warmer-looking than the rather austere grey of the granites that are so common around the Aberdeen area. The mercat cross stands in the village square and dates back to 1670. In comparison to this traditional piece of local architecture, a large and very ostentatious Gothic arch celebrates a visit by Queen Victoria in 1861.

Fettercairn Distillery stands on the village outskirts and tours round it are available. The original building was established in 1820. To the north you will find the estate of Fasque, which is open to the public. This was the home of William Gladstone, four times Prime Minister. Many of the rooms have changed little since the house was built in the 1820s and there is a wealth of Victorian artefacts, especially in the kitchens.

*Leave by the **B974** on the Cairn o' Mount road and head towards Banchory. Just before the town, turn right at a minor road (to Kirkton of Durris) and follow this along the southern bank of the River Dee. Turn left at the **A957** to reach Crathes. Turn right at the **A93** and then left at an unclassified road to Drum Castle.*

Fasque House in Fettercairn; one-time home to Prime Minister William Gladstone

## 3 Drum Castle,
Aberdeenshire

The old Tower of Drum was built in the 13th century with walls 12 feet (4m) thick. Beside it the relatively 'modern' 17th-century house has particularly interesting domestic rooms. The buildings stand in the Old Wood

**FOR CHILDREN**

Aberdeen makes an ideal base for a family holiday, with many parks, beaches and activity centres that will delight children, the Satrosphere, a kid-friendly exhibition where science becomes fun, and Storybook Glen which feature children's nursery rhyme characters. A visit to Doonies Farm at Nigg is always popular. Here, you can see Shetland ponies, cattle, sheep and pigs, and there is a picnic and play area.

of Drum, a remnant of the ancient Caledonian Forest, and many large oaks, pines and wild cherry trees still flourish here, while a walled garden houses a collection of historic roses. Nearby Garlogie Mill Power House Museum features a unique beam engine and associated displays.

The splendid gardens surrounding Crathes Castle

▶ *Return to the **A93** and turn right. Turn right at the entrance to Crathes Castle.*

### 4 Crathes Castle, Aberdeenshire

This L-shaped tower house was built in the 16th century and contains notable interior decoration. The painted ceilings are exceptionally fine – these date from the late 16th century and very early 17th century and feature ancient and mythical heroes such as Hector, Alexander the Great and King Arthur. The gardens are within yew hedges that are about 300 years old, and contain some excellent examples of topiary.

**SCENIC ROUTES**

As the B974 makes its way over the hills to Banchory, it passes the Cairn o' Mount, a massive roadside cairn that has been added to over the centuries by generations of travellers. The road crosses over a fine heather moor and there is a very wide panoramic sweep from the cairn over the moors and the low-lying land known as the Howe of the Mearns towards the sea.

The vibrantly painted ceiling at Crathes Castle

▶ *Continue on the **A93** for 3 miles (5km) to Banchory.*

### 5 Banchory, Aberdeenshire

Situated at the confluence of the River Dee and the Water of Feugh, Banchory is a pleasant little Highland town and is a good base from which to explore the area. There is a local history museum in Bridge Street, which includes displays on the prolific composer of traditional Scottish tunes, Scott Skinner. The town also hosts an annual festival of Scottish music each May.

Close to the village, the Bridge of Feugh spans a little gorge and has become a very popular place from which to watch salmon leaping their way upstream.

This is good farming country and numerous old farm buildings survive.

*i* ***Bridge Street***

▶ *Continue on the **A93** to Kincardine O'Neil.*

### 6 Kincardine O'Neil, Aberdeenshire

This small village gained early importance for its position at the Deeside side of the Cairn o' Mount route, and a ferry crossed the river here, later

superseded by a bridge in the 13th century. This is one of Deeside's oldest villages and it has a very fine ruined church, built in 1233 and associated with a hospice for travellers.

**FOR HISTORY BUFFS**

To the north of Kincardine O'Neil lies the village of Lumphanan, where Macbeth is said to have been killed, and to its southwest stands the Peel Ring of Lumphanan, one of the region's earliest earthworks. It dates from the 13th century and the buildings that were stationed on the mound were protected by a wide ditch.

▶ *Continue on the **A93** and turn right at the **B9119**. Turn left at the car park for the Burn o' Vat.*

**7 Burn o' Vat,** Aberdeenshire
The area around the Vat has been laid out with paths to guide visitors round the many examples showing how the landscape was formed during the Ice Age, about 12,000 to 15,000 years ago. Huge rivers and streams carried vast quantities of rock debris down from the ice-covered mountains and as they did so carved out gullies and gorges and dumped the debris on the low-lying land to the east. The Burn o' Vat itself is a huge bottle-shaped pot-hole that was worn out of the solid rock by the rushing water. It is some 65 feet (20m) in diameter, and its base is filled with sand and gravel.

Lochs Davan and Kinord lie to the east. These are 'kettle holes', formed where huge stranded blocks of ice eventually melted. There are a number of pleasant walks round Loch Kinord and on the northern shore of the loch is the Kinord cross-slab, a 9th-century granite Celtic cross.

The district known as Cromar, which lies to the north and east of the Vat, has numerous monuments that indicate its occupation by ancient peoples over a long time. One unusual structure is the Culsh Earth House, which was found at Culsh Farm, on the B9119, after Tarland. This was probably a storehouse built over 2,000 years ago.

The 18th-century Bridge of Feugh spanning the River Feugh, from which visitors can watch salmon leaping below

▶ *Continue on the **B9119** heading northeast. Turn left at the **A97** in order to reach Kildrummy Castle.*

**8 Kildrummy Castle,** Aberdeenshire
Before reaching Kildrummy, Glenbuchat Castle is passed at a bend in the River Don. This 16th-century castle was built above the ravine of

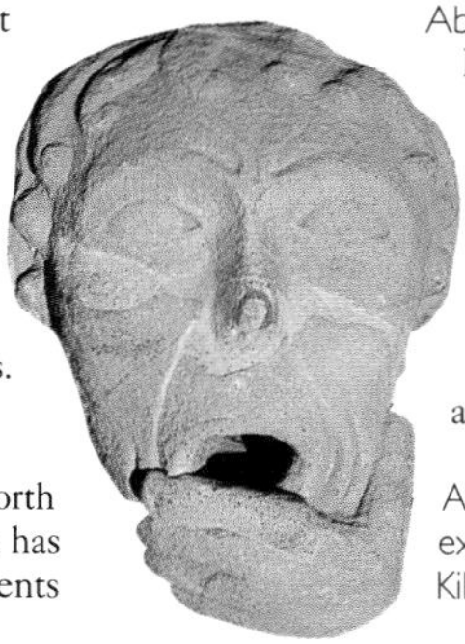

Artefact found during excavations at Kildrummy Castle

the Water of Buchan by John Gordon, and above the door of the southwest tower he had carved the rather philosophical inscription 'nothing on arth remains bot faime'.

The great medieval castle of Kildrummy lies on raised ground near the River Don. This was once one of the north's most important castles and, although now in ruins, many of its surrounding walls still stand. It survived numerous sieges but in 1306, when Robert the Bruce's brother was defending it against English attack, he was betrayed by a smith named Osbarn. Legend has it the gold he was promised for his treachery was poured down his throat, molten!

► *Continue on the **A97**, then turn right on to the **A944**, which leads to Alford.*

**9 Alford,** Aberdeenshire
This is the home of the Grampian Transport Museum, where visitors can enjoy such diverse exhibits as horse-drawn vehicles, vintage cars, a road roller and even a huge snow plough. One very unusual vehicle is the steam-driven car called the 'Craigievar Express', built by the local postman at Craigievar in 1895. It has three wheels and he used it to carry the post on his round.

The village was the terminus of a railway line from Aberdeen and the former station of the Great Northern Scottish Railway now houses a museum. A narrow-gauge railway runs to Haughton House Country Park and Murray Park. Alford's former cattle market has been preserved and now houses a Heritage Centre.

*i* *Railway Museum, Station Yard (seasonal)*

► *Continue on the **A944** and turn left at the **B993**. Turn left at a minor road to enter Monymusk, 9 miles (14km).*

**10 Monymusk,** Aberdeenshire
This quiet little village, sited just off the main road, has a splendid Norman church dating back to the 12th century when an Augustinian priory was also built. The village is laid out very neatly in the fashion of a planned 'estate village', with a little grassy area in its centre.

A former toll house stands at the junction of the B993 and the road into the village.

► *Return to the **B993** and turn left. Turn right at a minor road to Craigearn, then right again to Castle Fraser.*

**11 Castle Fraser,** Aberdeenshire
The castle, topped with the usual turrets and towers of the Scots baronial style, originated as a rectangular tower in the mid-15th century. Later additions and alterations transformed it into a handsome mansion house. The Round Tower gives an excellent view of the rest of the building and in particular all the different designs of small towers that decorate the upper part of the building. The pleasant gardens are well worth visiting.

► *Turn left after leaving the castle grounds and follow the unclassified road to the **B977** where a right turn is taken. Turn left at the **A944** to return to Aberdeen.*

**RECOMMENDED WALKS**

There are many popular walks in this area and most tourist information centres have leaflets with information on them, including forest walks, in their area. Places of particular interest include Burn o'Vat, Haughton House Country Park and the West Gordon Way (which passes near Alford).

Exhibit from the Grampian Transport Museum, Alford

# THE HIGHLANDS & ISLANDS

Nowhere else in Britain can match the Scottish Highlands and Islands for sheer splendour. The grand mountains, heather-clad hillsides and indented coastline (complete with some of Britain's best beaches) make this classic touring country.

The west coast, with its long broken coastline, provides the most dramatic scenery. Communities are few and far between in some districts, leaving the land to the sheep, the cattle and the midges. The east coast and the Great Glen are more populated and offer better facilities.

This historic region abounds with tales and legends of saints and Picts, of Viking invaders and endlessly warring native clans. It is a long history, much of it bloodied with battles, and it has left the countryside rich in antiquities, and burial chambers, standing stones, brochs, forts and castles which can be seen wherever people found land to settle. However, in the last 200 years, the proportion of Scots living in the Highlands and Islands has more than halved. Many people have been forced off the land, as during the infamous Highland Clearances, which spanned the mid-18th to the late 19th centuries, when landowners chose to evict their tenants, destroy their homes, and turn the land over to more profitably exploitable tenants – sheep. Many joined the population drift to the Central Belt of Scotland, where work was to be found. But many Highland communities are now finding that their population is rising again, as more 'incomers' discover the high quality of life.

The view towards the Isles of Rum and Eigg from Arisaig

Visitors will find that certain events in Scottish history crop up again and again as they tour round the region. The Highland Clearances, the feuding between the clans, the Jacobite Uprising of 1745, the boom and slump of the herring industry: these and other landmarks in Scotland's history shaped the country and have been well recorded in many monuments, large and small.

Above all, it is the people that make up the country and those who live and work in the Highlands and Islands are having to adapt to great changes. Many rely on the land for a living, but new skills are being learned, new trades taken up and new visitors welcomed to the delights of this part of Scotland.

**Tour 19**
West of the Highland 'gateway' of Fort William, great fingers of land stick out into the sea. These peninsulas are home to scattered crofting communities that are linked by narrow twisting roads offering new views round every corner. Road conditions dictate that progress will not be fast, but that is no drawback when travelling through one of the least visited parts of the mainland, where each bay and glen is worthy of unhurried exploration.

Passenger boat leaving Iona for Staffa

**Tour 20**
The length of this tour reflects the paucity of major cross-country routes in the Highlands and the extent to which the sea lochs bite into the west coast. This is the Highlands at its best, with giant mountains providing the backdrop to some unforgettable beaches. Inland, the Great Glen carves a wide gash through the fabric of the land, and this route has been followed over the millennia by successive waves of settlers, hunters, missionaries, soldiers – and even sailors!

**Tour 21**
Two cross-country routes link the eastern village of Bonar Bridge with more dramatic west coast scenery. Europe has few wildernesses left, but as visitors approach the uninhabited moor and mountain area of Inverpolly, they can get some feeling of just how starkly beautiful (and inhospitable!) the Highland landscape can be. However, the rich harvest from the sea provides many communities with a good livelihood and helps maintain the Highland crofting traditions.

**Tour 22**
Much of this long tour around the top of Scotland follows the narrow, populated coastal fringe. There seems to be almost no limit to the number of beautiful sandy beaches to be found here, and many of them will be deserted. Caithness, set in a much gentler landscape than Sutherland, has something of a timeless quality about it, especially in the farming areas, and it is rich in prehistoric antiquities that continue to puzzle archaeologists to this day.

**Tour 23**
In many ways, Easter Ross and the Black Isle are very different from the rest of the region. This is particularly good farming country, with large prosperous farms and bustling towns. The blend of gentler Highland landscape with the facilities of seaside resorts makes this district popular with families and those seeking a relaxed tour through pleasant countryside.

**Tour 24**
Skye, the 'Misty Isle', draws to its shores visitors eager to see the rugged grandeur of the Cuillin Hills and to experience a place where time passes more slowly than on the mainland. The island is so steeped in tradition and history, and has such splendid scenery that it lures visitors back time and again.

**Tour 25**
With its interior composed largely of mountain, moorland and bog, Mull's coastline roads link villages, harbours, farms and castles. The sea is never far away, and with a coastline some 300 miles (480km) long the views towards the sea are as fine as they are varied.

Kittiwakes on Handa's cliffs

TOUR
19

# The Road To The Isles

Fort William is often referred to as the Gateway to the Highlands, and although not essentially a tourist resort, it does have a wealth of services and shops for books, tartans, tweeds and outdoor wear. Just outside the town lies Ben Nevis, at 4,406 feet (1,344m), Britain's highest mountain.

**2/3 DAYS • 195 MILES • 315KM**

ITINERARY

| | |
|---|---|
| **FORT WILLIAM** | ▶ **Banavie (4m-6km)** |
| BANAVIE | ▶ **Glenfinnan (16m-26km)** |
| GLENFINNAN | ▶ **Loch nan Uamh (14m-23km)** |
| LOCH NAN UAMH | ▶ **Arisaig (6m-10km)** |
| ARISAIG | ▶ **Morar (6m-10km)** |
| MORAR | ▶ **Mallaig (3m-5km)** |
| MALLAIG | ▶ **Kinlochmoidart (31m-50km)** |
| KINLOCHMOIDART | ▶ **Acharacle (7m-11km)** |
| ACHARACLE | ▶ **Glenbeg (12m-19km)** |
| GLENBEG | ▶ **Kilchoan (11m-18km)** |
| KILCHOAN | ▶ **Strontian (29m-47km)** |
| STRONTIAN | ▶ **Lochaline (18m-29km)** |
| LOCHALINE | ▶ **Ardgour (30m-48km)** |
| ARDGOUR | ▶ **Fort William (8m-13km)** |

*i* *Cameron Centre, Cameron Square*

### SPECIAL TO...

The Ben Nevis Hill Race, which takes place on the first Saturday in September each year, attracts competitors from far and wide. Starting from close to sea level, this gruelling race to the summit and back is only for the fittest of athletes. The record time is 1 hour, 25 minutes and 34 seconds.

► *Leave by the **A82** (to Inverness), then turn left at the **A830** (to Mallaig). Turn right at the **B8004** to the Caledonian Canal's locks at Banavie, 4 miles (6km).*

### RECOMMENDED WALKS

There are good walks to be enjoyed in this area and local tourist information centres have guidebooks giving details of many of them. Glen Nevis, which is below Ben Nevis and easily reached from Fort William, provides a walk with waterfalls to see on the way. The Caledonian Canal's footpath provides good level walking for families.

**1 Banavie,** Highland

Northeast of Fort William, on the way to Banavie, are the impressive ruins of 13th-century Inverlochy Castle, on the banks of the River Lochy. It has massive round towers at the corners and the walls are 10 feet (3m) thick.

The Caledonian Canal runs through the Great Glen from Corpach (just southwest of Banavie) to Inverness, a total distance of 60 miles (97km). It was built between 1803 and 1822 by Thomas Telford so that boats could avoid the treacherous waters round Cape Wrath; the political decision to build the canal was hastened by the government's fear of Napoleon's naval strength. Although some commercial boats still use this beautifully sited waterway, most of the craft on it are motor cruisers or yachts. Neptune's Staircase, the most spectacular part of the canal, is at Banavie. This is a series of eight locks that raise boats a total height of 64 feet (20m) in a distance of only 1,500 feet (460m).

Neptune's Staircase: a series of eight locks on the Caledonian Canal

A short walk along the towpath leads to the basin and sea lock at Corpach, with its neat 'pepper pot' lighthouse. From this point there is an excellent view of Loch Linnhe, the surrounding hills and Ben Nevis.

Near by is the Treasures of the Earth, a stunning array of sparkling crystal and gemstones in simulated cave scenes.

► *Return to the **A830**. Turn right and follow the road to Glenfinnan.*

**2 Glenfinnan,** Highland

On the fateful afternoon of 19 August, 1745, Charles Edward Stuart raised the Stuart standard here and rallied more than a thousand armed supporters to the Jacobite cause. His father was proclaimed King James VIII of Scotland and III of England and Ireland and this historic act

### BACK TO NATURE

The grandeur of the scenery derives from the area's fascinating geology and the Great Glen Fault that runs right through the Highlands along a line joining Fort William and Inverness. Loch Linnhe and the Caledonian Canal lie along this great gash in the earth's surface, produced as the two sides of the glen moved past each other. The very occasional earth tremors indicate that the fault has not yet stopped moving!

Steam train crossing the Glenfinnan viaduct

started the tragic chain of events known in Scots history as the 'Forty-Five'. The army, though initially successful in moving far into England, was eventually defeated at Culloden, near Inverness, on 16 April, 1746, a defeat that did much to change the history of Scotland. The NTS Visitor Centre has a good display explaining the events surrounding the arrival of the prince and the raising of the standard. The nearby tall and slender monument at the head of Loch Shiel is Scotland's most famous memorial to the Jacobite cause.

The Fort William to Mallaig road runs parallel to the railway line for much of the way. The line's most spectacular structure is the Glenfinnan Viaduct with its 21 arches; the local railway station has a little museum depicting the history of the line.

*i* *NTS Visitor Centre (seasonal)*

▶ *Follow the **A830** for 14 miles (23km) to Loch nan Uamh.*

### 3 Loch nan Uamh, Highland

After the battle of Culloden, Bonnie Prince Charlie made his way back to this area and, on 20 September, 1746, he sailed away from this loch on a ship bound for France. The spot from which he sailed is marked by the Prince's Cairn. He had a price of £30,000 on his head but no one betrayed his presence while on the run from government troops, so loyal were local people to the Jacobite cause.

▶ *Continue on the **A830** to Arisaig.*

### 4 Arisaig, Highland

This little seaside village has many sandy beaches near by which makes it popular with families in summer. Arisaig has a fine view of the islands of Rum and Eigg and boats sail from the small harbour to these and other local islands.

▶ *Continue on the **A830** to Morar.*

The Prince's Cairn at Loch nan Uamh

### 5 Morar, Highland

Loch Morar, with a depth of 1,017 feet (310m), is Britain's deepest inland water and the home of Morag, a 'monster' reputed to be related to Loch Ness's Nessie. The loch is a

**FOR CHILDREN**

Of the many fine beaches along this coast, particular mention should be made of the ones at Morar, north of Arisaig, and at Kentra Bay. There are not many wet-weather facilities in the area, but Fort William has the Lochaber Leisure Centre, which has a swimming pool and facilities for many sports including outdoor activities such as tennis.
There are also dry-ski slopes at the skiing area at Aonach Mor, just off the A82, east of Fort William.

### FOR HISTORY BUFFS

As the A861 descends to Acharacle, it passes a minor road (left) to Dalelia and this leads to a walk to the shores of Loch Shiel. This is the narrowest part of the loch and is almost completely blocked by Eilean Fhianain (St Finnan's Island), where St Finnan, a disciple of St Columba, built a chapel. The ruins survive, and legend has it that a curse has been placed on anyone daring to remove the bell Finnan brought from Ireland. The churchyard was the burial place of the chiefs of Clanranald. This was also the spot from which Charles Edward Stuart started his journey up Loch Shiel to Glenfinnan, where he raised the Stuart standard in 1745.

A landed catch of mixed shellfish

remarkable example of the effect of glaciers during the Ice Age. The ice here was 4,000 feet (1,220m) thick and gouged out the loch's basin to a depth of more than 1,000 feet (300m) below sea level.

After tumbling over the Falls of Morar, the River Morar flows over the Sands of Morar, notable for a wide expanse of pure white silica sand.

► *Continue on the* ***A830*** *to Mallaig.*

### 6 Mallaig, Highland

Before the arrival of the railway, Mallaig was a small crofting community with a few thatched houses. Today it is the home port of a substantial fishing fleet, host to the Marine World Aquarium down by the harbour, and a heritage centre by the station, as well as being the mainland terminal for many boats operating ferry services to the islands.

Day excursions from the harbour are also available in season and these give visitors the opportunity to visit Skye or Muck, Eigg, Rum and Canna.

The peninsula of Knoydart is another fascinating place accessible only by boat. Surrounded on three sides by sea and on the fourth by mountains, it is one of Scotland's few wilderness areas; it retains its character because it cannot be reached by road. This is wonderful walking country, where real peace and quiet can be enjoyed.

The West Highland Railway from Fort William was opened in 1894 in order to transport the west coast herring catches to the southern markets as quickly as possible, and although the fish-carrying role

Fishing boats in Mallaig's pretty harbour

of the line has diminished, it is still of vital economic and social importance to the area. It is also very popular with summer visitors, especially when steam trains are used, and it has been described as one of the world's most scenic railway journeys.

SCENIC ROUTES

The 'Road to the Isles' is the name given to the attractive route from Fort William to Mallaig, which passes through an ever-changing landscape of hills, forest and lochs. Another outstanding journey is the one along Loch Linnhe, giving good views of Ben Nevis and the hills of Glen Coe.

*Return along the **A830** to Lochailort. Turn right at the **A861** and follow to Kinlochmoidart.*

**7 Kinlochmoidart,** Highland

To the right of the road stand the Seven Men of Moidart, seven beech trees planted early in the 19th century in tribute to the seven men who landed here with Bonnie Prince Charlie in 1745. The area around Loch Moidart is beautifully wooded with a large natural oak and birch forest; holly, cherry and ash are also common. Today these trees are protected, but in previous centuries they were used for charcoal burning or for making lime. An old lime kiln stands opposite the car-park at the Seven Men of Moidart. After climbing out of Kinlochmoidart, look out for a group of four cairns by the roadside. These are on an old 'coffin route' and mark where coffins were laid to give their bearers a rest while carrying their burden over the trackless hills to the local churchyard.

*Continue on the **A861** for 7 miles (11km) to Acharacle.*

The remains of tragic Castle Tioram

**8 Acharacle,** Highland

This small village, which makes a pleasant base from which to explore the surrounding area, is approached by crossing the Old Shiel Bridge.

To the west lies Kentra Bay with its fine sandy beaches, and Castle Tioram, a 14th-century castle standing on a tidal island in Loch Moidart. Though an empty ruin, it was not destroyed in battle, but put to the torch by its owner, the chief of Clanranald, during the 1715 Jacobite uprising. He did this to prevent it falling into the hands of his enemies.

*Continue on the **A861** to Salen, then turn right at the **B8007** and follow it to Glenbeg.*

**9 Glenbeg,** Highland

One mile (1.5km) southeast of the village is the RSPB Glenborrodale site, with its stunning landscape and wildlife. Further along the road the little bay of Camas nan Geall nestles beneath the steep slopes of Ben Hiant. In the field at the back of the bay there is an 18th-century burial site and a Bronze-Age standing stone which has a number of carvings on it; the evocative remains of a small settlement can also be seen here.

*Continue on the **B8007** for 11 miles (18km) to Kilchoan.*

**10 Kilchoan,** Highland

This little settlement of scattered houses makes a good base for exploring the western end of the Ardnamurchan peninsula; it also has a summer season ferry service to Tobermory on the island of Mull. Close to the settlement stands 13th-century Mingary Castle (not open). This was originally the seat of the MacIains and later the Campbells of Ardnamurchan, who held it for the king during the Jacobite rising in 1745.

Beyond Kilchoan is Ardnamurchan Point, the most westerly point on the British mainland. The view from here encompasses the Inner Hebrides and the islands of Barra and South Uist. Its lighthouse was built in the 1840s by Alan Stevenson, one of the three brothers who followed their father in designing lighthouses. The building is constructed of pink granite from the Ross of Mull and the design was influenced by Egyptian architecture.

*i Pier Road (seasonal)*

▶ *Return to Salen along the* ***B8007****, then turn right at the* ***A861*** *to Strontian.*

**11 Strontian,** Highland
The modern portion of this village lies near the main road while the older part is to be found on the western side of the Strontian River. From 1722 to 1904, this was the site of mines extracting lead, zinc and silver, but the most lasting contribution the village gave to science was through the discovery here in 1764 of the mineral strontianite. The examination of this mineral led to the discovery of the metal element strontium, used in fireworks. Its radioisotope, Strontium 90, is used in nuclear power sources. The former mining area is now a source of barytes, which is used in drillers' 'mud' as a lubricating agent for the drilling mechanism on North Sea oil rigs.

Ariundle Oakwood Nature Reserve lies to the north of the Strontian River and has a collection of fine oaks and Scots pines. A pleasant nature trail can be followed through the reserve.

*i Strontian (seasonal)*

▶ *Continue on the* ***A861****, then turn right at the* ***A884****. Follow this to Loch Aline and then continue to the village of Lochaline.*

**12 Lochaline,** Highland
Peaceful Loch Aline, which slices into the broad peninsula of Morvern, seems a rather incongruous place to have a modern mine, but close to the village is a source of very pure silica sand which is used in the production of high quality glassware. Behind the village, in the graveyard of Keil Church, stands a tall 15th-century Celtic cross, known as the Morvern Cross. Lochaline has a ferry service to Fishnish on Mull.

At the head of the loch stand Kinlochaline Castle (not open) and Ardtornish House, which has extensive gardens that are well worth visiting. To the south of the mansion stands 14th-century Ardtornish Castle, an imposing building on the coast that still acts as an important landmark to seafarers travelling down through the Sound of Mull.

▶ *Return on the* ***A884*** *to the junction (right) with the* ***B8043****. Cars should follow this unclassified road until the* ***A861*** *is met and then turn right and follow this road to Ardgour. Vehicles pulling caravans should avoid the* ***B8043*** *and instead continue on the* ***A884*** *to its junction with the* ***A861****; then turn right to Ardgour.*

**13 Ardgour,** Highland
The small village of Ardgour has developed at this important crossing over Loch Linnhe. The old jetty here was built by Thomas Telford in 1815, at about the same time as the lighthouse, which still acts as a prominent landmark.

▶ *Take the Corran ferry across Loch Linnhe at the Corran Narrows. At the other side turn left at the* ***A82*** *and return to Fort William, 8 miles (13km).*

The distinctive landmark of Ardgour lighthouse and Corran ferry on Loch Linnhe

# The Western Highlands

The fort at Fort Augustus, built by General Wade in 1730, was named after William Augustus, Duke of Cumberland, who brutally suppressed the Highlanders after the Battle of Culloden in 1746. In 1867 the fort became a Benedictine school; today it is in private ownership, and Fort Augustus is a popular base for cruisers on the Caledonian Canal.

**3 DAYS • 301 MILES • 484 KM**

ITINERARY

| | |
|---|---|
| **FORT AUGUSTUS** | ▶ Invergarry (7m-11km) |
| INVERGARRY | ▶ Shiel Bridge (36m-58km) |
| SHIEL BRIDGE | ▶ Kyle of Lochalsh (15m- 24 km) |
| KYLE OF LOCHALSH | ▶ Plockton (7m-11km) |
| PLOCKTON | ▶ Lochcarron (19m -31km) |
| LOCHCARRON | ▶ Applecross (18m-29km) |
| APPLECROSS | ▶ Shieldaig (26m-42km) |
| SHIELDAIG | ▶ Torridon (8m-13km) |
| TORRIDON | ▶ Kinlochewe (11m-18km) |
| KINLOCHEWE | ▶ Gairloch (20m-32km) |
| GAIRLOCH | ▶ Inverewe Gardens (7m-11km) |
| INVEREWE GARDENS | ▶ Corrieshalloch Gorge (39m-63km) |
| CORRIESHALLOCH GORGE | ▶ Strathpeffer (29m-47km) |
| STRATHPEFFER | ▶ Beauly (12m-19km) |
| BEAULY | ▶ Cannich (17m-27km) |
| CANNICH | ▶ Drumnadrochit (12m-19km) |
| DRUMNADROCHIT | ▶ Fort Augustus (18m-29km) |

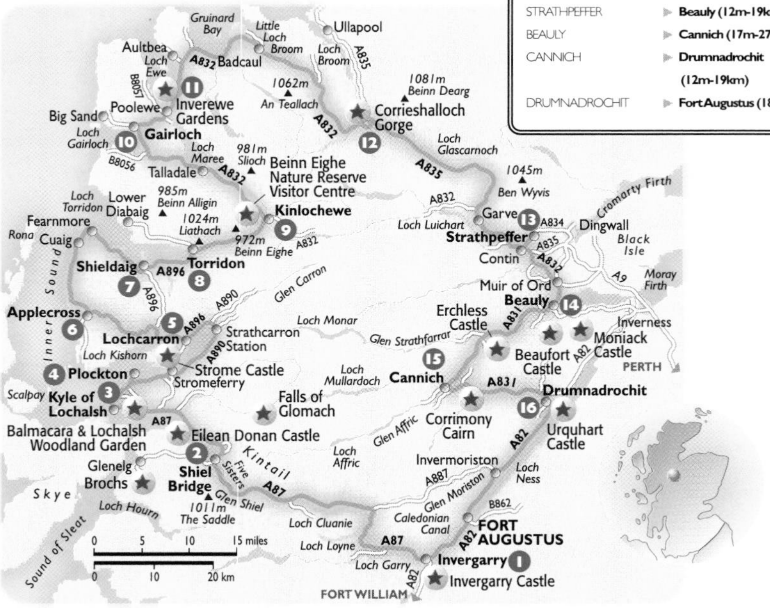

Eilean Donan Castle, resurrected from the rubble in 1912

*[i] Car Park (seasonal)*

▶ *Head southwards on the **A82** for 7 miles (11km) to Invergarry.*

**1 Invergarry,** Highland
This rather sleepy-looking village was the home of an important clan, the MacDonnells of Glengarry. To the south, within the grounds of a hotel, lie the ruins of Invergarry Castle; three castles have stood here, the last one having been burnt in 1746 by Cumberland because Charles Edward Stuart stayed here before and after the battle of Culloden. Just to the north of Invergarry stands the roadside Well of Seven Heads, a gruesome reminder of the slaying of seven MacDonnell brothers who had murdered their dead brother's two sons. The full story of this gory event is recorded on a monument inscribed in Gaelic, English, Latin and French.

▶ *Leave by the **A87** (to Kyle of Lochalsh) and follow this for 36 miles (58km) to Shiel Bridge.*

**2 Shiel Bridge,** Highland
The imposing entry to Shiel Bridge is by the magnificent Glen Shiel, with the group of mountains known as the Five Sisters of Kintail to the north. The mountains are seen to great advantage at Mam Ratagan, just a little to the west of Invershiel on the Glenelg road. Like many communities in this region, Shiel Bridge is a collection of houses at an important junction, in this case at the head of Loch Duich. Along the northern shore of the loch stands Eilean Donan Castle, which dates back to 1220. Shelled by a British frigate in 1719 during an abortive Jacobite rising, it lay in ruins until rebuilding started in 1912. It is now one of the Highlands' most popular and beautiful castles and is said to be the most photographed castle in Scotland.

There is an unmanned NTS centre at Strath Croe, to the northeast of Shiel Bridge, with useful wildlife displays explaining the natural history of this wild and beautiful area. A very rough cross-country path from Strath Croe leads to the Falls of Glomach where the water of the Allt a' Ghlomaich tumbles 750 feet (230m).

▶ *Continue on the **A87** to Kyle of Lochalsh.*

**3 Kyle of Lochalsh,** Highland
This bustling industrial village is the terminus of the railway line from Inverness. The controversial bridge to the Isle of Skye that replaced the ferries is reached by the A87. The western part of this peninsula lies within the NTS's Balmacara estate; 1 mile (1.5km) beyond the village of Reraig, Lochalsh House Woodland Garden is on the left. This boasts a fine collection of mature trees, and is developing more exotic species of plants such as bamboo.

*[i] Car Park (seasonal)*

▶ *Leave by the unclassified road that leads northwards to Plockton.*

**FOR HISTORY BUFFS**

To the west of Shiel Bridge lies Glenelg. The route to it has long been of strategic importance, hence the 18th-century military road and the (ruined) Bernera Barracks. It was used by Samuel Johnson and James Boswell in 1773 and is now followed by many summer visitors heading for the Kyle Rhea ferry to Skye. South of the village are two brochs, Dun Telve and Dun Trodden, built as defensive structures about 2,000 years ago, when they were over 40 feet (13m) high and had stairs and galleries built into their walls.

**4 Plockton,** Highland
With palm trees growing by the shore of Loch Carron, Plockton exudes the kind of peace and quiet that has attracted generations of painters; indeed, many would regard it as one of the northwest coast's loveliest villages. The sheltered position also provides a much-needed haven for yachts sailing along the west coast.

► *Return along the approach road to Plockton and turn left to head eastwards towards Stromeferry, following the shore of Loch Carron. Turn left when the* ***A890*** *is met. Follow to just beyond Strathcarron railway station then turn left on to the* ***A896*** *to Lochcarron.*

**5 Lochcarron,** Highland
Lochcarron is essentially a long string of houses (and a few hotels) along the shore of the sea loch. To its south is Strome Castle, once a stronghold of the MacDonnells of Glengarry, but destroyed by the MacKenzies in 1602. It commands a fine view of Skye. Just west of the village is Loch Kishorn, a deep and sheltered loch where enormous oil rigs were once built.

*i* *Main Street (seasonal)*

► *Continue on the* ***A896*** *but turn left at the head of Loch Kishorn to Applecross. This road is definitely not for caravans, but the* ***A896*** *from Loch Kishorn to Shieldaig and the minor road from Shieldaig to Applecross are suitable.*

**6 Applecross,** Highland
Applecross was one of the country's most isolated communities until the coastal road from Shieldaig was built in the 1970s. The traditional route, over the 2,053-foot (626m) pass of Bealach na Ba (Pass of the Cattle), one of the highest roads in Britain, was a formidable obstacle to many vehicles and it is often closed by snow in winter.

**RECOMMENDED WALKS**

A low-level walk runs behind Liathach, with a detour to the corrie north of Ben Eighe, Coire Mhic Fhearchair, which has three buttresses towering over a small loch. Take care, as this is very exposed country and inexperienced hikers should not attempt it.

An Irish monk, Maelrubha, landed at Applecross in the AD 670s and founded a monastery which was later destroyed by Vikings. The local church has an ancient cross slab 9 feet (3m) high, with a Celtic cross inscribed. This and others inside the church may date back to Maelrubha's time. An old chapel stands in the graveyard and two rounded stones in front of it mark the resting place of Maelrubha.

► *Head north on the unclassified road out of Applecross to Shieldaig. Turn left at the* ***A896****, then bear left to enter Shieldaig.*

**7 Shieldaig,** Highland
This charming village consists of a row of whitewashed houses standing along the loch's shore. Once famous for its herring fishing (its name is Norse for herring bay), it now relies more on tourism to maintain its livelihood.

Opposite the harbour lies the small wooded Shieldaig Island. From around Shieldaig there are wonderful views of some of the Highlands' best scenery. The mountains that run north from Loch Kishorn to Loch Maree are composed of red Torridonian sandstone, some 750 millions years old. However, around Shieldaig the rocks are a highly altered variety called gneiss which has been eroded to provide a low, smooth, platform above which the giant Torridon Mountains soar.

**SPECIAL TO...**

Many west coast fishing boats catch prawns and lobsters and local hotels often have wonderfully fresh seafood dishes on their menus. The shellfish, including delicious scallops, are particularly good.

▶ *Continue on the **A896** for 8 miles (13km) to Torridon.*

## 8 **Torridon,** Highland

The houses huddled together in the village are dwarfed by the mass of 3,360-foot (1,024m) Liathach, a mountain to be attempted only by experienced mountainwalkers as its ridge is very narrow and exposed. Composed of Torridonian sandstone, its name means the Grey One, as four of its seven tops are formed from grey-white quartzite rock.

An NTS countryside centre is situated just by the main road and this has displays and audio-visual presentations on the local geology and wildlife. Near by, there is a small Deer Museum; many breeds of deer may be spotted near here and can even be found wandering around the village itself.

Sitting on the top of the world, looking north to Torridon village

*i* *NTS Centre (seasonal)*

▶ *Follow the **A896** for 11 miles (18km) to Kinlochewe.*

## 9 **Kinlochewe,** Highland

This village stands at the head of Loch Maree, which was once called Loch Ewe, hence the name of the village. To its west lies the Beinn Eighe National Nature Reserve and the reserve's Aultroy Visitor Centre is just along the A832 from the village. Further on is an interesting nature trail which climbs to a fine view over the loch towards Slioch, the 3,217-foot (980m) high mountain that dominates the surrounding district. Loch Maree is one of the country's finest lochs and is steeped in history. The tiny Isle Maree was once a sacred place of the Druids, who are said to have introduced oak trees, significant religious symbols in the Celtic culture. In the 7th century, St Maelrubha came and set up his cell here and, for similar reasons, planted holly trees. In later centuries, paganism was practised here and rites involving the sacrifice of a bull occurred on the island as late as the 17th century.

The Loch Maree Hotel has a large boulder outside it on which is a Gaelic inscription celebrating a visit by Queen Victoria.

*Leave Kinlochewe on the* ***A832*** *for 20 miles (32km) to Gairloch.*

### 10 **Gairloch,** Highland

This widely scattered crofting and fishing community is the district's main centre and it has developed into a popular place for holidays as it combines fine scenery with long stretches of sandy beach. Fishing is important here and the harbour is well worth visiting when the boats come in. The fishing industry, crofting and other aspects of local life form important displays at the local Gairloch

Exotic and more common plants at Inverewe Gardens

FOR CHILDREN

Gairloch has some of the best beaches in the western Highlands. As well as the beach at the village, there are good ones near by, at Big Sand (to the west) and Red Point (further away to the southwest). For wet-weather activity, there is a swimming pool at Poolewe. The Gairloch Leisure Centre has facilities for sports as diverse as climbing, archery, badminton and short tennis. These are some of the few indoor activities in the region that may have to be considered if the weather is bad.

Heritage Museum, which was developed from a farmstead with a cobbled courtyard.

*i* *Auchtercairn (seasonal)*

*Continue on the **A832** to Inverewe Gardens, just beyond the village of Poolewe.*

**11 Inverewe Gardens,** Highland

In 1862 Osgood MacKenzie started a long labour of love when he began transforming an area of barren ground here into one of Britain's most remarkable gardens. Conifers were planted to form shelter belts, wet land was drained, soil was carried in on men's backs, and in 60 years the local people had created a garden that gives great pleasure to over 100,000 visitors each year. Inverewe lies at the same latitude as Siberia, but here, bathed by the warm Gulf Stream, it boasts palms, magnolias, rhododendrons and many other beautiful plants.

On a summer's day Loch Ewe is a peaceful place, a far cry from the days of World War II when it was a convoy station for ships bound for Russia or Iceland. Aultbea (a little further along the road) was the depot's HQ and remains of gun emplacements have been kept as reminders of the district's role in those dangerous days. Look out for information boards near Aultbea's pier.

*i* *NTS Centre (seasonal)*

*Continue on the **A832** to the **A835**. Turn left and continue for less than a mile (1.5km).*

**12 Corrieshalloch Gorge,** Highland

Much of the Highland landscape was sculpted by the movement of ice during the last Ice Age. Often the ice smoothed the land, but at Corrieshalloch Gorge its meltwater flowing down the River Broom gouged out this spectacular rugged gorge about one mile (1.5km) long. A narrow bridge crosses the chasm with the water plunging over the Falls of Measach some 150 feet (45m) below – this is not the place for vertigo sufferers! The bridge was built by Sir John Fowler, joint designer of the Forth Rail Bridge, but this is hardly on the same scale and there is a limit to the number of people permitted on the bridge at one time.

The busy fishing port of Ullapool lies further down Loch Broom. It was founded in 1788 by the British Fisheries Society to take advantage of the huge shoals of herring found in the nearby seas. It is an important ferry terminal for Stornoway; cruises to the Summer Isles are also available from the harbour.

*Head southeast on the **A835** towards Inverness. Turn left at Contin on to the **A834** to Strathpeffer.*

**13 Strathpeffer,** Highland

Strathpeffer prospered as a spa in the 19th century after springs (four sulphur and one chalybeate) were developed. The Victorian hotels and large villas date from the spa's heyday and today the hotels still do a brisk trade, catering mainly for bus tours. The spa water can be sampled in a small building by the Square but beware – its taste is even more pungent than its smell! Local handicrafts can be bought at the small shops now occupying the old railway station buildings.

At the northern end of the village is the Eagle Stone, a Pictish stone also said to celebrate a victory of the Munros over the MacDonalds. To the east, the prominent hill of Knockfarrel affords fine views over the district.

*i* *The Square (seasonal)*

*Return along the **A834** to the **A835** and turn left. Turn right at the **A832** and at Muir of Ord take the **A862** southwards to Beauly.*

**14 Beauly,** Highland

Mary, Queen of Scots is supposed to have come here in 1564 and taken a liking to the place; tradition has it she described it as a '*beau lieu*' (beautiful place), hence its name. However, it is more likely Beauly derives from the name given to the 13th-century priory around which the town was built. Beauly Priory was founded in 1230 and the present ruins date from the 13th to the 16th centuries. In 1572 Lord Ruthven obtained royal permission to strip the lead off the roof and by 1633 the building was in a ruinous condition. The town's 'modern' planned layout (built around 1840) features a wide market square and a grid street pattern.

There are many castles in the area. To the southeast is Moniack Castle, which makes wine from local produce; to the south is Beaufort Castle (not open), built about 1880 in Scots baronial style; and near the road to Cannich is Erchless Castle (not open), described in the 19th century as 'modernised, yet still a stately old pile'.

*Leave on the **A862** (to Inverness) and turn right at the **A831** and continue to Cannich.*

**15 Cannich,** Highland
Cannich stands at the head of Strathglass, a glen not normally on tourist routes. The lower part of the glen has an impressive narrow gorge (at An Druim) and there are a number of hydro-electric power stations here.

To the west of Cannich lie some very beautiful glens – Glen Affric, Glen Cannich and Glen Strathfarrar. These make for good walks as the scenery can be spectacularly wild in places: Scots pines are being regenerated and there are chances of seeing red deer. Corrimony Cairn is found just off the Cannich to Drumnadrochit road. This is about 4,000 years old and has a central grave chamber which can be reached by crawling through the passageway. Standing stones ring the cairn and the large capstone lying on top of it has small circular indentations called 'cup marks' on it. Further along this narrow road, the standing stone known as Mony's Stone can be found, as well as the walled rectangular graveyard of Clach Churadain (St Curadan's Cemetery).

► *Continue on the **A831** for 12 miles (19km) to Drumnadrochit.*

Loch Ness's most famous resident

**16 Drumnadrochit,** Highland
Huge numbers of visitors come here hoping to see the Loch Ness monster. The loch is only 2 miles (3km) wide at this point but about 750 feet (230m) deep and many 'sightings' have been reported. In the AD 600s, St Adamnan told how Columba drove back a monster when it was about to attack a swimmer. Frequent scientific expeditions have failed to prove that a monster exists; however, even sceptical visitors should keep a loaded camera handy! Two Loch Ness Centres (the 'official Loch Ness 2000' and the 'original') in Drumnadrochit have exhibits connected with Nessie, including possible photographs of the beast herself.

Just outside the village stands Urquhart Castle. The site may have been fortified in the Dark Ages but the present structure dates back to the 13th century. Its commanding position in the Great Glen gave it immense military importance and part of it was blown up in the late 17th century to prevent it falling into the hands of Jacobites. Further south, the road passes a cairn erected to John Cobb, who died on the loch in 1952 while attempting to set a new world speed record; he achieved the remarkable speed of 206mph (331kph) before the accident.

Brooding Urquhart Castle

The village of Foyers can be seen on the opposite shore of the loch. In 1896, Britain's first major commercial hydroelectric power station was built here to provide energy for an aluminium works. These buildings can still be seen though the factory has long since closed. Today, a large pump-storage scheme produces electricity using the water of Loch Mhor, which is on the moorland above the village.

► *Head south on the **A82** and return to Fort Augustus.*

**SCENIC ROUTES**

As a detour, the narrow and twisty road from Torridon to Lower Diabaig is highly recommended as there are splendid views of Loch Torridon. In addition, the small picturesque lochside settlements of Inveralligin and Lower Diabaig are worth seeing.

# The Wild West

This tour really does reveal the wide, wild expanse of the Highlands landscape. It begins at Bonar Bridge, named after the first bridge to be built over the Kyle of Sutherland at this point, designed by Thomas Telford but later destroyed by a flood. The village at Ardgay lies on the other side of the bridge.

**2 DAYS • 172 MILES • 277KM**

| ITINERARY | |
|---|---|
| **BONAR BRIDGE** | ▶ **Knockan Cliff (36m-58km)** |
| KNOCKAN CLIFF | ▶ **Inchnadamph (11m-18km)** |
| INCHNADAMPH | ▶ **Lochinver (13m-21km)** |
| LOCHINVER | ▶ **Kylesku (27m-43km)** |
| KYLESKU | ▶ **Scourie (12m-19km)** |
| SCOURIE | ▶ **Kinlochbervie (16m-26km)** |
| KINLOCHBERVIE | ▶ **Lairg (46m-74km)** |
| LAIRG | ▶ **Bonar Bridge (11m-18km)** |

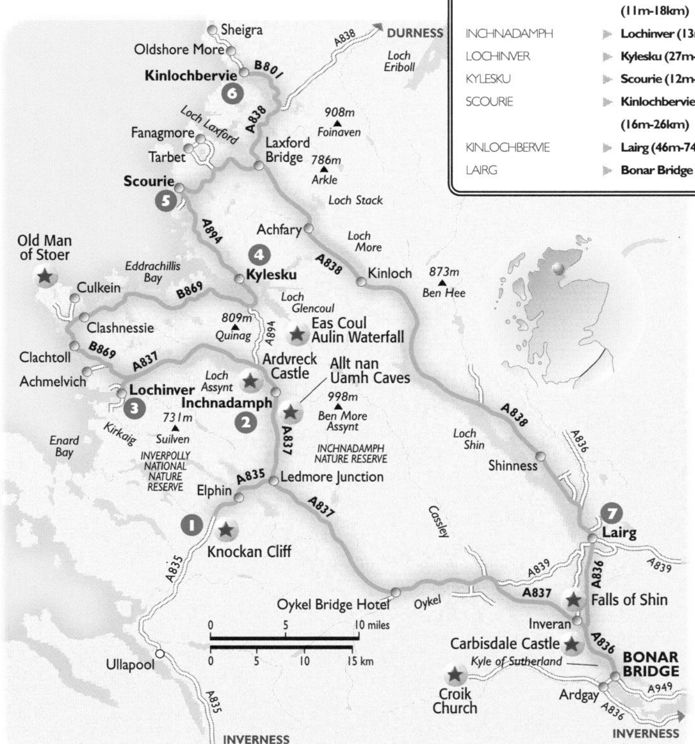

Inverpolly National Nature Reserve, as viewed from Cul Mor

**FOR HISTORY BUFFS**

To the west of Bonar Bridge, a narrow road leads through Strathcarron to Croick Church. This was designed by Thomas Telford in 1827 for what was then a well-populated district. However, in 1845, during the infamous Highland Clearances, the landowner tried to evict the people. Three attempts were made to throw the 18 families out of their homes and eventually they were forced to gather at this church with only a few possessions. They stayed there for a week, sheltering under blankets, and recorded their plight by scratching messages on the church's window panes.

*Leave by the **A836** and turn left at the **A837**. Continue on this road as far as Ledmore Junction, then turn left on to the **A835** to the Nature Trail at Knockan Cliff.*

**FOR CHILDREN**

As an unusual treat, why not spend a night in a castle? Carbisdale Castle is now used to house a youth hostel, complete with statues, paintings and beautiful woodwork, and will delight many children.

**1 Knockan Cliff,** Highland
The geological trail at Knockan Cliff provides a wonderful view of the district's unique landscape. Tall and isolated sandstone mountains rise steeply from the boggy moorland which is based on the very old rock known as Lewisian gneiss. This wilderness is part of the Inverpolly National Nature Reserve, which preserves this strange and fascinating landscape and the indigenous flora and fauna. The walks are spectacular, but only for prepared and experienced walkers. At

one point on the trail, you can stand beside the world-famous Moine Thrust where a huge slab of land (running from Loch Eriboll on the north coast all the way to the island of Islay) moved many miles westward, resulting in the geologically older rock coming to rest on the younger rock.

Much of Inverpolly is covered with wet heath, its main plants being heather, cottongrass and deergrass. The myriad boggy areas and little pools give shelter to bog myrtle and unusual plants such as the carnivorous sundew. Deer roam the land, spending summer in the high corries, but moving down to sheltered places during the winter. Otters, wild cats, pine martens and badgers can also be seen in the district. In good weather, this is the Highlands at its best; in bad weather, you won't see anything!

▶ *Return along the **A835** to Ledmore Junction. Turn left at the **A837** and follow this to Inchnadamph, 11 miles (18km).*

**2 Inchnadamph,** Highland
A hotel and a few houses stand near the road at the Inchnadamph Nature Reserve in an area popular with anglers. This is limestone country and the Allt nan Uamh caves near the valley of the River Traligill were used by late Stone Age people. Some of the earliest traces of habitation in Scotland have been found here, presumably attracted by the better soil and the 'ready-made' houses. Near the roadside houses, a cairn stands as a memorial to the two geologists, Benjamin Peach and John Horne, who unravelled the mysteries of the local landscape.

Beyond the settlement lies Loch Assynt, its dark pine-clad islands in stark contrast to the grassy hillsides. By its shore stands the ruin of Ardvreck Castle. In 1650 the Marquis of Montrose (well known for his exploits against the religious dissenters known as Covenanters) fled here. Neil Macleod imprisoned him and dispatched him to Edinburgh to be barbarously hanged, drawn and quartered. Although Macleod expected a bounty of £20,000 for Montrose, he was paid in oatmeal – 56,000 pounds (25,000kg) of it!

Calda House, which stands near the castle, was built in 1695 but was burned to the ground in somewhat mysterious circumstances in 1737.

▶ *Continue on the **A837** for 13 miles (21km) to Lochinver.*

The ruins of Ardvreck Castle on the shores of Loch Assynt

**3 Lochinver,** Highland
This is Assynt's main village and an important fishing port specialising in whitefish and shellfish. The life and history of the area is told in the village's Assynt Visitor Centre. During the summer it is popular with visitors, walkers and fishermen. A local place of interest is the Highland Stoneware factory, which produces high-quality hand-painted pottery.

From north of Lochinver, there are magnificent views of Suilven, at 2,399 feet (731m), one of Britain's most spectacularly shaped mountains. From this direction it rises as a huge dome of reddish-brown sandstone above the platform of the much lighter-coloured gneiss. The Vikings called it Sul Fhal, the Pillar Mountain, but the Gaelic name is Caisteal Liath, which translates as 'the Grey Castle'. It is regarded by many Scots as one of the country's most attractive hills; however, it is not one of the district's most-climbed hills as the moorland walk-in – although enjoyable – is quite long.

The tranquil harbour of Lochinver

[i] *Kirk Lane (seasonal)*

▶ *Leave by the* ***A837*** *and turn left at the* ***B869****. Continue on this road to the* ***A894****, then*

FOR CHILDREN

The area north of Lochinver has some wonderful sandy beaches, many of which can be relatively quiet even at the height of summer. Some of the best-known ones are at Achmelvich, Clachtoll and Clashnessie, all of which have sheltered bays and are very clean.

Crated local fish ready for export

RECOMMENDED WALKS

To the south of Lochinver, a path follows the River Kirkaig to the Falls of Kirkaig; further on, at Fionn Loch, there is a very good view of Suilven.

*turn left to reach the bridge at Kylesku. The **B869** is a narrow twisting road with many steep hills and it is unsuitable for caravans. An alternative route for caravans is the **A837** from Lochinver to Skiag Bridge and then left at the **A894**.*

**4 Kylesku,** Highland

The Kylesku Bridge, a graceful concrete construction that has won many accolades, crosses Loch a' Cháirn Bhàin with a view towards the pointed peak of Quinag, which dominates the southern shore.

To the east, the loch splits into two arms and boat trips are available on Loch Glencoul to visit seals and herons and to get a view of the remote waterfall Eas-Coul-Aulin. This is Britain's highest waterfall at over 650 feet (200m) high.

The car park on the northern side of the bridge offers excellent views of Quinag, the huge mountain that lies between Kylesku and Loch Assynt. It has seven peaks, the highest being 2,653 feet (809m). Like many of the neighbouring hills, it has a base of gneiss, but for the most part is sandstone; a few of the peaks have quartzite caps. Its name comes from the Gaelic Cuinneag, meaning a churn or pail.

SCENIC ROUTES

There are many beautiful stretches of road on this tour, including the route from Lochinver to Kylesku. Keen photographers may take days to travel this route as there are so many places where the views of the sea are quite outstanding. One particular detour north of Lochinver that is worth exploring is to follow the narrow roads to the Rhu Stoer lighthouse (built in 1870) or to Culkein. At the northern end of the Stoer peninsula is the Old Man of Stoer, a tall sandstone sea stack that stands just offshore.

▶ *Continue on the **A894** for 12 miles (19km) to Scourie.*

**5 Scourie,** Highland

This crofting community nestles comfortably in a sheltered hollow. It is a popular centre from which to tour the district and many walkers, fishermen and other visitors find this a charming base. Despite its northerly position, palm trees grow in the garden of Scourie Lodge.

The local landscape has earned the description 'knob and lochan' (a lochan is a small loch) as the undulating gneiss landscape is studded with little hillocks and countless pools. Where peat bogs have developed, these are used as a source of fuel and many of the villagers spend time during the early

The Kylesku Bridge spanning Loch a' Cháirn Bhàin

Crofters' cottages in Scourie, where a more traditional way of life still persists

summer cutting peat and stacking it to dry before taking them home for the winter.

To the north is Loch Laxford, a haven for seabirds and seals. Summer cruises on the loch are available from Fanagmore.

**BACK TO NATURE**

**The rocks in the Scourie and Laxford area are some of the oldest in Europe and may date back over 2,700 million years. They have undergone many changes and some indication of the complexity of the folding and flow of the rocks can be seen at the massive road cuttings at Laxford Brae, just after the A838 leaves Loch Laxford.**

▶ *Continue on the* ***A894*** *to Laxford Bridge and turn left at the* ***A838****. Turn left at the* ***B801*** *which ends at Kinlochbervie, a distance of 16 miles (26km).*

### 6 Kinlochbervie, Highland

In the 1960s this crofting village began its transformation into one of Scotland's most important modern harbours. Nowadays many boats, a large proportion of them originally from the more traditional fishing ports of the east coast of Scotland, land substantial catches of cod, haddock, whiting and many other varieties here.

The minor road beyond Kinlochbervie leads to the little community of Sheigra, passing glorious coastal scenery at crofting townships such as Oldshoremore (where there is also a superb beach). The 13th-century manuscript of the *Haakon Saga* records the fact that King Haakon anchored at Oldshoremore in 1263 when he commenced his invasion of Scotland.

The view to the east is dominated by the impressive hills of Ben Stack, Arkle and Foinaven.

▶ *Return along the* ***B801*** *and the* ***A838*** *to Laxford Bridge and turn to the left. Continue along the* ***A838****, then turn right at the* ***A836*** *to reach Lairg.*

### 7 Lairg, Highland

Lairg was established beside the River Shin in one of the few areas of decent arable land in Sutherland. This district was once quite well populated, but after the Clearances many of the displaced people emigrated to America or the British colonies. The Ferrycroft Countryside Centre features the history and archaeology of the area. Further down the river are the Falls of Shin with a visitor centre. This is a good salmon river and fish must climb the falls in order to return to their spawning grounds upstream. In days of old, poachers used to come to the falls so that they could spear or shoot the fish as they attempted to leap the falls.

[i] *Ferrycroft Countryside Centre (seasonal)*

A tapestry depicting the notorious Highland Clearances of the 18th century

▶ *Leave by the* ***A836*** *and follow it back to Bonar Bridge.*

**RECOMMENDED WALKS**

**Try the walk to Sandwood Bay: the path starts at Blairmore between Oldshoremore and Sheigra. Sandwood Bay abounds in legends, including the ghost of a 'bearded sailor' and visits by mermaids!**

# Northern Highlights

This tour traces the most northerly point of Scotland, visiting many wide, sandy – and largely empty – beaches. Dornoch is its starting point, with a fine bay and championship golf course. Its attractiveness is enhanced by its sandstone buildings and a spacious centre dominated by the cathedral.

**2/3 DAYS • 269 MILES • 433KM**

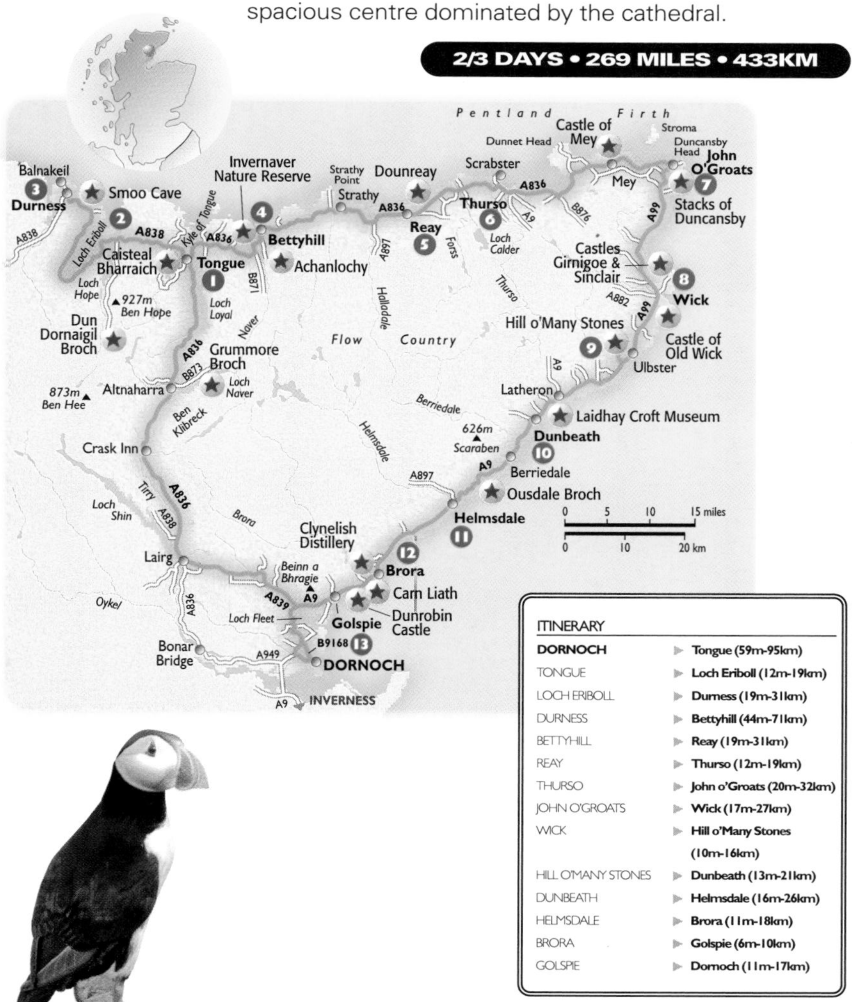


| ITINERARY | |
|---|---|
| **DORNOCH** | ▶ **Tongue (59m-95km)** |
| TONGUE | ▶ **Loch Eriboll (12m-19km)** |
| LOCH ERIBOLL | ▶ **Durness (19m-31km)** |
| DURNESS | ▶ **Bettyhill (44m-71km)** |
| BETTYHILL | ▶ **Reay (19m-31km)** |
| REAY | ▶ **Thurso (12m-19km)** |
| THURSO | ▶ **John o'Groats (20m-32km)** |
| JOHN O'GROATS | ▶ **Wick (17m-27km)** |
| WICK | ▶ **Hill o'Many Stones (10m-16km)** |
| HILL O'MANY STONES | ▶ **Dunbeath (13m-21km)** |
| DUNBEATH | ▶ **Helmsdale (16m-26km)** |
| HELMSDALE | ▶ **Brora (11m-18km)** |
| BRORA | ▶ **Golspie (6m-10km)** |
| GOLSPIE | ▶ **Dornoch (11m-17km)** |

The wide, sandy estuary of the Kyle of Tongue

[i] *The Square*

▶ *Leave by the **A949** and turn right when the **A9** is met. Turn left at the **A839** and follow it to Lairg. Leave Lairg by the **A836** and follow it to Tongue.*

**1 Tongue,** Highland
Tongue occupies a marvellous position overlooking the wide sandy estuary of the Kyle of Tongue. To the west of the village stands the ruin of Castle Varrich, or Caisteal Bharraich, a 14th-century stronghold of the MacKays on a site that may have been used by an 11th-century Norse king. Nearby Tongue House (not open) used to be the home of the chiefs of the MacKay clan.

▶ *Leave by the **A838** and follow it for 12 miles (19km) to Loch Eriboll.*

**2 Loch Eriboll,** Highland
This is one of the north coast's deepest and most sheltered sea lochs and it was used during World War II by convoys of ships waiting to sail across the North Atlantic. The sailors knew this rather desolate place as 'Loch 'Orrible'!

On the eastern side of the loch, a spit runs out to the rocky promontory of Ard Neackie on which are the very substantial remains of four lime kilns which were constructed around 1870.

▶ *Continue on the **A838** for 19 miles (31km) to Durness.*

**3 Durness,** Highland
This is a popular stopping point for visitors, not only for the local scenery, but also to enjoy the huge expanses of sandy beaches at the village and at neighbouring Balnakeil.

Durness is situated in a limestone area and is best known for Smoo Cave. The main cavern is huge – about 200 feet (60m) long and 110 feet (35m) wide – and is easy to enter. Beyond this, a second cave has a 'swallow hole' in its roof and a stream, the Allt Smoo, tumbles 80 feet (25m) into it. A third cave can only be entered by boat.

To the west of the village lies beautiful Balnakeil Bay which has a wide sweep of sand backed by tall grass-covered dunes. The site of the ruined church near by may date back to the 8th century when St Maelrubha of Applecross was in this district. The southern wall of the church contains the tomb of the murdered Donald

### BACK TO NATURE

The variety of good habitats, the plentiful supply of fish and the low human population have encouraged huge numbers of seabirds to nest along the coast. Particular places of interest include Faraid Head (near Durness) for puffins; Duncansby Head for many different types of cliff-nesting seabirds; Dunnet Bay for sea duck, divers and gulls in winter; and Golspie for sea duck and in particular eider. Loch Fleet is home to many birds, especially waders, so keen birdwatchers may wish to make a detour off the A9 and follow the southern shore of the loch before returning to Dornoch.

MacLeod, reckoned to be responsible for 18 deaths. It is said that he was so worried that his remains would be dug up after burial by families seeking revenge, he offered a local landowner a huge sum of money to reserve this tomb where he thought his bones might be safe. In many ways, the Balnakeil Craft Village is a memorial to days gone by. It was planned by the Ministry of Defence as an 'early warning station' but by the time it was built the technology was obsolete so the buildings were abandoned. They were subsequently taken up by craftsmen and women and their families who together have built up one of the Highlands' most fascinating communities. Crafts such as marquetry, knitting, pottery and woodturning are represented here and each of the craft shops has a display where the high-quality goods can be viewed.

Cape Wrath is reached by ferry and bus from the Kyle of Durness. The headland at Cape Wrath, the northwestern tip of mainland Britain, rises 360 feet (110m) from the sea and is topped by a lighthouse built by the grandfather of Robert Louis Stevenson, in 1828. Between the cape and the kyle is a vast expanse of peat bog known as the Parph and this comes to an abrupt end at the coast which has the highest cliffs on the mainland, the biggest being Clo Mor, which is over 600 feet (180m) high.

### BACK TO NATURE

While the attention of most visitors will be focused on the coast, the landward scenery should not be ignored as the peat bogs from Loch Loyal eastward are regarded as being of world importance. This is the Flow Country, a wilderness relatively undisturbed by humans for 6,000 or more years. It is home to such rarities as the freshwater pearl mussel, insectivorous plants such as the sundew and to birds – including 70 per cent of Europe's breeding population of greenshanks. Golden eagles, short-eared owls and peregrines all treat this as their hunting and breeding ground. Unfortunately, this beautiful and very desolate region is threatened by intensive forestry, often planted for tax advantages rather than from a wish to grow a worthwhile crop, and a great debate is still continuing on how to preserve this fine example of Scotland's natural heritage for future generations.

A potter at work at Balnakeil Craft Village

*i* *Durine, Durness (seasonal)*

▶ *Return along the **A838** to Tongue, then follow the **A836** along the coast to Bettyhill.*

**4 Bettyhill,** Highland
Bettyhill was founded by people displaced during the Clearances and the name derives from Elizabeth, Countess of Sutherland, wife of the duke who was responsible for many of the region's evictions. The local Strathnaver Museum is housed in a church built in 1774 and in the churchyard stands the Farr Stone, a good example of early Christian Celtic sculpture. The museum has features on the local

Dramatic Smoo Cave near Durness

clearances as Strathnaver was one of the centres of the evictions. To the south of Bettyhill stand the remains of the clearance village of Achanlochy, where seven families were thrown out of their homes.

The village stands close to the River Naver and looks over sandy Torrisdale Bay, on the southern side of which is the Invernaver Nature Reserve. Its flora is of an unusual mix as blown shell-sand has mixed with the otherwise acid soil and supports a wide variety of plants, including dwarf juniper, thrift, alpine bistort and creeping willow.

[i] *Clachan, Bettyhill (seasonal)*

▶ *Continue on the **A836** to Reay.*

**5 Reay,** Highland

The original Reay was buried in sand in the early 18th century, but the village was rebuilt and the local church dates from 1839 when the new community was being re-established. Reay has given its name to the 'Reay Country', the great inland tract of deer 'forest', though it should be noted that when the word 'forest' is used to describe a hunting ground, it does not necessarily imply that there are many trees there!

Today, Reay is best known for the hemispherical dome of the nearby nuclear reactor at Dounreay. In 1955 construction of the Dounreay Fast Reactor was begun in order to produce electricity. In 1974 the Prototype Fast Reactor began operating. Neither of these plants now produce electricity, but the site houses the UKAEA Exhibition Centre.

▶ *Continue on the **A836** for 12 miles (19km) to Thurso.*

**6 Thurso,** Highland

Thurso began life as a fishing settlement and the fishermen's houses can be seen above the harbour. However, it developed rapidly in the early 19th century when huge quantities of Caithness 'flags' were exported. These are the flat slabs of local sandstone that were in demand for pavements in the greatly expanding towns and cities of Britain and other countries. The flags are so plentiful here that even local fences are constructed with them.

The ruins of Old St Peter's Kirk in Thurso

Thurso expanded dramatically as a result of the building of the reactors at Dounreay, but it still has a number of substantial sandstone buildings and these help to retain its homely character. The ruined 17th-century Thurso Castle (fenced off) overlooks the harbour and beyond it is Harold's Tower, erected over the grave of Earl Harold, the 12th-century ruler of parts of Caithness, Orkney and Shetland.

The Thurso Heritage Museum contains a wide variety of interesting artefacts, including the Ulbster Stone (a Pictish sculptured stone), and also an important collection of rocks and fossils collected by Robert Dick in the 19th century.

Northwest of Thurso, on the A836, is the village of Mey. The Castle of Mey was the summer residence of the late Queen Mother.

[i] *Riverside (seasonal)*

▶ *Continue on the **A836** for 20 miles (32km) to John o' Groats.*

**7 John o' Groats,** Highland

This is often thought to be mainland Britain's most northerly point, but in fact Dunnet Head (to the west) holds that distinction. However, it is the country's most northerly village and therefore either the start or finish of the ever popular John o' Groats to Land's End long-distance walks. The village was named after Jan de Groot, a Dutchman who started a ferry service from here to Orkney in the 16th century.

Near by, Duncansby Head, the northeastern tip of the mainland, has cliffs 210 feet (64m) high and a lighthouse. With care, the cliff tops can be followed to view the pinnacles called the Stacks of Duncansby and other sea stacks and cliffs that the sea has carved out of the sandstone.

The Last House in John o' Groats, erroneously thought to be Britain's most northerly point

*i County Road (seasonal)*

▶ *Leave by the **A99** to Wick.*

**8 Wick,** Highland

Wick has been an important anchorage at least since the days of the Vikings; its name means 'bay'. Three castles testify to its strategic importance. The 12th-century castle of Old Wick stands to the south of the town; further north, the 15th-century Castle Girnigoe and 17th-century Castle Sinclair remain, though reduced to spectacular clifftop ruins.

Wick is still an important and busy place, with a fine harbour that was originally built for the once-prosperous herring industry. An earlier harbour was built at Pulteneytown by Thomas Telford in 1806 to encourage evicted crofters to take up fishing. Wick's Heritage Centre, on Bank Row, is in the heart of a district of old buildings associated with the fishing industry, and has displays on the history of the town and the herring industry. On High Street stands Wick's old parish church, with the ruined 13th-century chapel of St Fergus in its grounds.

*i Whitechapel Road, off High Street*

▶ *Remain on the **A99**. Turn right at a signposted unclassified road to the Hill o' Many Stones.*

**9 Hill o' Many Stones,** Highland

This intriguing fan-shaped array of 22 rows of stones dates back to the early Bronze Age, and is a type of monument unique to northern Sutherland (though they are similar to ones found in Brittany). Their purpose is still an unresolved mystery though it has been said that this could be some sort of ancient computer used to predict the movement of heavenly bodies.

### FOR HISTORY BUFFS

Pictish brochs can be found in many places on this tour. The most substantial ones near the route are Cairn Laith (south of Brae) and Ousdale Broch (north of Helmsdale). Good ones further off the route are Dun Dornaigil (south of Loch Hope) and Grummore Broch (north of Loch Naver).

▶ *Continue on the **A99** and **A9** for 13 miles (21km) to Dunbeath.*

**10 Dunbeath,** Highland

Dunbeath was the home of Highland writer Neil Gunn, whose books include *The Silver Darlings*. The local Heritage Centre (housed in the school that Gunn attended) has displays on the lives of crofters and the history of the district. Laidhay Croft Museum, just north of the village, occupies a traditional longhouse and barn steading worked up until 1968. Parts of this thatched building may date back to the late 18th century though most of it is mid-19th-century.

### RECOMMENDED WALK

From the Dunbeath Heritage Centre head towards the viewpoint overlooking the harbour and village, then proceed to cross the old bridge. Turn left after the bridge onto a footpath which leads past the old meal mill and continues to the remains of a broch. Nearby is Ballachly, where the ancestors of local author Neil Gunn (1891–1973) farmed.

▶ *Continue on the **A9** for 16 miles (26km) to Helmsdale.*

**11 Helmsdale,** Highland
Set on the River Helmsdale, at the seaward end of the attractive Strath of Kildonan, this was where some of the most infamous acts of the Clearances were carried out by Patrick Sellars on behalf of the Countess of Sutherland. The story of these sad days is admirably told in Helmsdale's Timespan Heritage Centre. This award-winning exhibition also has displays relating to the Kildonan 'gold rush' of 1868–9. Although gold was never found in economically viable quantities, some people still find that panning in the river will often reward with small flakes of the metal.

*Continue on the **A9** to Brora.*

**12 Brora,** Highland
Brora has the unusual distinction of having had a small coal mine based on a seam 'only' 125 million years old and, of course, a great distance from the country's main coalfields in the Midland Valley.

Today, one of its most notable industries is the Clynelish Distillery, Sutherland's only malt whisky distillery; tours are available.

*Continue on the **A9** to Golspie.*

**13 Golspie,** Highland
This small resort lies beneath the wooded slope of Beinn a' Bhragaidh, and near its summit is perched a statue of the first Duke of Sutherland, who was known as the 'Leviathan of Wealth'. Between the years 1810 and 1820 he was responsible for the eviction of some 15,000 tenants from their homes, in order to use the land for lucrative sheep farming. The scars of these times are still visible all over Sutherland. Ruined croft buildings stand and decay where families were forcibly moved from their land.

A rather unusual shop in the village is the Orcadian Stone Company, which sells examples of rocks, minerals and fossils. It also has a fine exhibition of these natural treasures.

The Dukes of Sutherland built nearby Dunrobin Castle on a site that has been fortified for many centuries. The present castle dates mainly from the 13th century but much of it was built between 1835 and 1850. Queen Victoria described it as a 'mixture of an old Scotch castle and a French château' and it does have a certain fairy-tale look about it. The gardens are extensive and contain a museum with interesting Pictish stones, an ice-house (for storing perishable food) and an 18th-century doocot.

South of Golspie, the main road crosses the head of Loch Fleet, over a huge earthen embankment known as The Mound. This was constructed in 1816 by Thomas Telford, partly to support the new road heading northwards, but also to reclaim the upper reaches of the loch. Today, this section is colonised by alder and willow and has been classed as a National Nature Reserve. The River Fleet runs through a sluice at the end of the embankment and at certain times of the year salmon may be seen there waiting for the gate to open so they can continue their journey.

Above: Panning for gold in the Kildonan Burn, Helmsdale
Right: The fairy-tale Dunrobin Castle, one of Queen Victoria's favourite places

*Continue on the **A9**, then turn left at the **B9168** in order to return to Dornoch, 11 miles (17km).*

**SCENIC ROUTES**

The superb coastal scenery, both cliffs and beaches, make this tour very attractive, especially along the north coast and near the high headlands in the northeast. The Strath of Kildonan is a fine drive for those wanting a detour.

# Easter Ross & the Black Isle

Away from the dramatic Highlands scenery of previous chapters, this tour takes in gentler countryside and coastal roads. The tour begins in Dingwall, a town which has enjoyed a chequered history, having been a Viking settlement and later a market town with the status of a royal burgh.

**2 DAYS • 107 MILES • 173KM**

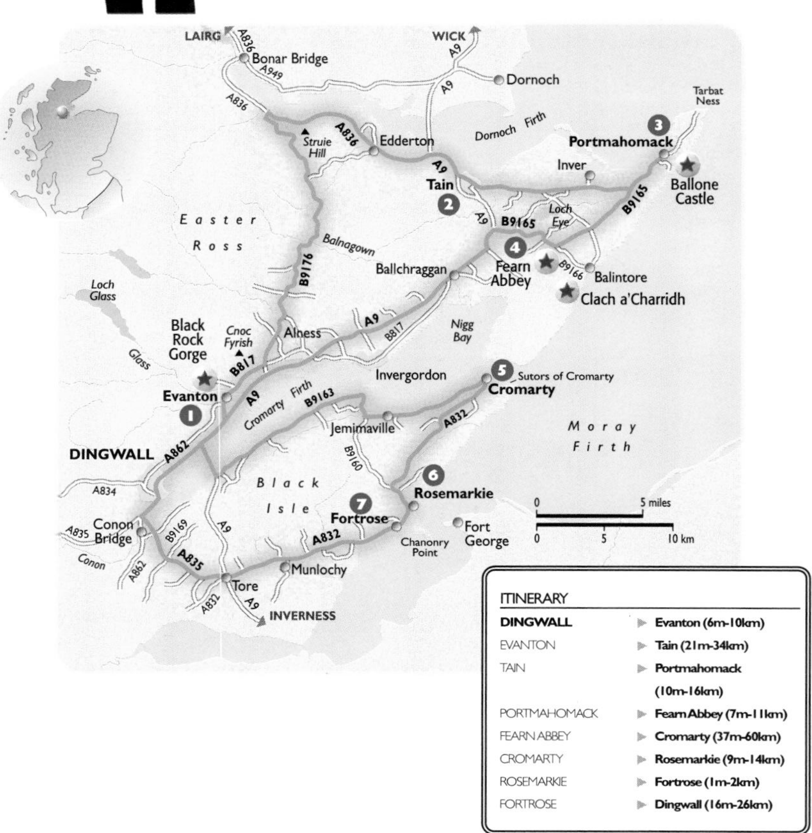


ITINERARY

| | |
|---|---|
| **DINGWALL** | ▶ **Evanton (6m-10km)** |
| EVANTON | ▶ **Tain (21m-34km)** |
| TAIN | ▶ **Portmahomack (10m-16km)** |
| PORTMAHOMACK | ▶ **Fearn Abbey (7m-11km)** |
| FEARN ABBEY | ▶ **Cromarty (37m-60km)** |
| CROMARTY | ▶ **Rosemarkie (9m-14km)** |
| ROSEMARKIE | ▶ **Fortrose (1m-2km)** |
| FORTROSE | ▶ **Dingwall (16m-26km)** |

*Leave by the **A862**. Join the **A9** heading northwards, then turn left at the **B817** to Evanton.*

**SCENIC ROUTES**

The sea views are particularly striking especially when driving past the firths' narrowest parts. One of the best known views is found on the Struie road; as this road descends there is a viewpoint on the right overlooking the Kyle of Sutherland.

### 1 Evanton, Highland

From the road, a curious monument will be seen on the summit of Cnoc Fyrish, the hill just beyond Evanton. This is a folly built in 1782 by General Sir Hector Munro to help alleviate local unemployment. The general had served in India and this monument is a replica of an Indian gate. Down by the Foulis Ferry, an 18th-century rent house is now at the heart of the Storehouse of Foulis attraction. Its features include imaginative history and wildlife exhibitions and an audio-visual theatre, and outside there is a display of traditional fishing vessels and a shoreline walk.

*Continue on the **B817** and turn left at the **B9176** (the Struie road). Turn right at the **A836** and join the **A9** for Tain. Bear left after 2 miles (3km) to enter Tain.*

### 2 Tain, Highland

Tain's name comes from the Norse word 'thing', meaning a parliament, as a Viking colony was established in this district. Later, the town's patron, St Duthus, was born here (in AD 1000) and he established a chapel just outside the town. He died in Ireland, but his remains were brought back and interred in the 14th-century St Duthus' Church. The town subsequently became a place of pilgrimage and James IV often travelled here, thus increasing its prestige and importance.

Tain's history was blotted, however, when it became an administrative centre for the Clearances. It was here that orders for the appropriation of the crofters' land were made. The deeds were carried out from the Tolbooth that still stands in the High Street, and it was within this building that crofters were imprisoned if they refused to obey the eviction notices. The Tolbooth is Tain's finest building; it was built between 1706 and 1733 with fine conical roofs on top of the turrets, and replaced an earlier tolbooth of 1631.

At Castle Brae, the Tain Through Time exhibition describes the history of the town; the centre also includes St Duthus' Church.

The Glenmorangie Distillery, renowned for its single malt whisky, lies on the outskirts of town.

Stained-glass window at St Duthus' Church, Tain

**RECOMMENDED WALKS**

The walk at Evanton to see the Black Rock Gorge is worthwhile, as is the nerve-racking walk over the narrow bridge at the gorge. Walks to lighthouses or looking points are usually interesting: try Tarbat Ness (a circular walk from Portmahomack via the coastal path that goes past Ballone Castle) or the look-out at the top of the Sutors of Cromarty.

Publicans' copper measures, Tain Museum

The fishing village of Portmahomack

FOR HISTORY BUFFS

The great Pictish cross slab, known as Clach a'Charridh, stands above the seaside village of Shandwick, near Balintore. It occupies its original position, and the face looking out to sea is engraved with a cross, angels and a beast. The other side has fivel panels, one of which shows a Pictish beast.

*Continue on the **B9165** and turn left at the **A9**. Cross the Cromarty Firth, then turn left at the **B9163** to Cromarty.*

*Leave by the minor road to Portmahomack. Turn left at the **B9165** to enter the village.*

**3 Portmahomack,** Highland
This pleasant lobster-fishing village sits in a broad bay with views across the Dornoch Firth. Just by the main street, an ornate Victorian cast-iron fountain celebrates the introduction of 'gravitation water' to the village in 1887 (water had previously come up from a well). Another unusual structure is the tower of the local church, which is domed.

Beyond the village, a minor road leads to a lighthouse at Tarbat Ness. To the east of Portmahomack the restored Ballone Castle (private) is passed on a walk from the village to the lighthouse.

*Return along the **B9165** for 7 miles (11km) to Fearn Abbey.*

**4 Fearn Abbey,** Highland
The original abbey was founded in the 13th century and is unfortunately best known for the collapse of its roof in 1742, which killed 42 people. This had been prophesied by the Brahan Seer, Coinneach Odhar. The 16th-century clairvoyant had the gift of the 'second sight' and during his life he gave many warnings of unhappy events that were to happen. Many of these came true and his penultimate prophecy, telling of the infidelity of the Countess of Seaforth's husband, led to him being burned alive in a barrel of tar. His last prophecy, made just before he died, foretold of the extinction of the Seaforth family. That took place in the early 19th century. Brahan, where he came from, is an estate to the south-west of Dingwall.

BACK TO NATURE

Both the Dornoch and the Cromarty Firth are good for birdwatching, particularly for waders when the tide is out. Since the district projects some distance into the North Sea it is the first landfall for many migratory birds and Tarbat Ness is often a temporary resting place for visiting birds on their migratory routes. The best times of year are April, May, August and October, particularly when the winds are from the east.

**5 Cromarty,** Highland
Cromarty stands at the entrance to the Cromarty Firth, a passage dominated by the headlands of the Sutors of Cromarty and the North Sutor on the opposite shore. This is an important anchorage and was used during both world wars. Today, the firth has an oil rig fabrication site and these massive rigs dominate the sheltered waters.

The village was once important as it was on the main route north from Inverness which ran along the coast and used a series of ferries across the various stretches of water. The village declined after the fishing failed and after it was decided that the railway route was to go on the other side of the firth. The most outstanding building from more prosperous times is the Town House, built in the 18th century. This contains the courthouse and has been opened as a visitor centre.

Cromarty's most notable inhabitant was Hugh Miller, whose cottage has been preserved by the National Trust for Scotland. Miller was a stonemason by trade but he never lost his childhood curiosity for collecting fossils and interesting rocks. He helped to popularise geology as he avoided the jargon of the professionals and

> **FOR CHILDREN**
>
> There are many fine beaches along the coast, including those at Cromarty, Fortrose, Portmahomack and Tain. As wet-weather alternatives, there are swimming pools in Alness, Dingwall and Tain. In addition, Alness has a sports hall and both Dingwall and Invergordon have sports centres.

he wrote a widely read series of articles entitled *The Old Red Sandstone*, published in 1841. However, Miller had strong religious ideas that contradicted his scientific findings and his writings were furiously attacked by the religious bigots of the day. His thatched cottage, built in the early 18th century, contains mementoes of his life. Within the house is an example of the fossil fish named after him, *Pterichthys milleri*, and outside stands a sundial that he carved himself.

► *Leave by the* ***A832*** *and follow it to Rosemarkie.*

### 6 Rosemarkie, Highland

With red sandstone houses and a red sandy beach to match, attractive Rosemarkie sits at the mouth of the Moray Firth opposite Fort George. St Moluag founded a monastic school here in the 6th century and a Pictish stone in the local churchyard is said to mark the saint's resting place. Other carved stones are among the exhibits in the local museum in Groam House, which has special displays on the Picts and the Brahan Seer. The Fairy Glen, reputedly the home of a witch, runs inland from the village and there are two waterfalls further up this nicely wooded valley.

The remains of Fortrose's medieval cathedral

► *Continue on the* ***A832*** *for 1 mile (2km) to Fortrose.*

### 7 Fortrose, Highland

Fortrose's main attraction is its medieval cathedral, which has an octagonal clock tower and a detached Chapter House. The local bishopric was originally at Rosemarkie, but it moved to Fortrose in the early years of the 13th century and work on the new cathedral was started at that time, although it was not completed until the 15th century. A treasure trove of over 1,000 medieval coins was discovered buried in the green in 1880.

The harbour is well sheltered but is now mainly used by pleasure craft. From the village, a narrow neck of land stretches out into the Moray Firth to Chanonry Point where there is a lighthouse. It was here that the Brahan Seer was burned to death, and a monument has been set up to celebrate this rather remarkable man.

► *Continue on the* ***A832*** *to the Tore roundabout. Join the* ***A835*** *and turn right at the* ***A862*** *to return to Dingwall.*

Fortrose cathedral: detail

# Over the Sea to Skye

Skye is the most scenically spectacular island of the whole of the British Isles, with glorious mountain landscapes. The gateway to Skye, Kyleakin, is guarded by the ruin of Castle Moil, a small Norse keep. The village is crowded during the summer months as this is the terminus of the railway line from Inverness.

**2/3 DAYS • 244 MILES • 392KM**

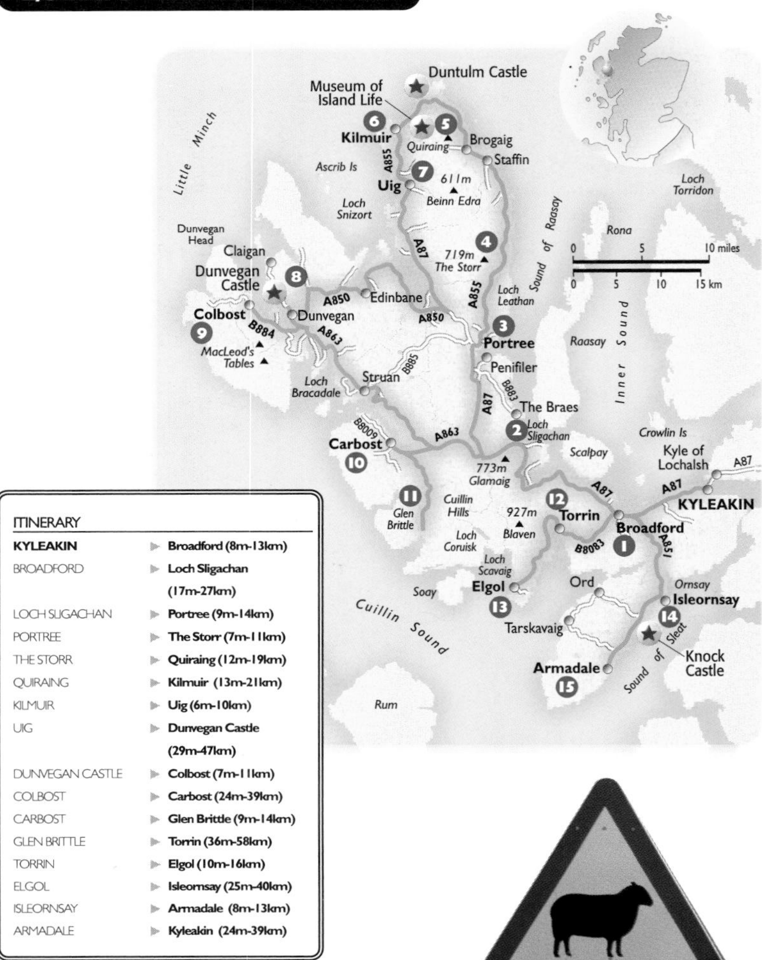


ITINERARY

| | |
|---|---|
| **KYLEAKIN** | ▶ **Broadford (8m-13km)** |
| BROADFORD | ▶ **Loch Sligachan (17m-27km)** |
| LOCH SLIGACHAN | ▶ **Portree (9m-14km)** |
| PORTREE | ▶ **The Storr (7m-11km)** |
| THE STORR | ▶ **Quiraing (12m-19km)** |
| QUIRAING | ▶ **Kilmuir (13m-21km)** |
| KILMUIR | ▶ **Uig (6m-10km)** |
| UIG | ▶ **Dunvegan Castle (29m-47km)** |
| DUNVEGAN CASTLE | ▶ **Colbost (7m-11km)** |
| COLBOST | ▶ **Carbost (24m-39km)** |
| CARBOST | ▶ **Glen Brittle (9m-14km)** |
| GLEN BRITTLE | ▶ **Torrin (36m-58km)** |
| TORRIN | ▶ **Elgol (10m-16km)** |
| ELGOL | ▶ **Isleornsay (25m-40km)** |
| ISLEORNSAY | ▶ **Armadale (8m-13km)** |
| ARMADALE | ▶ **Kylealkin (24m-39km)** |

▶ *Leave by the **A850** and follow it for 8 miles (13km) to Broadford.*

**1 Broadford,** Highland
This widely scattered crofting community lies beneath the Red Hills, a group of rounded granite mountains. This is a good base for the south of the island.

*i Car Park (seasonal)*

▶ *Continue on the **A87** to the Sligachan Hotel at the head of Loch Sligachan.*

**2 Loch Sligachan,** Highland
This is an idyllic base for any visitor, and especially for those who come to walk in the Cuillin Hills. The campsite by the shore must surely have one of the finest locations of any site in Britain – opposite towering 2,536-foot (773m) Glamaig, and with a view across the Inner Sound towards the mainland. A stroll from the road leads to an old bridge over the River Sligachan from which the Cuillin Hills can be seen to greater advantage.

The Cuillin Hills, reflected in the waters of Loch Sligachan

▶ *Continue on the **A87** for 9 miles (14km) to Portree.*

**3 Portree,** Highland
This is the island's capital and although the islanders themselves might think of it as a busy place, the pace of life follows the generally relaxed Highland pattern. This is certainly a most picturesquely positioned town, with its well-sheltered harbour nestling at the foot of wooded hills.

The town's name, Port an Righ, or 'king's port', celebrates the visit here in 1540 by James V in his attempt to persuade local chiefs that they should swear allegiance to him. He brought 12 ships with him to help them make up their minds!

*i Bayfield House, Bayfield Road*

▶ *Leave by the **A855** and continue for 7 miles (11km) to The Storr (after Loch Leathan).*

FOR HISTORY BUFFS

South of Portree, the B883 road leads to the settlement of Braes, where a monument celebrates the battles between local crofters and the police in 1882. The locals had asked their laird, Lord MacDonald, for extra land on which to graze their animals. He refused, even though the crofters were prepared to pay, and they decided to withhold their rents. Court orders were then taken out against them but the orders were seized and torn up when the sheriff's officers tried to deliver them.
In a further confrontation, the local police were helped by 50 policemen from Glasgow (and backed up by naval ships standing by with troops aboard should the 'trouble' spread). These events caused a public outcry about the way in which landowners treated crofters and this led to legislation being passed which guaranteed fair rents and security of tenure.

The Old Man of Storr on the Isle of Skye

**4 The Storr,** Highland
As the road heads northwards it runs beneath a steep escarpment, the highest point of which is The Storr, 2,363 feet (719m) high. To the right of this can be seen the tall pinnacle called the Old Man of Storr which is 160 feet (49m) tall. This is the site of Britain's most spectacular example of landslipping; the jumble of boulders, screes and pinnacles indicates where chunks of the mountain have slipped as the weak underlying clays and limestones collapsed under the weight of the overlying lavas.

> **SCENIC ROUTES**
>
> In good weather the whole of this tour passes through scenery which is truly memorable. Perhaps the most dramatic parts are north of Portree when the Old Man of Storr is seen with Loch Fada in the foreground, and also going down Glen Brittle and seeing the massive northern corries of the Cuillin Hills.

▶ *Continue on the **A855** for 12 miles (19km) to the Quiraing.*

**5 Quiraing,** Highland
To the northwest of the crofting community of Staffin, another escarpment indicates the site of a massive landslip. This is known as the Quiraing and is best approached on foot from the Staffin to Uig road. Nature has produced some strange shapes here, and some of the features have been given names like the Table, the Prison and the Needle.

▶ *Continue on the **A855** for 13 miles (21km) to Kilmuir.*

**6 Kilmuir,** Highland
This scattered crofting community is home to the Skye Museum of Island Life, which has a number of attractive thatched cottages that have been restored to show how people lived in these small houses a century ago. Near by, a tall monument in the local graveyard marks the grave of Flora MacDonald. She has a very special place in Scottish history as the woman who helped Bonnie Prince Charlie escape after Culloden. He had fled to South Uist but found the island crawling with hundreds of government soldiers, all of them keen to capture a man with a price of £30,000 on his head. Flora disguised the prince as her maidservant, Betty Burke, and smuggled him across to Skye, from where he was able to reach the Scottish mainland and make his escape to safety in France.

To the north of Kilmuir stand the ruins of Duntulm Castle, built in the early 17th century by the MacDonalds. It stands on a crag, protected by cliffs and steep slopes on the three seaward sides and a dry ditch on the landward side.

▶ *Continue on the **A855** to Uig.*

Flora MacDonald's grave at Kilmuir

### 7 Uig, Highland

This little port is the terminus for the ferries that serve Lochmaddy on North Uist and Tarbert on Harris, so the harbourside can be busy around sailing times. A little tower overlooks the harbour and though it looks rather old, it is in fact a Victorian folly dating back to the 19th century.

▶ *Leave by the **A87** and turn right at the **A850**. Follow this to Dunvegan Castle.*

### 8 Dunvegan Castle, Highland

The home of the chiefs of Clan MacLeod was built as a keep in the 14th century with its only entrance through the sea gate. Within the castle is the famous 'fairy flag', said to have been given to a MacLeod chief by his fairy wife. The faded and tattered flag is of Eastern origin and according to the legend it will protect the clan if it is waved at moments of great danger. Also on display is the drinking horn of chieftain Sir Rory Mor: this can hold the equivalent of two bottles of wine, and it is claimed that he could drain it in one draught!

On the other side of Loch Dunvegan stand the two flat-topped hills called MacLeod's Tables. Their name recalls a chieftain bragging to a Lowlander of the size of his dining table; to prove his boast he entertained his guest on one of the summits.

*i* *2 Lochside, Dunvegan (seasonal)*

#### BACK TO NATURE

Common seals and great grey Atlantic seals are found in Loch Dunvegan and boat trips to the seal colonies are available from Dunvegan. Golden eagles and white-tailed sea eagles may also be seen in the locality. The latter are the subject of a re-introduction programme in Scotland. In spring, the flower-rich meadows can be a colourful sight and alpine species are sometimes found growing beside the road in upland areas.

#### RECOMMENDED WALKS

Skye offers countless opportunities for walking – provided the weather is kind! One straightforward walk starts at Claigan, which is north of Dunvegan. This follows the shore and leads to a little 'coral' beach. The Old Man of Storr can be reached from a roadside path but the path is steep and there is a lot of loose scree in places. The landscape here is unique and the view is a fine reward indeed. The Cuillin Hills should certainly not be attempted by walkers with little hillwalking experience, but there are low-level walks that are easier. The best advice is to buy one of the local walking guides which are widely available.

View of the ferry loading at Uig

The Cuillin Hills seen above Loch Scavaig, near Elgol

▶ *Leave by the **A863**, then turn right at the **B884** to Colbost.*

**9 Colbost,** Highland
The little Croft Museum here has a thatched cottage and a display of 19th-century furniture and farming implements. If you have never smelled a peat fire burning then here is your chance!

> FOR CHILDREN
>
> The moors and lower hills of Skye provide good terrain for pony-trekking and there are facilities at Struan (south of Dunvegan on the A832), Penifiler (south of Portree) and Uig. However, it must be remembered that Skye's weather can be very mixed.

▶ *Return along the **B884** and turn right at the **A863**. Turn right at the **B8009** and follow this to Carbost.*

**10 Carbost,** Highland
This is the site of the Isle of Skye's only distillery, the Talisker Distillery. The peat fires used to dry the grain gives the whisky its distinctive smokey flavour.

▶ *Return along the **B8009** and turn right at the minor road that takes you down Glen Brittle.*

**11 Glen Brittle,** Highland
Many of the Cuillin Hills' lower slopes are covered with loose scree, while the upper parts are bare rock with little or no vegetation – the preserve of experienced hillwalkers. For walkers trying to capture all the 'Munros' (Scottish hills with a peak over 3,000 feet/914m high), their most difficult obstacle is usually the Inaccessible Pinnacle on Sgurr Dearg, which involves climbing a pinnacle at the top of the mountain. Definitely not for casual walkers, who would be best advised to stick to easier walks in the area.

The foot of the glen is often busy with walkers and climbers who are here to scale the hills. Looking up and around, there are marvellous views of the jagged hills with their long steep scree slopes.

▶ *Return to the **B8009** and turn right. Turn right at the **A863** and continue to Sligachan, then turn right at the **A87**. Follow this to Broadford, then turn right at the **B8083** in order to reach Torrin.*

**12 Torrin,** Highland
Torrin is best known for its fine view of the 3,043-foot (927m) mountain Blà Bheinn (or Blaven) and its precipitous rocky ridge known as Clach Glas. The latter entices the experienced climber. A couple of quarries near by are sources of the white Skye marble.

▶ *Continue on the **B8083** and follow it to Elgol.*

**13 Elgol,** Highland
Elgol, overlooking Loch Scavaig, has a small jetty from which there is one of the best views of the Cuillin Hills. From here it is possible to appreciate the shape of the complex, with a ring of hills surrounding Loch Coruisk. Boat trips to Loch Coruisk are available from Elgol. Looking in the other direction, the breathtaking view over the sea encompasses the islands of Soay, Rum, Canna and Eigg.

▶ *Return along the **B8083** as far as Broadford, then turn right at the **A87**. Turn right again at the **A851** to Isleornsay.*

**SPECIAL TO...**

Crabs are often landed by fishing boats at small jetties (for example at Elgol) or just on a suitable beach, so keep a lookout for local boats coming inshore. Many of the small boats make special deliveries to local hotels once they have landed their catch, so the food could hardly be fresher. Many people on Skye speak Gaelic and road signs and other notices are written in English and Gaelic.

### 14 Isleornsay, Highland

The village lies a little off the main road. At the road end is a headland on which there is an inn, a pier and a view towards the tidal island of Ornsay. The wilderness of Knoydart stands opposite, on the other side of the Sound of Sleat. Further south lies Knock Bay and above this is a rocky mound on which stands Knock Castle. Its ivy-covered ruins are sometimes called Castle Camus. It was built in medieval times by the MacDonalds of Sleat and its best known occupant was a lady known as Mary of the Castle.

► *Continue on the **A851** for 8 miles (13km) to Armadale.*

### 15 Armadale, Highland

Armadale can be a busy little place at times as it has a car ferry connection with Mallaig, but it is really a very picturesque spot in a sheltered bay. Close to the village stands the Clan Donald Centre. This is in the grounds of the now partly ruined Armadale Castle, which was built in 1815 and has interesting displays on the history of the MacDonalds. There are also gardens and woodland trails in the grounds. This part of Skye, known as Sleat, is sometimes called the 'Garden of Skye' because of its luxuriant coastal vegetation. Dr Johnson visited Armadale in 1773 and was duly impressed by what he saw of the fine gardens here, commenting that the planting of the gardens 'proved that the present nakedness of the Hebrides is not wholly the fault of Nature'.

An alternative route back to Isleornsay (instead of taking the A851) is via Tarskavaig on the western side of Sleat. This route gives really superb views over to Soay and Rum. There are also fine unspoiled beaches at Tarskavaig Bay and Ord.

► *Return along the **A851** towards Broadford. Turn right at the **A87** to return to Kyleakin.*

Isolated church and graveyard on the road to Elgol

# Spanish Gold & Celtic Crosses

Mull is an island of great beauty and emptiness. Its capital, Tobermory, can be a busy place in the summer, with Main Street thronged with cars, caravans and visitors, while its bay is usually full of pleasure boats. In 1588 a galleon of the Spanish Armada sank in the bay, and rumours of sunken gold still abound.

**1/2 DAYS • 143 MILES • 231KM**

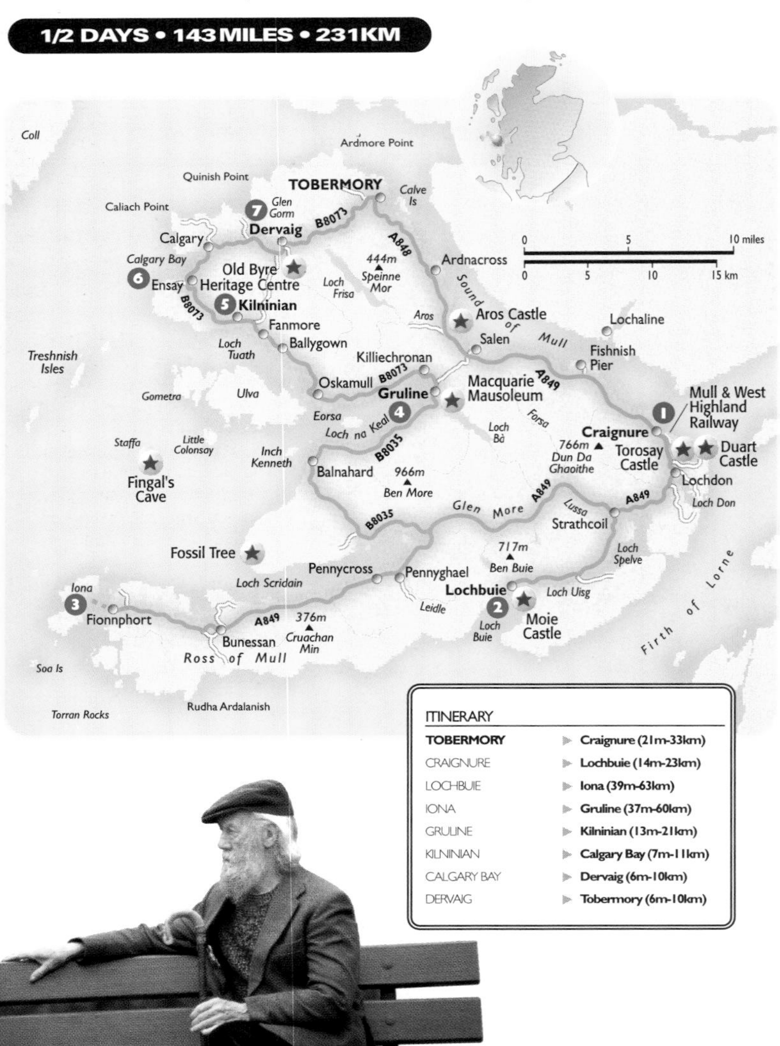


| ITINERARY | |
|---|---|
| **TOBERMORY** | ▶ **Craignure (21m-33km)** |
| CRAIGNURE | ▶ **Lochbuie (14m-23km)** |
| LOCHBUIE | ▶ **Iona (39m-63km)** |
| IONA | ▶ **Gruline (37m-60km)** |
| GRULINE | ▶ **Kilninian (13m-21km)** |
| KILNINIAN | ▶ **Calgary Bay (7m-11km)** |
| CALGARY BAY | ▶ **Dervaig (6m-10km)** |
| DERVAIG | ▶ **Tobermory (6m-10km)** |

**FOR HISTORY BUFFS**

Just north of Salen stands the ruined tower of Aros Castle. Like Duart Castle further down the coast, this commands a fine view over the Sound of Mull and was an important bastion of the powerful Lords of the Isles, the rulers of this region of Scotland from the 14th to the 16th centuries.

Torosay Castle gardens: statue details

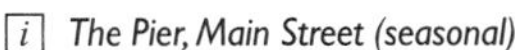

*i* *The Pier, Main Street (seasonal)*

► *Leave by the* ***A848*** *to Salen, then continue along the coast on the* ***A849*** *to Craignure.*

**1 Craignure,** Argyll & Bute

This is the island's main ferry terminal and the first place in Mull that most visitors will see. Torosay Castle stands close to Craignure and visitors can reach it by driving further down the road, strolling along a forest walk from Craignure or taking a trip on the miniature railway. The castle is not a fortified structure, but a Victorian mansion built in 1856; it has extensive gardens designed by Sir Robert Lorimer and a 'statue garden' with 19 Italian figures. A little further down the coast stands the stronghold of Duart Castle. This was originally built in the 13th century by the MacDougalls but later passed into the hands of the Macleans. Much of the present structure comprises their 14th-century additions.

View of the colourful harbour front, Tobermory

► *Follow the* ***A849*** *to Strathcoil, then turn left at the unclassified road to Lochbuie.*

**2 Lochbuie,** Argyll & Bute

The minor road down to Lochbuie is narrow and winding and passes through a well-wooded glen and a landscape that is quite different from the open moorlands so common in much of Mull. At the shore, the wide bay is ringed by hills and to the east stands the fenced-off ruined tower of Moy Castle, which featured in the 1940s film *I Know Where I'm Going*. The castle has a special dungeon off the dining room. It is a pit filled

### BACK TO NATURE

Compared to many islands off the west coast, Mull has considerable areas of native woodland as well as plantations. Look for woodland birds here, while golden eagles and buzzards prefer rocky crags. Offshore, sea birds, including guillemots, can be seen while others feed unobtrusively along the shoreline.

with water to a depth of 9 feet (3m) with a stone sticking up in the middle of the pool; this is where the poor prisoner sat – in total darkness! The fertile land at the head of the loch earned the estate the name the 'Garden of Mull'. Behind Lochbuie House stands a reminder of a very early settlement, a stone circle with nine uprights and three outlying monoliths.

▶ *Return to the **A849** and turn left. Follow this road to Fionnphort and take the ferry over to Iona. Cars should be left at Fionnphort.*

**3 Iona,** Argyll & Bute
The small island of Iona is a magnet for summer visitors, and is a place of great historic and spiritual significance. Part of Scotland's history is re-created in its abbey, now painstakingly reconstructed using traditional materials. The historic importance of Iona stems from the arrival here in AD 563 of the Irish missionary Columba, who established a monastery. The island became a religious centre and its influence spread throughout Scotland and into England, but it suffered at the hands of the Viking raiders in the 8th century. A Benedictine abbey was founded around the start of the 13th century and the oldest part of the abbey dates from that time. Until the time of the Reformation, there were over 300 crosses standing near the abbey but many were broken during those turbulent times and only a few massive examples now remain as beautifully carved memorials to the skills of the early craftsmen.

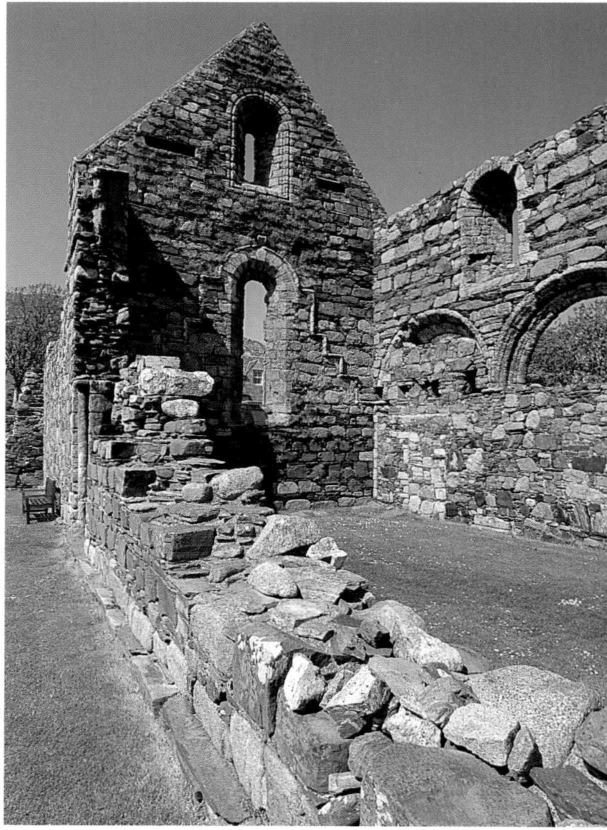

The ruined abbey on the Isle of Iona

Apart from the abbey, there are a number of other buildings worth looking at, including the ruined Augustinian nunnery and St Oran's Chapel. The chapel is the oldest building on Iona. The story behind its name involves its troubled construction. The walls kept collapsing and to placate the evil spirit that was felt to be causing this problem, it was decided that a human sacrifice was needed to be placed under the foundations – Oran was the volunteer. The chapel is in the Reilig Oran – the graveyard of kings – where many of Scotland's early kings and queens, and a number of Irish, Norwegian and possibly French kings are buried.

▶ *Return to Fionnphort and follow the **A849** eastwards. Turn left at the **B8035** to reach Gruline.*

**4 Gruline,** Argyll & Bute
At Gruline, a narrow road (right) leads to the mausoleum of Major-General Lachlan Macquarie. Born locally, he followed a career in the British army before becoming Governor-General of New South Wales in Australia, a post he held from 1810 to 1820. In recognition of this connection, the building is maintained on behalf of the National Trust of Australia.

### BACK TO NATURE

Much of Mull has been built up by basalt lava flows from long-lost volcanoes and the island has some unique volcanic features that are worth seeing. The uninhabited peninsula on the northern side of Loch Scridain is aptly named 'The Wilderness' and on its southern shore is the world-famous McCulloch's Fossil Tree, a large conifer that was engulfed by lava. It can only be approached at low tide and then after a long walk, so careful preparation is needed for a visit.

▶ *Continue on the **B8035**, then turn left on to the **B8073** to reach Kilninian, 13 miles (21km).*

**5 Kilninian,** Argyll & Bute
There has been a little church here overlooking the sea since at least 1561 but the present structure was built in 1755. At the back of the church there are a number of large carved grave slabs from the early 16th century. Dun Aisgain is found a little further along the road, standing on a rocky knoll overlooking the sea. This defensive site still has some of its 6-foot (2m) thick walls intact, and has traces of the internal mural gallery that was built within it. The Dun is best approached from Burg.

### SCENIC ROUTES

Most of the coastal roads give fine views over the sea, especially the sections by Loch na Keal and Loch Tuath where there are excellent views of the offshore islands, the largest of which is Ulva, where the parents of Scots missionary David Livingstone came from.

▶ *Continue on the **B8073** for 7 miles (11km) to Calgary Bay.*

**6 Calgary Bay,** Argyll & Bute
This wide bay, with its sandy beach, is a popular stopping place for visitors. Few people live here now, but on the northern side of the bay there are deserted townships and an old pier. The builders of the pier took full advantage of the local geology when they used a prominent volcanic dike as one of the walls. The existence of this prominent vertical sheet of rock could have led to the name of the bay, as Calgary may have come from the Gaelic word Calagharaidh, meaning 'the haven by the wall'. The town of Calgary in Alberta, Canada, was named after the bay.

▶ *Continue on the **B8073** for 6 miles (10km) to Dervaig.*

**7 Dervaig,** Argyll & Bute
Dervaig is a very pleasant little community that was established as a 'planned village' in 1799. The village and its environs have been designated a conservation area and this is a good base from which to explore the north of the island, Calgary and Tobermory. The most obvious village landmark is the church's round tower, reminiscent of Irish churches. The building is relatively modern, having been constructed as recently as 1905. Two other local places of interest are the Mull Little Theatre and, a little further out of the village, the Old Byre Heritage Centre, where displays depict island life.

### FOR CHILDREN

There are a number of good beaches round the coast, notably at Calgary Bay, which is ideal for bathing, and Lochbuie. The narrow-gauge railway to Torosay Castle is always appealing to children (and adults). This is the country's only island railway and was originally built in 1984 to encourage reluctant walkers to go from Craignure Pier to Torosay Castle; however, it has become an attraction in its own right. It has four engines, two of them steam-powered.

▶ *Continue on the **B8073** and return to Tobermory.*

The Isle of Mull's steam railway from Craignure to Torosay Castle

# MOTORING IN SCOTLAND

## ACCIDENTS

In the event of an accident, the vehicle should be moved off the carriageway wherever possible. If the vehicle is fitted with hazard warning lights, they should be used. If available, a red triangle should be put on the road at least 165 feet (50m) before the obstruction, on the same side of the road.

If damage or injury is caused to any other person or vehicle you must stop, give your own and the vehicle owner's name and address and the registration number of the vehicle to anyone having reasonable grounds for requiring them. If you do not give your name and address at the time of the accident, report the incident to the police as soon as reasonably practicable, and in any case within 24 hours.

## BREAKDOWNS

Visitors who bring their cars to Scotland and are members of a recognised automobile club in their own country may benefit from the services that are provided free of charge by the AA. Car rental companies normally provide cover with one or other of the major motoring organisations in Britain. On motorways there are emergency telephones at the side of the hard shoulder at one-mile (1.5km) intervals.

In the event of a breakdown, the vehicle should be moved off the carriageway wherever possible. If the vehicle is fitted with hazard warning lights, they should be used. If you have one in the car, a red warning triangle should be placed on the road at least 165 feet (50m) before the obstruction and on the same side of the road.

## CARAVANS

### Brakes

Check that the caravan braking mechanism is correctly adjusted. If it is fitted with a breakaway safety mechanism, the cable between the car and caravan must be firmly anchored so that the trailer brakes act immediately if the two part company.

### Caravan and luggage trailers

Take a list of contents, especially if any valuable or unusual equipment is being carried, as this may be required on arrival in Britain.

A towed vehicle should be readily identifiable by a plate in an accessible position showing the name of the make of the vehicle and the production and serial number.

### Lights

Make sure that all the lights are working – rear lights, stop lights, numberplate lights, rear fog guard lamps and indicator flashers (check that the flasher rate is correct: 60–120 times a minute).

### Tyres

Both tyres on the caravan should be of the same size and type. Inspect them carefully: if you think they are likely to be more than three-quarters worn before you get back, replace them before you set off. If you notice uneven wear, scuffed treads or damaged walls, you should get expert advice on whether the tyres are suitable for further use.

Find out the recommended tyre pressures from the caravan manufacturer.

## CAR HIRE AND FLY/DRIVE

Drivers must hold, and have held for one year, a valid national licence or an International Driving Permit. The minimum age for hiring a car ranges from 18 to 25, depending on the model of car. With some companies, there is a maximum age limit of 70. You can arrange to pick up your car in one town and return it in another. If you are hiring a car, you can often get a good deal with a fly/drive package from the airline.

The larger car hire companies have desks at airports and branches in major towns. These may not be the cheapest; telephone around for the best deal.

## CHILDREN

The following restrictions apply to children travelling in private motor vehicles:

Children under 3 years: front seat – appropriate child restraint must be worn; rear seats – appropriate child restraint must be worn if available.

Children aged 3 to 11 and under 5 feet (1.5m) tall: front seat – appropriate child restraint must be worn if available; if not, adult seat belt must be worn. Rear seat – appropriate child restraint must be worn if available; if not, adult seat belt must be worn if available.

Children aged 12 or 13 or younger child 5 feet (1.5m) or more in height – front and rear seats – adult seat belt must be worn if available.

Note: under no circumstances should a rear-facing child car seat be used in a seat that is equipped with an airbag.

## CRASH (SAFETY) HELMETS

Visiting motorcyclists and their passengers must wear crash or safety helmets.

## DOCUMENTS

You must have a valid driver's licence or an International Driving Permit. Holders of permits written in a foreign language are advised to obtain an official translation from an embassy or recognised automobile association.

Non-EC nationals must have Green Card insurance.

**DRINKING AND DRIVING**
The laws regarding drinking and driving are strict and the penalties are severe. There is only one piece of advice: if you drink, don't drive.

**DRIVING CONDITIONS**
Traffic drives on the left and goes clockwise at roundabouts (traffic circles), with priority given to traffic already on the roundabout, ie approaching from your right. Speed-limit and destination signs use miles (one kilometre is roughly 5/8 of a mile).

Motorways link most major cities; service areas are indicated well in advance. Roads in some areas of Scotland are very narrow. See also **ROADS**.

**FUEL**
The fuels most widely available are petrol and diesel, with LPG (Liquid Petroleum Gas) found at only 1,400 outlets in the UK.

Most of the petrol sold in the UK is Premium Grade unleaded with an octane rating of 95. This is suitable for use in all cars made after 1992. Super Unleaded (more expensive) has an octane rating of 97. This may provide improved performance in modern cars with electronic ignition and fuel injection systems.

Petrol stations are usually self-service and are mostly around towns and on motorways and major roads. Most motorway service stations and some on busy roads and in large towns open 24 hours, or at least late into the night. Most accept credit cards.

Fuel costs vary; generally the further north you go the more expensive it becomes. Lowest prices are at supermarket filling stations.

**INSURANCE**
Fully comprehensive insurance, which covers you for some of the expenses incurred after a breakdown or an accident, is advisable.

**LIGHTS**
You must ensure that your front and rear side lights and rear registration plate lights are lit at night. You must use headlights during the day when visibility is seriously reduced and at night on all unlit roads and those where the street lights are more than 600 feet (185m) apart.

**ROADS**
Roads in Scotland are generally good. In the Highlands and Islands of Scotland, however, and in some country areas, the roads can often be quite narrow. Single-track roads have passing places at regular intervals – pull into these only if they are on your left; stop level with those on your right and the oncoming traffic will make the detour. Never hold up faster traffic approaching from behind; stop at suitable places and allow following vehicles to overtake.

When driving within the larger cities and towns, try to travel outside the main rush hours of 8–9.30am and 4.30–6pm.

**ROUTE DIRECTIONS**
Throughout the book the following abbreviations are used for Scottish roads:
A – main roads
B – local roads
unclassified roads – minor roads (unnumbered).

**SEAT BELTS**
Seat belts are compulsory for drivers and front seat passenger. Passengers travelling in the rear of the vehicle must wear a seat belt if fitted.

**SPEED LIMITS**
Speed limits for cars are 70mph (112kph) on motorways and dual carriageways; 60mph (96kph) on other roads; 30mph (48kph) in built-up areas, unless otherwise indicated.

**TOLLS**
Tolls are levied on certain bridges and tunnels.

**WARNING TRIANGLE/ HAZARD LIGHTS**
If the vehicle is fitted with hazard warning lights, they should be used in the event of a breakdown or accident. If available, a red triangle should be placed on the road at least 165 feet (50m) before the obstruction and on the same side of the road.

**FERRIES**
Several of the routes in this book are on islands and can only be reached by ferry. Ferries can also be used to link some of the drives, avoiding long road journeys.

Scotlands premier ferry operator is Caledonian MacBrayne Ltd. Timetables for all routes are available on their website www.calmac.co.uk, and bookings can be made online or tel: 08705 650000.

Island Rover and Hopscotch Tickets can provide the most economical way to use Calmac ferries. Details can be found on the website.

Several independent ferries offer alternatives to Calmac on some of the routes. Tour 9 – Western Ferries (tel: 01369 704452; www.western-ferries.co.uk) offer a shorter and more frequent crossing from Hunters Quay in Dunoon.

It is possible to take a ferry shortcut from Tour 19 to Tour 24. Calmac operate a summer car ferry from Mallaig to Armadale in Skye. Other options include taking the community-run summer ferry (tel: 01599 522273; www.skye-ferry.co.uk) from Kylerhea on Skye to Glenelg on the mainland, leading on to Tour 20 at Shiel Bridge.

Calmac operate two ferry services to the Isle of Mull. The main route is from Oban to Craignure, with a shorter crossing between Tobermoray and Kilchoan on the Ardnamurchan Peninsula. Using that crossing, it is possible to make a connection between Tour 25 and Tour 19.

# FESTIVALS AND EVENTS

## JANUARY

### Ne'er Day (New Years Day)

Hogmanay celebrations (see December) continue throughout the night and the next day.

### Fire Festivals

Found throughout Scotland, fire festivals date back to pagan celebrations of the winter solstice. One of the most spectacular is in Stonehaven (see Tour 18), where townspeople gather just before midnight. On the stroke of 12 they light giant fireballs and march down the High Street swinging them around their heads, eventually hurling them into the sea from the harbour.

**For information:**
www.hogmanay.net/events/stonehaven

### Burns Night

This is a celebration of the birthday of Scotland's National Poet, Robert Burns, and suppers are held in his honour country-wide on or around 25 January. Traditionally the meal consists of haggis, neeps (turnip) and tatties (potatoes), washed down with whisky. The haggis is ceremonially brought into the room, preceded by a piper, and Burns' *Address to the Haggis* is recited before it is served. After-dinner entertainment consists of speakers, singers and music, with a few recitations of his more famous works, notably *Tam O'Shanter* and *Holy Willie's Prayer*. (See Tour 1 for 'Burns Country'.)

### Celtic Connections

Inaugurated in 1992, this excellent showcase of the finest Celtic music is now the biggest winter festival of its kind in the world. International musicians feature on the programme alongside performers from the Celtic countries.

**For information:**
tel: 0141 353 8000
www.celticconnections.com

## FEBRUARY

### Glasgow Film Festival

Featuring over 100 films and events, this is a relatively new festival but one that is likely to become exceedingly popular. (For Glasgow, see Tour 10.)

**For information:**
www.glasgowfilmfestival.org.uk

### The Fastern Eve Hand Ba'

This game in the Borders town of Jedburgh (see Tour 6) has been played annually in its present form since 1700 and is almost without rules. Hundreds participate but there are only two teams – the 'Uppies' and the 'Doonies'. They play a series of games throughout the day with a leather ball tied with ribbons that is thrown in the air at the market cross. The 'Uppies' have to throw the ball over the castle wall to score while the 'Doonies' goal is the Jedwater. Tradition has it that the original game was played using the severed head of an English general. Fastern Eve is the Tuesday before Ash Wednesday, Scotland's Mardi Gras or Shrove Tuesday.

**For information:**
www.jedburgh-online.org.uk/traditions.asp

## MARCH

### Whuppity Scoorie

This ancient festival was originally held to mark the arrival of spring. Nowadays it is schoolchildren who keep it going. Starting at 6pm with the ringing of a bell, they run round St Nicholas' church, Lanark, whirling balls of paper on the end of strings. After going round a few times and making as much noise as they can, the local community council throw some coins on the ground and the youngsters scramble to pick them up. There's also a week-long festival of storytelling, music and children's events.

**For information:**
tel: 01355 26100

### StAnza Scotland's Poetry Festival

The old university town of St Andrews (see Tour 13) is home to the only regular festival dedicated to poetry. The guests include world-class poets and writers, performing in a variety of historical and atmospheric venues.

**For information:**
www.st-andrews.ac.uk/standrews/stanza/

## APRIL

### Edinburgh International Harp Festival

Concerts, workshops and training courses are all on offer in this celebration of Scotland's oldest instrument. It features some of the finest players the country has to offer, as well as a selection of international artistes. (For Edinburgh, see Tour 7.)

**For information:**
www.harpfestival.co.uk

### Melrose Sevens

The Scottish Borders are famous for their enthusiasm for the game of rugby. While seven-a-side rugby is now played around the world, it was Melrose Rugby Club that first introduced it in 1883 as a fund raiser. Rugby Sevens can be found throughout the area, but the one at Melrose (see Tour 6) is the best and attracts thousands of spectators.

**For information:**
www.melroserugby.bordernet.co.uk

### Girvan Cycle Race

Over the Easter holiday weekend each year some 100 riders participate in one of the best cycle road races in Britain. It is split into four separate stages, each taking in some of the most spectacular scenery in the southwest of Scotland. (For Girvan, see Tour 2.)

**For information:**
www.girvanrace.info

**Easter Eggstravaganza**
It's Easter Sunday and over 6,000 eggs are hidden in the maze at historic Traquair House (see Tour 5), making this the biggest egg hunt in the Borders. There's a special hunt for the under fives.
**For information:**
tel: 01896 830323
www.traquair.co.uk

**Scottish Grand National**
This is the premier event in the Scottish National Hunt horseracing calendar and the culmination of the two-day Scottish Grand National Festival at Ayr (see Tour 1.)
**For information:**
www.ayr-racecourse.co.uk

**Dundee Jazz Festival**
The City of Discovery, Dundee (see Tour 12) presents an extravaganza of local musicians alongside a cast of internationally acclaimed stars like Martin Taylor and Maggie Bell.
**For information:**
www.jazzdundee.co.uk

**Spirit of Speyside Whisky Festival**
This festival provides a grand opportunity for whisky lovers to tour around 50 of the world-famous distilleries in Speyside (see Tour 15) and enjoy tasting sessions, a gala dinner, a ceilidh and exhibitions.
**For information:**
www.spiritofspeyside.com

**MAY**

**Highland Games**
You'll find Highland Games in every country to which Scots have emigrated in any numbers, but there's nothing like the atmosphere of the games in their home country. Tests of skill and strength include tossing the caber, tug-of-war and the throwing of various weights, from hammers to haggis. There are also the gentler skills of bagpipe playing and Highland dancing. Hundreds of events take place across Scotland between May and September.
**For information:**
www.albagames.co.uk or www.visitscotland.com (site search for Highland Games)

**Girvan Folk Festival**
Girvan (see Tour 2) has the best small festival in the country. Set in this little fishing town, with it's picturesque harbour against a backdrop of Ailsa Craig and the Firth of Clyde, it has a long history of showcasing the artists who will become the big names of tomorrow – Billy Connolly, Altan, Mary Black and Dolores Kean have all appeared over the years.
**For information:**
http://girvanfolkfestival.com

**Wigtown Book Town Spring Festival**
First of two intimate literary festivals in this delightful time warp of a town – a book lover's haven (see Tour 2).
**For information:**
www.wigtownbookfestival.com

**Moniaive Folk Festival**
Moniaive (see Tour 3) is one of Scotland's most picturesque villages and is well known for its colony of artists, musicians and writers. The festival is a series of concerts and competitions, with continually running sessions featuring visiting musicians in both of the hotels.
**For information:**
tel: 01848 200474
www.moniaive.com

**The Loch Shiel Spring Festival**
Mostly classical music is performed in the intimate settings of small hotels and village halls, as far apart as Ardnamurchan and Glenfinnan (see Tour 19).
**For information:**
www.lochshielfestival.com

**Traquair Mediaeval Fayre**
The oldest continuously inhabited house in Scotland (see Tour 5) hosts this successful annual event, which has jousting, a medieval masked theatre and early music at its heart. A living history encampment, with medieval traders, minstrels and jesters, is also there and visitors can see demonstrations of ancient crafts like tapestry, bookbinding and the art of the scribe.
**For information:**
tel: 01896 830323
www.traquair.co.uk

**Dumfries & Galloway Arts Festival**
This 10-day feast of culture spans May and June and has venues across the region (see Tours 2 and 3), from theatres to hotel lounges. There's music, dance, theatre, literary events, children's entertainment and visual arts, with performers from home and abroad.
**For information:**
tel: 01387 260447
www.dgartsfestival.org.uk

**Spring Fling**
In an area (see Tour 6) literally swarming with artists and craftspeople, this open-door arts and crafts event is the only one of its kind in Scotland, with over 100 (and the number is growing) studios open for the weekend. From traditional artists like sculptress Elizabeth Waugh and illustrator Clare Melinsky, both at Langholm, to off-the-wall chainsaw carver Rodney Holland of Moniaive and the philosophising glass worker Ed Iglehart at Palnackie, this is a five-star event and one not to be missed. An accompanying booklet provides maps and tours and suggests good places to eat.
**For information:**
tel: 01387 262084
http://artandcraftsouthwest scotland.com

**JUNE**

**Glasgow Jazz Festival**
A superb selection of internationally acclaimed artists is booked each year for the showcase concerts, but what really makes this event buzz is the rapidly expanding fringe. You'll

find gigs in coffee shops, hotels and bars, and lots of superb local musicians can be heard. (For Glasgow, see Tour 10.)
**For information:**
tel: 0141 552 3552;
www.jazzfest.co.uk

**Riding the Marches**
Common riding festivals can be found across the southern part of Scotland from June to August and most involve a horseback parade led by a standard bearer, who may be called the Coronet or, in Galashiels, the Braw Lad. The riders follow the marches (boundaries) of the burgh in a territory-marking ceremony dating back to more troubled times. You'll find ceremonies in most of the towns of the Scottish Borders (see Tour 7), and in Sanquhar, Lanark (both Tour 4), Annan and Musselburgh. In Dumfries (see Tour 3) the ceremony is part of the week-long Guid Nychburris (Good Neigbours) Festival.
**For information:**
www.guidnychburris.co.uk

## JULY

**Tarbert Seafood Festival**
Tarbert is a tranquil, west coast, fishing village and it hosts one of the few remaining seafood festivals in Scotland. The Seafood Queen and Princesses arrive in Tarbert harbour by fishing boat, their coronation signifying the start of the festivities. There's lots of music, street entertainers, amusements for the children and a traditional boat rally. But it's the food that is paramount. Loch Fyne is famous for it's seafood and you can sample it all here, as well as pick up tips on how best to cook it.
**For information:**
www.seafood-festival.com

**Glasgow River Festival**
On- and off-river activities abound at this celebration of the Clyde, past, present and future. Venues are the SECC, Science Centre and the Tall Ship at Glasgow Harbour. It's a great event for all the family over the city's traditional Fair Holiday weekend. (For Glasgow, see Tour 10.)
**For information:**
www.glasgowriverfestival.co.uk

**The Wickerman Festival**
Inspired by the 1973 cult movie of the same name, starring Edward Woodward, this alternative music festival takes place at East Kirkcarswell Farm, Dundrennan, near Kirkcudbright (see Tour 3). Apart from the eclectic selection of music, the highlight is the 30-foot-high (9m) reconstruction of the wickerman that is sacrificed on Saturday night when it is set alight.
**For information:**
tel: 01738 450442;
www.thewickermanfestival.co.uk

**Scottish Traditional Boat Festival**
For a couple of days in early July, the little harbour at Portsoy plays host to around 80 traditional boats, and visitors can enjoy demonstrations and exhibitions about seafaring, alongside all kinds of entertainments, food, music and craft events.
**For information:**
tel: 01261 842951
www.thebpl.co.uk

**Newcastleton Traditional Folk Festival**
The planned village of Newcastleton in the Scottish Borders, with its delightful squares, is host to one of the most enduring small festivals in Scotland. No big names are booked here, although you may see a few of them wandering about and in the sessions. What is on offer is a relaxed, friendly atmosphere, lots of competitions, ceilidhs and sessions with the music going on into the wee hours. Probably the longest-running small festival in Scotland.
**For information:**
tel: 013873 76254
http://newcastleton.com

**Edinbane Festival**
Edinbane is a small township on the Isle of Skye (see Tour 24). This non-profit festival started from the launch party for a CD and just grew from there. Now it's a mixture of village party, music festival and a showcase for young talent. Local band the Peatbog Faeries are an impressive example of the new wave of young Celtic musicians.
**For information:**
www.edinbane-festival.com

## AUGUST

**Edinburgh International Festival**
Scotland's famous arts festival runs for three weeks in August and presents theatre, classical music, opera and dance of the highest quality, with performers from around the world.
**For information:**
tel: 0131 473 299
www.eif.co.uk

**The Fringe**
An event that developed as an adjunct to the Edinburgh International Festival has now eclipsed the main event. It showcases less mainstream – often controversial – theatre, hugely popular comedy shows, concerts and children's events. Throughout the festival, street entertainers throng the city and there's a vibrant atmosphere.
**For information:**
tel: 0131 226 0026
www.edfringe.com

**Edinburgh International Book Festival**
This is the largest event of its kind, and runs as part of the Edinburgh Festival. A tented village is erected in Charlotte Square Gardens in the World Heritage-listed New Town and there, over the course of the festival, some 600-plus events are on offer, including meeting some of the world's top-selling writers. (For Edinburgh, see Tour 7.)
**For information:**
tel: 0131 718 5666
www.edbookfest.co.uk

**Edinburgh Military Tattoo**
For three weeks in August, Edinburgh Castle is alive with the sound of massed pipe and drum bands and other military bands from around the world. The programme also features spectacular displays, such as precision motorcycle teams, Cossack dancers, martial arts exhibitions and gymnastics.
**For information:**
tel: 08707 555118
www.edinburgh-tattoo.co.uk

**The Burryman**
The origins of this ancient pagan festival, held annually in South Queensferry, are lost in time, and even Sir Walter Scott was unable to cast any light on them. In its present form it dates back only as far as the 1930s. The Burryman, a strange figure wrapped in strips of flannel with spikey burrs (the hooked fruit of the burdock plant) stuck on to form a thick matting, leads a parade for 7 miles (11km) around the town.
**For information:**
www.ferryfair.co.uk

**Marymas**
The festival of Marymas dates back to the Middle Ages and was traditionally held to celebrate the feast of the Virgin. A few areas in the North, including Inverness and Caithness, still hold Marymas Fairs, but it's Irvine (see Tour 1) in the southwest that has the finest. It has been run by Irvine Carters Society since at least the early 18th century. Although the trade of horse carters no longer exists, the society is still around. The main part of the festival is the Marymas Parade, which has no motorised vehicles. Marymas Folk Festival, which runs as part of the celebrations, is one of the oldest in Scotland.
**For information:**
www.marymass.org or
www.irvinefolkclub.co.uk/festival.html

**Speyfest**
The Morayshire village of Fochabers (see Tour 15) is the base for this annual pan-Celtic festival, held over four days, which features performances from some of the biggest names in traditional folk music.
**For information:**
www.speyfest.com

**SEPTEMBER**
**Dundee Flower and Food Festival**
Three days of superb garden and floral displays, cookery demonstrations, craft stalls, children's activities, competitions and fashion shows, all contained in marquees in the superb grounds of Camperdown Country Park. (For Dundee, see Tour 12.)
**For information:**
tel: 01382 434940;
www.dundeeflowerandfoodfestival.com

**UCI Mountain Bike World Cup**
Scotland has some of the finest mountain-biking trails in the world and the world's finest mountain-bikers come to the Nevis range at Fort William (see Tour 19) for the British leg of the international UCI series. They compete for this prestigious prize in a series of downhill, 4-cross and cross-country events.
**For information:**
tel:0 131 557 3012;
www.fortwilliamworldcup.co.uk

**Wigtown Book Town Festival**
Scotland's official book town (see Tour 2) presents the second of two annual events and provides visitors with the opportunity to meet a wide variety of authors, sample some great Scottish music, spend a fortune in the town's bookshops and visit the most southerly malt whisky distillery in Scotland.
**For information:**
www.wigtownbookfestival.com

**OCTOBER**
**The Royal National Mod**
This is the premier showcase of talent from the Gaelic-speaking community, as well as a major showcase of Gaelic-related products and services. A different venue is chosen each year.
**For information:**
tel: 01463 709705
www.the-mod.co.uk

**Tunnock's Tour of Mull Rally**
Most of the roads on the beautiful island of Mull (see Tour 25) are single track with hairpin bends, steep drops and big hills. Cars compete against the clock in this superb spectator event.
**For information:**
www.2300club.org

**DECEMBER**
**Hogmanay**
Traditionally Scotland's premier festival, with people holding open house throughout the night to welcome friends, neighbours and even complete strangers. Visitors would carry a bottle – usually whisky – and sometimes also a lump of coal, enjoy a wee dram with their hosts and perhaps have something to eat, before moving on to the next house. While the tradition of 'first footing' continues, in many of the larger communities it has been overshadowed by street parties. The Hogmanay Celebration in Edinburgh (see Tour 7), in Princes Street Gardens, is the finest in the world. Images of the celebration, with crowds of people listening to bands performing on an open-air stage against a backdrop of Edinburgh Castle, are beamed around the world.
**For information:**
tel: 0131 529 3914
www.edinburghshogmanay.org

Page 164: A piper at the Edinburgh Military Tattoo

# ACCOMMODATION AND RESTAURANTS

Following is a selection of hotels (🏨) and restaurants (🍴) which can be found along the routes of each tour. The price brackets given below are intended as a guide only; check details before visiting.

**Accommodation Prices**
Hotel prices are divided into three price brackets:
**Expensive £££** – over £100
**Moderate ££** – £60–£100
**Budget £** – under £60
These are the rates for a double room for one night, and the price will usually include breakfast.

**Restaurant Prices**
Meal prices are divided into three price brackets:
**Expensive £££** – over £31
**Moderate ££** – £15–£30
**Budget £** – under £15

**AA Hotel Booking Service**
A free, fast and easy way to find a place to stay for your short break or holiday.
Tel: 0870 5050505 (lines open every day, 24 hours a day)
Email: accommodation@aabookings.com or book online at www.theaa.com/hotels

**TOUR 1**
**AYR** South Ayrshire
🏨 **Carrick Lodge ££**
46 Carrick Road (tel: 01292 262846; fax: 01292 611101).
8 rooms.

🏨 🍴 **Enterkine Country House £££**
Annbank By Ayr (tel: 01292 520580; fax: 01292 521582).
*British and French cuisines are served in this stylish country house, such as home-smoked venison and lamb noisette.*
6 rooms.

🏨 🍴 **Fairfield House Hotel £££**
12 Fairfield Road (tel: 01292 267461). *Modern cooking based on simple combinations, plus great sunsets over the isle of Arran.*
44 rooms.

🏨 **Savoy Park ££**
16 Racecourse Road (tel: 01292 266112; fax: 01292 611488).
19 rooms.

🍴 **Fouters Bistro ££**
2a Academy Street (tel: 01292 261391). *Modern Scottish cuisine, such as breast of Gressingham duck followed by caramelised orange tart. Closed Sun, Mon, 4–11 Jan.*

**TURNBERRY** South Ayrshire
🏨 🍴 **Malin Court £££**
On A719 (tel: 01655 331457; fax: 01655 331072). *Modern British and traditional Scottish cuisine in a coastal setting, offering such dishes as pan-fried breast of duck with lavender and raspberry sauce. Fixed-price four course menu or concise carte.*
18 rooms.

🏨 🍴 **Westin Turnberry Resort Hotel £££**
(tel: 01655 331000). *Scottish/French cuisine, such as rack of Dornoch lamb with braised puy lentils and natural juices.*
221 rooms.

**MAYBOLE** South Ayrshire
🏨 🍴 **Ladyburn ££**
By Maybole (tel: 01655 740585; fax: 01655 740580). *Traditional French cuisine served in a 16th-century dormer dower house. Reservations essential.*
8 rooms.

🏨 **Willow Bank ££**
96 Greenock Road (tel/fax: 01475 672311).
30 rooms.

**TROON** South Ayrshire
🏨 🍴 **Lochgreen House £££**
Monktonhill Road, Southwood (tel: 01292 313343). *One of Scotland's finest restaurants, within an award-winning country house hotel. The seafood is specially recommended.*
40 rooms.

**TOUR 2**
**NEWTON STEWART**
Dumfries & Galloway
🏨 **Bruce ££**
88 Queen Street (tel/fax: 01671 402294).
20 rooms.

🏨 **Creebridge House ££**
Off A75 (tel: 01671 402121; fax: 01671 403258).
18 rooms.

🏨 🍴 **Kirroughtree House £££**
Minnigaff (tel: 01671 402141). *Seared Solway scallops with maple and chive sauce is the house speciality. The local lamb is also tasty.*
17 rooms.

**WIGTOWN** Dumfries & Galloway
🏨 🍴 **The Bladnoch Inn ££**
Bladnoch (tel/fax: 01988 402200.
*À la carte menu of traditional Scottish dishes prepared from fresh, locally sourced ingredients.*
4 rooms.

**ISLE OF WHITHORN**
Dumfries & Galloway
🍴 **The Steam Packet Inn £–££**
Harbour Row (tel: 01988 500334). *Fine harbour views add to the enjoyment of the food, which specialises in seafood straight from the boats. Closed 25 Dec.*

**PORTPATRICK** Dumfries & Galloway
🏨 🍴 **Fernhill ££**
Off A77 (tel: 01776 810220; fax: 01776 810596).
*Dine overlooking one of the most picturesque fishing harbours in Scotland. The food, a mixture of British and European cuisine, is always perfect.*
23 rooms.

🏨 🍴 **Knockinaam Lodge £££**
Knockinaam Bay, near Portpatrick. (tel: 01776 810471; fax: 01776 810435). *One of the most elegant Victorian dining*

*rooms in the south. The modern-focused food, in an area famed for its cuisine, is about as good as eating can get.*
9 rooms.

**STRANRAER** Dumfries & Galloway

**Corsewall Lighthouse Hotel £££**
Corsewall Point, Kirkcolm (tel: 01776 853220; fax: 01776 854231). *Eat in a lighthouse, perched on the rocky coastline at the end of a single-track road. It's a bit of a drive to get there, but the food makes the trip worthwhile. Book in advance.*
9 rooms.

**North West Castle ££**
Seafront (tel: 01776 704413; fax: 01776 702646).
72 rooms.

**TOUR 3**

**DUMFRIES** Dumfries & Galloway

**Cairndale ££**
English Street (tel: 01387 254111; fax: 01387 250555).
91 rooms.

**Travelodge £**
Annan Road, Collin (tel/fax: 01387 750658).
40 rooms.

**Abbey Cottage Tea Rooms £**
26 Main Street, New Abbey (tel: 01387 850377). *For light lunches and afternoon teas.*

**CASTLE DOUGLAS** Dumfries & Galloway

**Imperial £**
35 Kings Road (tel: 01556 502086; fax: 01556 503009).
12 rooms.

**Urr Valley Country House £**
Ernespie Road (tel: 01556 502188; fax: 01556 504055).
19 rooms.

**Carlo's £**
211 King Street (tel: 01556 503977). *Family-run establishment offering well-cooked Italian standards.*

**Designs £**
179 King Street (tel: 01556 504552). *Fabulous restaurant with an organic slant, downstairs in a shop of the same name. Probably the most popular lunch spot in town.*

**Plumed Horse £–££**
Main Street, Crossmichael (tel: 01556 67033). *Serious and creative French cuisine, utilising the best local fish, beef, game and seafood. Closed Mon, Sun dinner, 25–26 Dec, 2 weeks in Jan, 2 weeks in Sep.*

**KIRKCUDBRIGHT** Dumfries & Galloway

**Arden House Hotel ££**
Tongland Road (tel: 01557 330544; fax: 01557 330742).
9 rooms.

**Harbour Lights £–££**
32 St Cuthberts Street (tel: 01557 332322). *Excellent home-cooked food. Daily 10–5, with extended hours in summer.*

**Selkirk Arms ££–£££**
Old High Street (tel: 01557 330402). *Modern British cooking with such delights as gâteau of prawns and cream cheese on a pear salad with red pepper sauce, or saddle of venison with a juniper reduction.*

**GATEHOUSE OF FLEET**
Dumfries & Galloway

**Cally Palace £££**
1 mile (1.5km) out of town (tel: 01557 814341; fax: 01557 814522). *Modern British cooking presented in grand style. Closed 3 Jan–3 Feb.*
56 rooms.

**Murray Arms ££**
Off A75 near clock tower (tel: 01557 814207; fax: 01557 814370).
12 rooms.

**MONIAIVE** Dumfries & Galloway

**Trigony House ££**
Closeburn (tel: 01848 331211; fax: 01848 331303).
8 rooms.

**TOUR 4**

**LANARK** South Lanarkshire

**Cartland Bridge ££**
Glasgow Road (tel: 01555 664426; fax: 01555 663773).
18 rooms.

**New Lanark Mill Hotel ££**
New Lanark World Heritage Site (tel: 01555 661345; fax: 01555 665738).
*Set in a former 18th-century cotton mill in Robert Owen's Utopian New Lanark, this restaurant serves a varied selection of the finest Clydesdale produce, cooked with a hint of Mediterranean influence.*
38 rooms.

**Popinjay ££**
Lanark Road, Rosebank (tel: 01555 860441; fax: 01555 860204).
38 rooms.

**BIGGAR** South Lanarkshire

**Shieldhill Castle £££**
Shieldhill Road, Quothquan (tel: 01899 220035; fax: 01899 221092). *Imaginative modern European cuisine, such as monkfish and scallop with turbot consommé, or wood pigeon with puy lentils and artichoke ravioli, and a superb wine list.*
16 rooms.

**Toftcombs Country House ££**
Peebles Road (tel: 01899 220142). *Modern British fare.*

**SANQUHAR** Dumfries & Galloway

**Blackaddie House ££**
Blackaddie Road (tel: 01659 50270; fax: 01659 50900).
10 rooms, plus 3 cottages.

**STRATHAVEN** South Lanarkshire

**Springvale Hotel £**
18 Lethame Road (tel: 01357 521131). *Modern Scottish cuisine, such as layered haggis gâteau and roast mallard with sweet red cabbage.*
14 rooms.

**Strathaven ££**
Hamilton Road (tel: 01357 521778; fax: 01357 520789).
22 rooms.

**HAMILTON** South Lanarkshire

**Holiday Inn Express £**
Strathclyde Country Park, off M74 (tel: 01698 858585; fax: 01698 852375).
120 rooms.

**TOUR 5**

**MOFFAT** Dumfries & Galloway

**Beechwood Country House ££**
Harthope Place (tel: 01683 220210; fax: 01683 220889).
*Closed 2 Jan–14 Feb.*
7 rooms.

**Black Bull Hotel £**
Churchgate (tel: 01683 220206; fax: 01683 220483).
12 rooms.

**The Star £**
44 High Street (tel: 01683 220156; fax: 01683 221524).
8 rooms.

**Well View £££**
Ballplay Road (tel: 01683 220184). *Daily changing six-course taster menu of classic European cuisine. Closed Mon–Sat lunch; reservations required.*

**WEST LINTON** Scottish Borders

**The Gordon Arms £**
Dolphinton Road (tel: 01968 660208; fax: 01968 661852).
4 rooms.

**PEEBLES** Scottish Borders

**Castle Venlaw Hotel £££**
Edinburgh Road (tel: 01721 720384). *Traditional British fixed-price menu, with an occasional Mediterranean influence.*
13 rooms.

**Peebles Hydro £££**
On A702 (tel: 01721 720602; fax: 01721 722999).
130 rooms.

**Tontine Hotel ££–£££**
High Street (tel: 01721 720892; fax: 01721 729732). *Scottish cuisine. Open all year daily.*
36 rooms.

**Cringletie House £££**
2 miles (3.2km) north on A703 (tel: 01721 725750). *Classic Scottish food with a modern touch, including the best seafood and seasonal game. Closed Jan–Feb.*

**INNERLEITHEN** Scottish Borders

**Traquair Arms Hotel ££**
Traquair Road (tel: 01896 830229; fax: 01896 830260).
15 rooms.

**GALASHIELS** Scottish Borders

**Woodlands House ££**
Windyknowe Road (tel: 01896 754722; fax: 01896 754892).
*Closed 25–26 Dec.*
10 rooms.

**TOUR 6**

**MELROSE** Scottish Borders

**Burt's ££**
Market Square (tel: 01896 822285; fax: 01896 822870). *Skilfully cooked Scottish ingredients include Border lamb, game and seafood. Closed 26 Dec.*
20 rooms.

**The Kings Arms £**
High Street (tel: 01896 822143; fax: 01896 823812).
8 rooms.

**Marmions Brasserie ££**
Buccleuch Street (tel: 01896 822245). *Lively contemporary bistro. Booking recommended.*

**Russell's Restaurant £**
28 Market Square (tel: 01896 822335). *Excellent home-baking, speciality teas and a selection of fresh and smoked salmon, cooked local meats and a changing menu of chef's specials.*

**The Ship Inn £**
East Port (tel: 01896 822191). *This pub serves good home-cooked lunches, and in summer you can eat in the garden.*

**JEDBURGH** Scottish Borders

**Glenbank Hotel £**
Castlegate (tel: 01835 862258; fax: 01835 863697).
6 rooms.

**Jedforest Hotel £££**
Camptown (tel: 01835 840222). *Sophisticated setting for inspired country house cooking, including braised beef with chestnut mash and Bordeaux wine sauce.*
12 rooms.

**Spreadeagle Hotel £**
20 High Street (tel: 01835 862870).
5 rooms.

**Simply Scottish ££–£££**
6–8 High Street (tel: 01835 864696). *Outstanding Scottish cuisine, particularly beef, lamb, fish and game dishes.*

**HAWICK** Scottish Borders

**Elm House £**
North Bridge Street (tel: 01450 372866).
15 rooms.

**LANGHOLM** Dumfries & Galloway

**Crown Hotel ££**
High Street (tel/fax: 013873 80247; fax: 013873 81128).
10 rooms.

**Eskdale Hotel £**
Market Place (tel/fax: 013873 80357).
15 rooms.

**ETTRICK** Dumfries & Galloway

**Tushielaw Inn £–££**
(tel: 01750 62205). *Good, wholesome pub food here includes Aberdeen Angus steaks, deep-fried haddock, grilled lamb, and – best of all – fresh trout from local lochs. Closed 1 Jan.*

**TOUR 7**

**EDINBURGH** City of Edinburgh

**Braid Hills £££**
134 Braid Road, Braid Hills (tel: 0131 447 8888; fax: 0131 452 8477).
68 rooms.

**Bruntsfield £££**
69–74 Bruntsfield Place (tel: 0131 229 1393; fax: 0131 229 5634).
73 rooms.

**Ibis ££**
Hunter Square (tel: 0131 240 7000; fax: 0131 240 7007).
99 rooms.

**Jury's Inn ££–£££**
43 Jeffrey Street (tel: 0131 200 3300; fax: 0131 200 0400).
186 rooms.

**Old Waverley £££**
43 Princes Street (tel: 0131 556 4648; fax: 0131 557 6316).
66 rooms.

**The Roxburgh £££**
38 Charlotte Square (tel: 0131 240 5500; fax: 0131 240 5555).
197 rooms.

**Atrium £–££**
10 Cambridge Street (tel: 0131 228 8882). *Stylish restaurant in the Traverse Theatre, serving modern brasserie-style dishes that combine Scottish produce with Mediterranean influences. Closed Sat lunch, Sun (except Aug), 25–26 Dec, 1–2 Jan*

**Bonars ££**
56 St Mary's Street (tel: 0131 556 5888). *Stylish setting; adventurous cooking.*

**Le Café St Honore £–££**
34 NW Thistle Street Lane (tel: 0131 226 2211. *Parisian-style bistro offering classic, good-value favourites. Closed 25–26 Dec, 3 days at New Year.*

**Duck's at Le Marche Noir £–££**
14 Eyre Place (tel: 0131 558 1608). *A historic tenement with rustic ambience is the setting for classic British and International food such as roast duck with butternut squash purée. Closed Sat–Mon lunch, 25–26 Dec.*

**Haldanes ££**
39A Albany Street (tel: 0131 556 8407). *Peaceful, city-centre restaurant serving modern Scottish food such as ravioli of scallops or maize-fed guinea fowl with sherry vinegar sauce. Closed Sat, Sun lunch, 25 Dec.*

**Martin Wishart £££**
54 The Shore, Leith (tel: 0131 553 3557). *One of Scotland's top chefs creates modern dishes based on a classic French theme at this chic waterfront restaurant, with such combinations as beef shin, veal sweetbreads and red wine jus. Closed Sun–Mon, bank hols, Sat lunch, 25 Dec.*

**Stac Polly ££–£££**
8–10 Grindlay Street (tel: 0131 229 5405); 29–33 Dublin Street (tel: 0131 556 2231). *A Scottish experience, complete with tartan and Highland music. Menus might include haggis, Cullen Skink and Aberdeen Angus beef fillet. Closed Sat and Sun lunch.*

**GULLANE** East Lothian
**Greywalls Hotel £££**
Muirfield (tel: 01620 842144). *Beautiful country house with an elegant restaurant serving such dishes as langoustine ravioli and Aberdeen Angus beef. Dinner only. Closed Nov–Mar.*
22 rooms.

**Golf Inn £–££**
Main Street (tel: 01620 843259). *Golf is the theme of the décor, but it's fish that majors on the menu, including gravadlax, roast monkfish tails with onion and garlic confit, and moules marinière.*

**La Potinière ££–£££**
Main Street (tel: 01620 843214). *Delightful cottage restaurant offering ambitious dishes on a concise modern British menu (just two choices for each course). Try Thai coconut soup, west coast scallops or roast venison. Closed Mon–Tue, Sun dinner Oct–Mar, Christmas.*

**NORTH BERWICK** East Lothian
**Macdonald Marine ££**
Cromwell Road (tel: 0870 400 8129; fax: 01620 894480).
83 rooms.

**Nether Abbey ££**
20 Dirleton Avenue (tel: 01620 892802; fax: 01620 895298).
15 rooms.

**DUNBAR** East Lothian
**Bayswell ££**
Bayswell Park (tel/fax: 01368 862225).
19 rooms.

**KELSO** Scottish Borders
**Ednam House £££**
Bridge Street (tel: 01573 224168; fax: 01573 226319). *Closed 25 Dec–10 Jan.*
32 rooms.

**White Swan £–££**
Abbey Row (tel: 01573 225800).
5 rooms.

**LAUDER** Scottish Borders
**Lauderdale ££**
1 Edinburgh Road (tel: 01578 722231; fax: 01578 718642).
10 rooms.

**TOUR 8**
**OBAN** Argyll & Bute
**Alexandra ££**
Corran Esplanade (tel: 01631 562381; fax: 01631 564497).
79 rooms.

**Columba ££**
North Pier (tel: 01631 562183; fax: 01631 564683).
48 rooms.

**Manor House Hotel ££**
Gallanach Road (tel: 01631 562087; fax: 01631 563053). *Top-quality Scottish fish and game are given a modern slant in such dishes as rack of lamb with herb crust or warm beef, red onion and stilton salad, and a delicious iced gingerbread and Cointreau parfait. Open all year daily.*
11 rooms.

**Eeusk ££–£££**
North Pier (tel: 01631 565666). *Dine on top-quality seafood, such as Loch Etive mussels and wild halibut, on one of Oban's piers overlooking the waters from where it came. Closed 25–26 Dec, 1 Jan.*

**CLACHAN-SEIL** Argyll & Bute
**Willowburn £££**
Island of Seil, half mile (1km) from Atlantic Bridge (tel: 01852 300276; fax: 01852 300597). *Closed Jan–Feb.*
7 rooms.

**Tigh an Truish Inn £–££**
(tel: 01852 300242). *Based on the finest local produce, the menu here includes such dishes as seafood pie, salmon, and steak and ale pie. Lunch only in winter. Closed 25 Dec, 1 Jan.*

**CRINAN** Argyll & Bute
**Crinan Hotel £–££**
At north end of Crinan Canal (tel: 01546 830261). *A great place for a bar lunch, with dramatic views across Loch Fyne, or dinner in the restaurant.*

**LOCHGILPHEAD** Argyll & Bute
**The Stag £–££**
Argyll Street (tel: 01546 602496; fax: 01546 603549).
18 rooms.

**INVERARY** Highland
**The Argyll ££–£££**
Front Street (tel: 01499 302466; fax: 01499 501207).
36 rooms.

**GLENCOE** Highland
**Glencoe ££**
On A82 in Glencoe village (tel: 01855 811245; fax: 01855 811687).
15 rooms.

**BALLACHULISH** Highland
**Ballachulish House ££**
Ballachulish (tel: 01855 811266; fax: 01855 811498). *The inventive, daily changing menus offer a selection of main dishes and some rather complex and ambitious choices.*
8 rooms.

**TOUR 9**
**PAISLEY** Renfrewshire
**Dean Park ££**
91 Glasgow Road (tel: 0141 886 3771; fax: 0141 885 0681).
118 rooms.

**DUMBARTON** West Dunbartonshire
**Dumbuck ££**
Glasgow Road (tel: 01389 734336; fax: 01389 742270).
22 rooms.

**HELENSBURGH** Argyll & Bute
**County Lodge Hotel £**
Old Luss Road (tel: 01436 672034; fax: 01436 671628).
7 rooms.

**Rosslea Hall Country House ££**
Ferry Road, Rhu (tel: 01436 439955). *Fine cuisine. Open daily; restaurant open for dinner only; bar lunches available.*
34 rooms.

**LOCH FYNE** Argyll & Bute
**Greggans Inn £££**
Strachur, on the shores of Loch Fyne (tel: 01369 860279; fax: 01369 860637). *Breathtaking views across the lake and a daily changing menu, using the best local produce from the land and loch.*
14 rooms.

**TIGHNABRUAICH** Argyll & Bute
**The Royal at Tighnabruaich £££**
Shore Road (tel: 01799 811239; fax: 01700 811300). *Another fine lochside restaurant with stunning views across the picturesque Kyles of Bute. The innovative menu includes peat-smoked haddock chowder, local scallops, monkfish in bacon, and clootie dumpling, a traditional Scottish pudding for dessert.*
11 rooms.

**DUNOON** Argyll & Bute
**Enmore £££**
Marine Parade, Kirn (tel: 01369 702230; fax: 01369 702148). *Closed 2–12 Jan.*
10 rooms.

**Lyall Cliff £**
141 Alexandre Parade, East Bay (tel/fax: 01369 702041). *Closed Nov–26 Dec.*
9 rooms.

**TOUR 10**
**GLASGOW** City of Glasgow
**Campanile Glasgow £–££**
10 Tunnel Street (tel: 0141 287 7700; fax: 0141 287 7701).
106 rooms.

**Ewington £££**
Balmoral Terrace, 132 Queens Drive, Queens Park (tel: 0141 423 1152; fax: 0141 422 2030).
43 rooms.

**Malmaison £££**
278 West George Street (tel: 0141 572 1000). *French brasserie food has been given a contemporary reworking in such dishes as confit of duck or seared foie gras; in the former crypt of a stylish old church conversion.*
72 rooms.

**One Devonshire Gardens £££**
1 Devonshire Gardens (tel: 0141 339 2001; fax: 0141 337 1663).
35 rooms.

**Tulip Inn ££**
80 Ballater Street (tel: 0141 429 4233; fax: 0141 429 4244).
114 rooms.

**Arisaig Restaurant and Bar ££–£££**
Merchant City, 24 Candleriggs (tel: 0141 552 4251). *A must for lovers of haggis, good whisky and for adventurous diners ready to try unusual Scottish treats such as kale, nettles and red seaweed. Closed Mon–Thu lunch, 26 Dec, 1 Jan.*

**Brian Maule at Chardon d'Or £££**
176 West Regent Street (tel: 0141 248 3801). *Cosmopolitan restaurant where chef Brian Maule adds a modern touch to classic French cuisine. Closed Sat lunch, Sun, 2 weeks Jan, 2 weeks summer.*

**Gamba ££**
225a West George Street (tel: 0141 572 0899). *Scottish seafood is the speciality here, with global influences flavouring such dishes as snapper with garlic gravy. Closed Sun, 25–26 Dec, 1–2 Jan.*

**Lux ££–£££**
1051 Great Western Road (tel: 0141 576 7576). *Exemplary cooking features some unusual combinations, such as pork fillet with mango salsa and coriander cream cheese mash, alongside popular traditional choices. Dinner only. Closed Sun, 25–26 Dec, 1–2 Jan.*

**Puppet Theatre ££**
11 Ruthven Lane (tel: 0141 339 8444). *Scottish/Mediterranean cuisine. Closed Mon.*

**Papingo £–££**
104 Bath Street (tel: 0141 332 6678). *Modern Scottish food, with such specialities as roast guinea fowl, tournedos of pork and roast rump of lamb. Closed Sun lunch, 25–26 Dec, 1–2 Jan.*

**Rococo ££–£££**
202 West George Street (tel: 0141 221 5004). *One of Glasgow's best restaurants, with traditional and contemporary-style dishes, such as boneless saddle of Normandy rabbit. Closed Sun, 1 Jan.*

**Ubiquitous Chip ££–£££**
12 Ashton Lane (tel: 0141 334 5007). *Glasgow institution that has served top-notch Scottish cuisine for more than 30 years. Unpretentious dishes include wild boar with paprika potatoes and Calvados vinaigrette and salmon with lime and vanilla mash. Closed 25 Dec, 1 Jan.*

**ABERFELDY** Perthshire & Kinross
**The Weem ££**
On B846 northwest (tel: 01887 820381; fax: 01887 8297020).
11 rooms.

**Farleyer Country House and Restaurant ££**
Farleyer House, Weem, near Aberfeldy (tel: 01887 820332). *Stylish and skilful French cuisine served in this former 16th-century dower house to Menzies Castle. The menu might include braised pig's trotter, or rosemary smoked pork cutlet with turnip and sage sponge and apple mash. Closed Mon in winter and 2 weeks in Feb.*
6 rooms.

**CRIEF** Perth & Kinross
**The Bank ££**
32 High Street (tel: 01764 656575). *In a former Victorian bank building, this restaurant offers simple but interesting British and French food showing great technical skill, such as Mull cheddar beignets, and saddle of venison with foie gras. Closed Mon, 24–26 Dec, 2 weeks mid-Jan. Lunch only on Sun.*

**LOCHEARNHEAD** Stirling
**Lochearnhead £**
(tel: 01567 830229; fax: 01567 830364). *Closed Dec–Mar.*
10 rooms.

**CALLANDER** Stirling
**Roman Camp Country House £££**
Off Main Street (tel: 01877 330003; fax: 01877 331533). *Innovative modern British food using quality Scottish produce in dishes such as breast of squab with truffle custard, or red mullet with goats' cheese risotto and ragout of squid.*
14 rooms.

**11 Park Avenue £–££**
11 Park Avenue (tel: 01241 853336). *Classy modern restaurant with the finest local ingredients shaping such dishes as warm salad of Skye scallops, and Gressingham duck with a crème de cassis and red wine sauce. Closed Sun, Mon, 1st week in Jan. Dinner only Tue–Thu and Sat.*

**ABERFOYLE** Stirling
**Fielbarachan Guest House £**
Lochard Road (tel: 01877 382536; fax: 01877 382536).
12 rooms.

**TOUR 11**
**STIRLING** Stirling
**Stirling Highland £££**
Spittal Street (tel: 01786 272727; fax: 01786 272829). *A former Victorian school is the setting for this restaurant, offering a safe but winning selection of dishes, such as Shetland salmon on lemon risotto with parsley cream. Closed Sat lunch.*
96 rooms.

**Terraces ££**
4 Melville Terrace (tel: 01786 472268; fax: 01786 450314).
17 rooms.

**River House ££**
Castle Business Park, Craigforth (tel: 01786 465577). *Mediterranean-style cuisine. Open all year daily.*

**DUNBLANE** Stirling
**Westlands Hotel £**
Doune Road (tel: 01786 822118; fax: 01786 822118).
5 rooms.

**Cromlix House £££**
Kinbuck (tel: 01786 822125). *Modern British cooking is based on traditional themes and uses luxury and seasonal produced, much sourced on the estate. Try the roast turbot with langoustine and vanilla sauce or the chicken and crab ravioli with lemongrass froth. Lunch by reservation only Oct–Apr. Closed 1–21 Jan.*
14 rooms.

**DOLLAR** Clackmannanshire
**Castle Campbell Hotel ££**
11 Bridge Street (tel: 01259 742519; fax: 01259 743742).
9 rooms.

**DUNFERMLINE** Fife
**Keavil House ££**
Crossford (tel: 01383 736258; fax: 01383 621600). *Modern brasserie food at this hotel's smart conservatory restaurant, Cardoon, might include Thai-roasted monkfish with lemongrass, coriander and mussel risotto.*
47 rooms.

**Pitbauchlie House £££**
Aberdour Road (tel: 01383 722282; fax: 01383 620738).
50 rooms.

**Town House Restaurant £–££**
48 Eastport (tel: 01383 432382). *International brasserie food has strong Mediterranean influences in dishes such as confit of duck with red onion marmalade or hot smoked salmon with polenta cake. Very lively in the evenings. Closed 26 Dec, 1 Jan.*

**LINLITHGOW** West Lothian
**The Champany Inn ££**
Near Linlithgow (tel: 01506 834532). *Famous for juicy steaks, sourced and prepared by their own butchery, but the menu also features lamb double loin chops, baked chicken with tarragon mousse and some seafood options. Closed Sat lunch, Sun, 25–26 Dec.*

**Livingston's £££**
57 High Street (tel: 01506 846565). *Intimate cottage restaurant with a menu that might include seared loin of tuna or Highland venison with bramble and honey sauce. Closed Sun, Mon, 2 weeks Jan, 1 week Jun, 1 week Oct.*

**TOUR 12**
**PERTH** Perthshire & Kinross
**Huntingtower £££**
Crieff Road (tel: 01738 583771; fax: 01738 583777). *The wood-panelled Oak Room is the setting for contemporary and traditional Scottish and French cuisine.*
34 rooms.

**Parklands Hotel £££**
2 St Leonards Bank (tel: 01738 622451; fax: 01738 622046). *Modern British cuisine features adventurous combinations and light saucing in dishes such as salmon and monkfish terrine and lamb with herb and garlic crust. Open Tue–Sat for dinner only.*
14 rooms.

**Woodlea £**
23 York Place (tel: 01738 621744; fax: 01738 621744). *No credit cards.*
12 rooms.

**63 Tay Street ££**
63 Tay Street (tel: 01738 441451). *Stylish modern restaurant with views of the River Tay and exciting dishes like Shanghai shellfish risotto, and Perthshire venison with braised red cabbage. Closed Sun, Mon, 1st 2 weeks Jan, last week Jun, first week Jul.*

**Let's Eat ££**
77–79 Kinnoull Street (tel: 01738 643377).
*Modern Scottish cuisine, such as fillets of Stornoway halibut, John Dory and brill. Closed Sun and Mon; also 2 weeks Jan and 2 weeks Jul.*

**DUNKELD** Perth & Kinross
**Royal Dunkeld Hotel ££**
Athol Street (tel: 01350 727322; fax: 01350 728989).
35 rooms.

**Kinnaird £££**
Kinnaird Estate (tel: 01796 482440). *One of Scotland's finest restaurants, serving creative, imaginative, classically based cuisine with a touch of excitement. The elegant dining room is at the heart of a vast country estate, with superb views.*

**BLAIRGOWRIE** Perth & Kinross
**Kinloch House Hotel £££**
Blairgowrie (tel: 01250 884237). *Formal, country-house dining on such delicacies as hare fillet with port wine sauce or a succulent Aberdeen Angus steak. Closed 17–29 Dec.*
18 rooms.

**The Royal Hotel ££**
53 Allen Street (tel: 01250 872226; fax: 01250 875905).
27 rooms.

**GLAMIS** Angus
**Castleton House ££**
Castleton of Essie (tel: 01307 840340; fax: 01307 840506). *Flawless dishes at this fine Victorian country house might include marbled Glen Isla venison terrine with truffled celeriac or pan-fried, home-reared Tamworth pork fillet with caramelised apples and muscovite sauce.*
6 rooms.

**BRECHIN** Angus
**Northern Hotel ££**
2 Clerk Street (tel: 01356 625400; fax: 01356 625219).
12 rooms.

**MONTROSE** Angus
**The George Hotel ££**
22 George Street (tel: 01674 675050; fax: 01674 471153).
26 rooms.

**Best Western Links ££**
Mid Links (tel: 01674 671000; fax: 01674 672698). *The hotel's trendy bistro has an exciting menu of dishes that combine complex combinations with sleek, minimalist presenatation. Choices might include Scottish smoked salmon roulade and roast monkfish with mussel cream.*
57 rooms.

**ARBROATH** Angus
**Hotel Seaforth ££**
Dundee Road (tel: 01241 872232; fax: 01241 877473).
19 rooms.

**Rosely Country House Hotel £**
Forfar Road (tel/fax: 01241 876828).
14 rooms.

**CARNOUSTIE** Angus
**Carnoustie House Hotel ££**
Carlogie Road (tel: 01241 853185; fax: 01241 856528).
17 rooms.

**Kinloch Arms ££**
27–29 High Street (tel: 01241 853127; fax: 01241 855183).
7 rooms.

**11 Park Avenue ££**
11 Park Avenue (tel: 01241 853336). *Friendly restaurant with a loyal local clientele, serving simple, well-cooked dishes such as seared sea bass fillet with scallop and butter sauce. Closed for lunch Tue–Thu and Sat. Closed Sun, Mon, 25 Dec, 1st week Jan.*

**DUNDEE** Dundee City
**Shaftesbury ££**
1 Hyndford Street (tel: 01382 224188).
12 rooms.

**Metro ££–£££**
Apex City Quay Hotel, 1 West Victoria Dock Road (tel: 01382 202404). *Cutting-edge cuisine, such as sea bass with truffle pommes purée and lime froth, on a seasonally changing menu of exciting contemporary creations. Try the tasting menus. Closed Sun, Mon.*

**The Tasting Rooms £**
5 South Ward Road (tel: 01382 669216; fax: 01382 641598). *This former jute warehouse presents a true taste of Scotland with an international twist. Top quality produce, fine wines and great coffee.*

**TOUR 13**
**ST ANDREWS** Fife

**Russell ££**
26 The Scores (tel: 01334 473447; fax: 01334 478279). *East coast produce features strongly on the menu in the Russell's intimate restaurant, where you might find duck breast with kumquat and red onion marmalade or seared fillet of Tay salmon on the menu. Closed Christmas.*
10 rooms.

**St Andrews Golf £££**
40 The Scores (tel: 01334 472611; fax: 01334 472188). *The hotel's restaurant offers honest, modern cooking based around fine Scottish produce.*
22 rooms.

**Scores £££**
76 The Scores (tel hotel: 01334 472451; restaurant: 01334 479475; fax: 01334 473947). *The Seafood Restaurant offers accomplished cooking in a stunning glass building by the bay. The kitchen, in full view of diners, turns out classic and daring combinations to a standard that earned it the title of AA Restaurant of the Year in 2005. Closed 25–26 Dec, 1 Jan.*
30 rooms.

**Inn at Lathones £££**
Largoward (tel: 01334 840494). *Modern Scottish cooking with international influences creates an interesting menu that might include scallops with pastrami, marinated sardine fillets with chilli dressing, Thai-flavoured crab cake or baked haddock and ginger salsa. Closed 25–26 Dec, 4–18 Jan.*

**Parkland Hotel ££**
Double Dykes Road (tel: 01334 473620). *Highly praised Scottish regional cuisine.*

**Road Hole Grill £££**
Old Course Hotel (tel: 01334 474371). *Sumptuous dining on traditional classics with a modern twist, such as roast Scottish lobster with scallop tortellini and bouillon or Angus beef with oxtail and wild mushrooms. Dinner only. Closed 24–28 Dec.*

**CRAIL** Fife

**Balcomie Links Hotel ££**
Balcomie Road (tel: 01333 450237; fax: 01333 450540).
14 rooms.

**The Golf Hotel £**
4 Hight Street (tel: 01333 450206; fax: 01333 450795).
5 rooms.

**ANSTRUTHER** Fife

**The Smuggler's Inn £**
High Street East (tel: 01333 310506; fax: 01333 312706).
6 rooms.

**Cellar Restaurant ££–£££**
24 East Green (tel: 01333 310378). *Renowned for its seafood: steamed John Dory fillets with rosemary beurre blanc; roast Pittenweem langoustines with herb and garlic butter; or crayfish bisque glazed with gruyère and cream. Closed Mon, Tue lunch, Christmas.*

**ELIE** Fife

**Golf ££**
Bank Street (tel: 01333 330209; fax: 01333 330381).
22 rooms.

**Sangsters ££–£££**
51 High Street (tel: 01333 331001). *With a commitment to top-quality local produce, this highly acclaimed restaurant offers a short menu of simple dishes such as slow cooked shoulder noisette of lamb or seared Isle of Mull scallops. Closed Mon, Tue & Sat lunch, Sun dinner and various holiday periods.*

**Ship Inn £–££**
The Toft (tel: 01333 330246). *On the waterfront of Elie Bay, you'll find a menu with excellent fresh fish, plus staples such as bangers and mash, haggis and prime steaks. Closed 25 Dec.*

**KINROSS** Perthshire and Kinross

**Kirklands Hotel ££**
20 High Street (tel/fax: 01577 863313).
8 rooms, plus 1 apartment.

**Windlestrae £££**
Windlestrae (tel: 01577 863217; fax: 01577 864733).
45 rooms.

**CUPAR** Fife

**Eden House £££**
2 Pitscottie Road (tel: 01334 652510; fax: 01334 652277).
28 rooms.

**Ostlers Close ££**
Bonnygate (tel: 01334 655574). *Friendly and cosy restaurant featuring well-balanced flavours and quality ingredients. Try the pan-fried mixed fish fillets with chervil sauce or roast roe venison with red wine sauce. Closed Sun–Mon, Tue–Fri lunch, 25–26 Dec, 1–2 Jan, 2 weeks in Oct.*

**TOUR 14**
**INVERNESS** Highland

**The Drumossie ££**
Old Perth Road (tel: 01463 236451; fax: 01463 712858).
44 rooms.

**Glendruidh Hotel £££**
Druid Glen, Old Edinburgh Road South (tel: 01463 226499; fax: 01463 710745).
5 rooms.

**Loch Ness House ££**
Glenurquhart Road (tel: 01463 231248; fax: 01463 239327).
21 rooms.

**Lochardil House ££**
Stratherrick Road (tel: 01463 235995; fax: 01463 713394).
12 rooms.

**Bunchrew House Hotel ££**
Bunchrew (tel: 01463 234917). *Modern Scottish cuisine with a French influence, in which local produce and home-grown herbs are handled with deft simplicity to produce such dishes as saddle of venison with juniper and rosemary sauce. Closed 22–28 Dec; may be closed for functions at other times.*

**Riverhouse £–££**
1 Greig Street (tel: 01463 222033). *Formal dining on the banks of the River Ness, with an open kitchen turning out innovative dishes such as seared shark with lemon, dill and pine pesto, spicy sausage and potato hash and sea bream with roasted celery, cherry tomatoes, mussels and crab. Closed Mon, Sun lunch.*

**Rocpool ££**
1 Ness Walk (tel: 01463 717274). *Lively, cosmopolitan atmosphere and international cuisine. Innovative dishes might include chilli crusted lamb cutlets with crisp polenta. Closed Sun, 25 Dec.*

**NAIRN** Highland

**Alton Burn £**
Alton Burn Road (tel: 01667 452051; fax: 01667 456697).
25 rooms.

**Boath House ££**
Auldearn (tel: 01667 454896; fax: 01667 455469). *Classic dishes blend with modern techniques to produce well-balanced, clear flavours in such dishes as roasted cannon of red deer saddle with a pear tarte Tatin and foie gras. Closed Mon–Wed lunch, Christmas.*
6 rooms.

**Braeval Hotel £**
Crescent Road (tel: 01667 452341).
10 rooms.

**Newton Hotel ££**
Inverness Road (tel: 01667 453144). *International cuisine features quality Scottish ingredients, with a focus on local game and seafood.*

**FORRES** Moray

**Cluny Bank Hotel £££**
69 St Leonard's Road (tel: 01309 674304; fax: 01309 671400).
9 rooms.

**Ramnee ££**
Victoria Road (tel: 01309 672410; fax: 01309 673392).
20 rooms.

**GRANTOWN-ON-SPEY** Highland

**Coppice £**
Grant Road (tel/fax: 01479 872688).
26 rooms.

**Culdearn House £££**
Woodlands Terrace (tel: 01479 872106; fax: 01479 873641). *British dishes such as roast guinea fowl with lemon and pistachio stuffing. The game and seafood are particularly recommended. Closed 30 Oct–28 Feb.*
7 rooms.

**Ravenscourt House Hotel ££**
Seafield Avenue (tel: 01479 872286; fax: 01479 873260).
7 rooms.

**CULLODEN** Highland

**Culloden House Hotel £££**
Culloden (tel: 01463 790461). *A modern translation of classic dishes, not to mention probably the best bowl of porridge in Scotland.*

**TOUR 15**

**ELGIN** Moray

**Laichmoray ££**
Maisondieu Road (tel: 01343 540045; fax: 01343 540055).
34 rooms.

**Mansion House Hotel ££**
The Haugh (tel: 01343 548811). *Innovative contemporary cooking artistically presented, with a focus on Scottish seafood, meat and game.*
23 rooms.

**Sunninghilll Hotel ££**
Hay Street (tel: 01343 547799; fax: 01343 547872).
19 rooms.

**LOSSIEMOUTH** Moray

**Skerry Brae Hotel £**
Stotfield Road (tel: 01343 812040; fax: 01343 813708).
19 rooms.

**FOCHABERS** Moray

**Spey Bay Golf Links Hotel £££**
Spey Bay (tel: 01343 820424; fax: 01343 829282).
10 rooms and 4 lodges.

**BUCKIE** Moray

**The Old Coach House Hotel ££**
26 High Street (tel: 01542 836266; fax: 01542 836361).
21 rooms.

**CULLEN** Moray

**Cullen Bay ££**
On A98 west of village (tel: 01542 840432; fax: 01542 840900).
14 rooms.

**Seafield Hotel and Restaurant ££**
19 Seafield Street (tel: 01542 840791; fax: 01542 840736). *Good use of local produce in dishes such as loin of venison with red onion tart and blackcurrant jus.*
18 rooms.

**Coasters Restaurant ££**
43–45 Castle terrace (tel: 01542 840252). *Traditional but innovative cooking. This is the place to try Cullen Skink, a rich, tasty soup whose main ingredient is smoked haddock.*

**PORTSOY** Aberdeenshire

**The Boyne Hotel £**
2 North High Street (tel/fax: 01261 842242).
12 rooms.

**Station Hotel £**
Seafield Street (tel: 01261 842327; fax: 01261 842975).
5 rooms.

**DUFFTOWN** Moray

**The Fife Arms Hotel ££**
2 The Square (tel: 01340 820220; fax: 01340 821137).
6 rooms.

**TOUR 16**

**BANFF** Aberdeenshire

**Banff Springs ££**
Golden Knowes Road (tel: 01261 812881).
35 rooms.

**Fife Lodge Hotel ££**
Sandyhill Road (tel: 01261 812436; fax: 01261 812636).
14 rooms.

**MACDUFF** Aberdeenshire
**The Waterfront Hotel £**
25 Union Road (tel: 01261 831661; fax: 01261 831662).
12 rooms.

**FRASERBURGH** Aberdeenshire
**Lonmay Old Manse £**
Lonmay, near Fraserburgh (tel/fax: 01346 532227).
3 rooms.

**The White Horse ££**
65 High Street, Strichen (tel: 01771 637218). *À la carte menu.*

**PETERHEAD** Aberdeenshire
**Carrick Guest House £**
16 Merchant Street(tel/fax: 01779 470610).
6 rooms.

**Palace ££**
Prince Street (tel: 01779 474821; fax: 01779 476119).
64 rooms.

**Waterside Inn ££**
Fraserburgh Road (tel: 01779 471121; fax: 01779 470670).
109 rooms.

**CRUDEN BAY** Aberdeenshire
**Kilmarnock Arms £££**
Bridge Street (tel: 01779 812213; fax: 01779 812153).
9 rooms.

**ELLON** Aberdeenshire
**Station Hotel ££**
Station Brae (tel: 01358 720209; fax: 01358 722855).
14 rooms.

**INVERURIE** Aberdeenshire
**Strathburn ££**
Burghmuir Drive (tel: 01467 624422; fax: 01467 625133).
23 rooms.

**The Swallow Kintore Arms £–£££**
83 High Street (tel: 01467 621367; fax: 01467 625620).
15 rooms.

**Thainstone House £££**
(tel: 01467 621643). *Local beef, game and seafood. Open all year daily.*

**HUNTLY** Aberdeenshire
**Castle ££**
Near castle ruins (tel: 01466 792696; fax: 01466 792641).
18 rooms.

**The Huntly Hotel £–££**
18 The Square (tel: 01466 792703; fax: 01466 792703).
10 rooms.

**TOUR 17**
**PITLOCHRY** Perthshire and Kinross
**Acarsaid ££**
8 Atholl Road (tel: 01796 472389). *Closed 4 Jan–10 Mar.*
28 rooms.

**Dundarroch ££**
Perth Road (tel: 01796 472292; fax: 01796 473284).
72 rooms.

**Pine Trees £££**
Strathview Terrace (tel: 01796 472121; fax: 01796 472460).
20 rooms.

**Donavourd House ££**
(tel: 01796 472100).
*Unpretentious country-house cooking with a short menu of simple classics, such as parmesan crusted chicken with buttered tagliatelle and mange tout. Dinner only. Closed Jan–Feb.*

**Green Park Hotel ££**
Clunie Bridge Road (tel: 01796 473248). *A scenic setting for the quality ingredients that go to make up the short daily menu of such dishes as duck confit with bean and chorizo stew. Dinner only.*

**Knockendarroch House Hotel ££**
Higher Oakfield (tel: 01796 473473). *British cuisine with European influences is strong on traditional cooking and local produce. Dinner only. Closed Nov–Feb.*

**KINGUSSIE** Highland
**Ardselma Guest House £–££**
The Crescent (tel/fax: 01540 661809). *Closed 6–31 Jan.*
3 rooms.

**The Scot House ££**
Newtonmore Road (tel: 01540 661351; fax: 01540 661111).
*Closed 6–31 Jan.*
9 rooms.

**The Cross £££**
Ardbroilach Road (tel: 01540 661166). *Good local produce – scallops, salmon, venison, salt marsh lamb – is prepared and presented with the deceptive simplicity of modern Scottish cuisine, which brings out all the flavours. Excellent wine list. Dinner only. Closed Tue.*

**AVIEMORE** Highland
**Aviemore Highlands ££**
Aviemore Mountain Resort (tel: 01479 810771).
171 rooms.

**BRAEMAR** Aberdeenshire
**Braemar Lodge £**
Glenshee Road (tel/fax: 013397 41627).
7 rooms.

**TOUR 18**
**ABERDEEN** Aberdeen City
**Allan Guest House £**
56 Polmuir Road, Ferryhill (tel/fax: 01224 584484).
3 rooms.

**Ardoe House £££**
Blairs, South Deeside Road (tel: 01224 867355). *A baronial mansion offering sophisticated European-influenced British dishes, such as roast loin of Highland venison with sloe gin and cranberry compote. Closed Sat lunch.*
117 rooms.

**Copthorne Hotel Aberdeen £££**
122 Huntly Street (tel: 01224 630404). *Scottish cuisine is served in this conveniently located hotel. Try the braised lamb rump with baby vegetables and herb mash. Closed Sat, Sun lunch; 25–26 Dec.*
89 rooms.

**Craighaar £££**
Waterton Road, Bankhead (tel: 01224 712275; fax: 01224 716362). *Closed 26 Dec, 1–2 Jan.*
55 rooms.

**The Mariner Hotel ££**
349 Great Western Road (tel: 01224 712275; fax: 01224 571621).
17 rooms, plus 8 in annexe.

**Maryculter House Hotel ££**
On B9077, off A90 south of Aberdeen (tel: 01224 732124). *Modern French cuisine, with a hint of Scottish, is served in this country house hotel with a fascinating history. Try the sliced beef fillet with shallot compote and bordelaise sauce. Dinner only. Closed Sun.*

**Norwood Hall ££–£££**
Garthdee Road, Cults (tel: 01224 868951). *Whether you choose a simple traditional steak or a complex concoction such as roasted sea bass with saffron linguine and coriander infusion, quality is assured in this imposing, richly furnished, Victorian mansion.*

**Patio Hotel ££**
Beach Boulevard (tel: 01224 633339). *International and Scottish fare. Open all year daily.*

**STONEHAVEN** Aberdeenshire
**Tolbooth ££**
Old Pier Road (tel: 01569 762287). *Former jail house situated on the harbour wall. Locally sourced seafood, some landed right outside the restaurant, is the house speciality. The standard of cooking has earned the Tolbooth the title AA Seafood Restaurant of the Year for Scotland.*

**BANCHORY** Aberdeenshire
**Burnett Arms ££**
25 High Street (tel: 01330 824944; fax: 01330 825553).
16 rooms.

**Raemoir House £££**
Raemoir (tel: 01330 824884; fax: 01330 822171).
20 rooms.

**Tor-na-Coille Hotel ££**
(tel: 01330 822242). *British and European food is served in the elegant dining room here, where the menu might include an aged fillet of Aberdeen Angus beef or perhaps local game and salmon. Dinner only Mon–Sat. Closed 24–28 Dec.*

**TOUR 19**
**FORT WILLIAM** Highland
**Imperial ££**
Fraser's Square (tel: 01397 702040; fax: 01397 706277).
34 rooms.

**Inverlochy Castle Hotel £££**
Torlundy (tel: 01397 702177). *A delicious range of interesting dishes based around simple combinations prepared from the finest of Scottish ingredients, and one of the best wine lists in the Highlands. They even have a supply of Cloudy Bay Sauvignon Blanc. Ben Nevis provides a majestic backdrop for this gracious hotel, set on the edge of a loch. Closed 6 Jan–1 Feb.*
17 rooms.

**Moorings Hotel**
Banavie (tel: 01397 772797). *Solid British and European choices feature on the menu in the spacious Jacobean dining room here. Ingredients, notably salmon, crab and lamb, are sourced locally and cooked in contemporary style. Dinner only.*
28 rooms.

**No 4 Cameron Square ££**
4 Cameron Square (tel: 01397 704222). *Modern British cuisine. Closed Sun lunch.*

**ARISAIG** Highland
**Arisaig ££**
On A830 opposite harbour (tel: 01687 450210; fax: 01687 450310). *Closed 24–26 Dec.*
13 rooms.

**MALLAIG** Highland
**Marine £**
Beside railway terminal (tel: 01687 462217; fax: 01687 462821). *Closed 25 Dec–1 Jan.*
19 rooms.

**TOUR 20**
**INVERGARRY** Highland
**Forest Lodge £**
South Laggan (tel: 01809 501219; fax: 01809 501476). *Contemporary Scottish dishes. Closed Nov–Apr.*
26 rooms.

**Glengarry Castle £££**
On the A82 beside Loch Oich (tel: 01809 501254; fax: 01809 501207). *Lochside dining on flavourful local game and fish: fillet of venison with juniper berry scented sauce, for example. Dinner only. Closed Nov–mid-Mar.*

**KYLE OF LOCHALSH** Highland
**Kyle Hotel ££**
Main Street (tel: 01599 534204; fax: 01599 534932).
31 rooms.

**Lochalsh £££**
Ferry Road (tel: 01599 534202; fax: 01599 534881).
40 rooms.

**PLOCKTON** Highland
**Haven Hotel £**
Innes Street (tel: 01599 544334). *Robust Scottish fare. Closed 20 Dec–1 Feb.*
15 rooms.

**APPLECROSS** Highland
**Applecross Inn £–££**
Shore Street (tel: 01520 744262). *Stunning food in a waterfront location. Try king scallops in garlic butter with crispy bacon on rice, oysters in tempura batter with sweet chilli sauce, and venison casserole.*

**GAIRLOCH** Highland
**Creag Mor £££**
Charleston (tel: 01445 712068; fax: 01445 712044).
17 rooms.

**Millcroft Hotel £**
Strath (tel: 01445 712376; fax: 01445 712091).
5 rooms.

**Myrtle Bank ££**
Low Road (tel: 01445 712004; fax: 01445 712214).
12 rooms.

**The Old Inn ££–£££**
Just off the A832 at southern end of village (tel: 01445

712006). *This former AA Pub of the Year overlooks the harbour, which provides some of the fresh seafood on the menu. Highland game also features.*

**ULLAPOOL** Highland
**The Ceilidh Place ££**
14 West Argyle Street (tel: 01854 612103). *Long-established, all-day bar with informal dining on locally landed fish. The menu might feature fillet of cod on garlic mash and rocket purée, or monkfish wrapped in bacon with sauerkraut and chorizo sausage. Closed 2 weeks mid Jan.*

**STRATHPEFFER** Highland
**Brunstane Lodge £**
Golf Road (tel: 01997 421261). *Closed 1–2 Jan.*
6 rooms.

**BEAULY** Highland
**Priory ££**
The Square (tel: 01463 782309; fax: 01463 782531).
34 rooms.

**DRUMNADROCHIT** Highland
**Polmaily House £££**
On Cannich road (tel: 01456 450343; fax: 01456 450813). *Closed 31 Oct–30 Dec.*
30 rooms.

**TOUR 21**
**LOCHINVER** Highland
**Albannach ££**
Baddidarrach (tel: 01571 844407). *A haven of gastronomy in the Scottish Highlands, with a daily-changing six-course menu combining French techniques with Scottish flavours. Try the cheese soufflé with red onion marmalade, or the beef with parsley mash and root vegetable parcel. Dinner only, served at 8pm. Closed mid-Nov to mid-Mar.*

**Inver Lodge £££**
Off A835 from village (tel: 01571 844496; fax: 01571 844395). *Contemporary slant to Scottish produce on a concise menu that might feature Inver Bay lobster thermidor, lamb cutlets with mint risotto and pear and rosemary jus, or halibut with butternut squash purée. Try the deep-fried ice-cream. Dinner only. Closed Dec–Mar.*
20 rooms.

**Polcraig Guest House £**
(tel/fax: 01571 844429).
10 rooms.

**SCOURIE** Highland
**Eddrachilles ££**
Badcall Bay (tel: 01971 502080; fax: 01971 502477). *Satisfying dishes here might include lemon and basil poached chicken breast or halibut with lime butter sauce. Dinner only. Closed Nov–Feb.*
12 rooms.

**KINLOCHBERVIE** Highland
**Kinlochbervie ££**
(tel: 01971 521275; fax: 01971 521438). *Closed 23 Dec–4 Jan.*
10 rooms.

**Old School Hotel £**
Inshegra (tel/fax: 01971 521383).
6 rooms.

**LAIRG** Highland
**Overscaig £**
Loch Shin, on A838 (tel: 01549 431203).
5 rooms.

**TOUR 22**
**DORNOCH** Highland
**2 Quail Restaurant & Rooms £££**
Inistore House, Castle Street (tel: 01862 811811). *There are only four tables, so booking is essential. The food is Highland cooking at its best: starters include Skye scallops with fresh pea purée and crispy bacon, followed by venison with celeriac dauphinoise and red wine jus, or Tournedo Rossini. Closed Sun, Mon, Christmas, 2 weeks Feb–Mar.*

**Burghfield House ££**
(tel: 01862 810212; fax: 01862 810404).
29 rooms.

**Dornoch Castle ££**
Castle Street (tel: 01862 810216; fax: 01862 810981). *Closed Nov–Mar.*
17 rooms.

**Eagle Hotel £**
Castle Street (tel: 01862 810008).
9 rooms.

**TONGUE** Highland
**Ben Loyal £**
Village centre (tel: 01847 611216; fax: 01847 611336). *The menu of ambitious modern Scottish cuisine majors on local game and seafood. The wild salmon gravadlax with deep-fried oysters, and brochette of local langoustines in Thai spice are recommended. Dinner only. Closed Nov–Mar.*
11 rooms.

**THURSO** Highland
**Park ££**
On A882 near town centre (tel: 01847 893251). *Closed 1–3 Jan.*
16 rooms.

**Station Hotel ££**
Princes Street (tel: 01847 892003).
30 rooms.

**MEY** Highland
**Castle Arms £**
On A836 (tel: 01847 851244; fax: 01847 851244).
8 rooms.

**WICK** Highland
**Mackay's ££**
Union Street (tel: 01955 602323; fax: 01955 605930). *Closed 1–2 Jan.*
27 rooms.

**BRORA** Highland
**Royal Marine Hotel ££**
(tel: 01408 621252). *Saddle of Sutherland venison with stewed plums is a great favourite, as is the excellent Cullen Skink. Elegant country house surroundings enhance the experience. Dinner only. Reservations essential.*

**TOUR 23**
**DINGWALL** Highland
**Kinkell House ££**
Easter Kinkell, Conon Bridge (tel: 01349 861270; fax: 01349 865902). *Local lamb, fish and pork. Open all year.*
9 rooms.

**TAIN** Highland
**Glenmorangie Highland Home at Cadboll £££**
Cadboll, Fearn (tel: 01862 871671). *Meals are served dinner-party style after social pre-dinner drinks. Consequently, there are no choices on the four-course menu, which features such dishes as wild duck breast marinated in whisky with beetroot and apple tartare. Dinner only, served at 8pm. Closed 23–26 Dec, 4–18 Jan.*

**GolfView Guest House £**
13 Knockbreck Road (tel: 01862 892856; fax: 01862 892172).
5 rooms.

**Mansfield House ££**
Scotsburn Road (tel: 01862 892052; fax: 01862 892260).
19 rooms.

**PORTMAHOMACK** Highland
**Caledonian £**
Main Street (tel: 01862 871345; fax: 01862 871757).
15 rooms.

**TOUR 24**
**PORTREE** Highland
**Almondbank £**
Viewfield Road (tel: 01478 612696; fax: 01478 613114).
3 rooms.

**Cuillin Hills £££**
Off A855 north of Portree (tel: 01478 612003; fax: 01478 613092). *Magnificent views from the dining room over Portree Bay to the Cuillin Hills beyond match the quality of the food served here, with traditional roasts alongside Continental choices such as grilled chicken with pancetta, and polenta with balsamic reduction. Dinner only (except Sun).*
25 rooms.

**Rosedale ££**
Beaumont Crescent (tel: 01478 613131; fax: 01478 612531). *Modern Scottish cuisine features local produce, particularly seafood, in such dishes as hake with a coriander crust and pink peppercorn sauce, or lamb with a sweet potato and black pudding crumble, served overlooking Portree harbour. Dinner only. Closed Nov–Nar.*
19 rooms.

**UIG** Highland
**Ferry Inn £**
On Portree road near ferry terminal (tel: 01470 544242). *Closed 25 Dec & 1 Jan.*
6 rooms.

**DUNVEGAN** Highland
**Atholl House ££**
(tel: 01470 521219; fax: 01470 521481). *Closed end Dec–Feb.*
9 rooms.

**Roskhill House £–££**
Roskhill, 3 miles (5km) south (tel: 01470 521317; fax: 01470 521827).
4 rooms.

**HARLOSH** Highland
**Harlosh House ££**
On A863 south of Dunvegan (tel: 01470 521367).
8 rooms.

**COLBOST** Highland
**Three Chimneys £££**
(tel: 01470 511258). *A simple whitewashed crofter's cottage sitting on the edge of a loch, serving food that is way off the scale in terms of quality. Try the citrus baked halibut with seared scallops, followed by hot marmalade pudding and Drambuie custard. Closed Sun lunch, 3 weeks Jan, 1 week Dec.*

**ISLEORNSAY** Highland
**Kinloch Lodge £££**
(tel: 01471 833214 & 833333; fax: 01471 833277).
*Closed 22 Dec–31 Jan.*
15 rooms.

**Duisdale Country House Hotel ££**
(tel 01471 833202). *A former hunting lodge with stunning views is the setting for classically inspired menus that make full use of the excellent local produce, including Black Douglas cheese, Lochcarron oysters and roast turbot with mussels. Dinner only.*

**Hotel Eilean Iarmain £££**
Isle of Skye (tel: 01471 833332). *Complex modern Scottish cuisine featuring local game and seafood. Dinner only, reservation required.*
16 rooms.

**TOUR 25**
**TOBERMORY** Argyll & Bute
**Western Isles ££**
(tel: 01688 302012; fax: 01688 302297). *Closed 17–28 Dec.*
28 rooms.

**Highland Cottage £££**
Breadalbane (tel: 01688 302030). *Local venison, beef, smoked haddock, crab and monkfish feature in the plain and simple dishes served in this relaxing restaurant. Dinner only. Closed mid-Oct to mid-Nov, Christmas and part of Jan–Mar.*

**Tobermory Hotel £–££**
53 Main Street (tel: 01688 302091). *Excellent cuisine using fresh local produce, strong on seafood but also featuring dishes such as apricot and rosemary stuffed pork loin. Dinner only. Closed Christmas.*

**PENNYGHAEL** Argyll & Bute
**Pennyghael ££**
Main road (tel: 01681 704288).
6 rooms.

**BUNESSAN** Argyll & Bute
**Argyll Arms £££**
On the waterfront (tel: 01681 700240).
9 rooms.

**DERVAIG** Argyll & Bute
**Druimard Country House £££**
On the Tobermoray to Dervaig road (tel/fax: 01688 400345). *A modern slant on locally sourced meat, game and seafood is presented on a short, daily, fixed-price menu, which might include Gressingham duck breast with lemon and asparagus risotto. Dinner only. Closed Nov–Mar.*
7 rooms.

Pages 178–9: Eating out in the Grassmarket area of Edinburgh

Petit Paris
38 40
ONE COURSE
INC. COFFEE
£5'00
Served
12 to 3pm
we are open from 12 to 3pM & 530pM. till Late

AURANT
Petit Paris
Restaurant
0131 226 2442
Petit Paris
Restaurant
0131 226 2442
ONE COURSE INC, Coffee

[i] Tourist Information Office
12 Tour Number

**TOUR INFORMATION**
The addresses, telephone numbers and opening times of the attractions mentioned in the tours, together with the telephone numbers of the Tourist Information Offices, are listed below.

## TOUR 1

For all telephone enquiries call 01292 678100. Personal callers can visit the following centres:

[i] 22 Sandgate, Ayr.

[i] Main Street, Largs (seasonal).

**1 Alloway**
Burns National Heritage Park (including Burns Cottage)
Murdoch's Lone. Tel: 01292 443700.
www.burnsheritagepark.com
*Open Apr–Sep, daily 10–5.30, Oct–Mar, Mon–Sat 10–5 (Sun noon–4).*

**3 Culzean Castle**
4 miles (6km) west of Maybole, off A77.
Tel: 0870 118 1945.
www.culzeanexperience.org
*Open Apr (or Good Fri if earlier)–Oct, daily 10.30–5.30; country park daily 9.30–sunset.*

**5 Kirkoswald**
Souter Johnnie's Cottage
Main Road. Tel: 01655 760603.
www.nts.org.uk
*Open Apr–Sep, Fri–Tue 11.30–5.*

**6 Maybole**
Crossraguel Abbey
2 miles (3km) south on the A77. Tel: 01655 883113.
www.historic-scotland.gov.uk
*Open Apr–Sep, Mon–Sat 9.30–6.30.*

**7 Mauchline**
Burns House Museum
Castle Street. Tel: 01290 550045.
*Open Apr–Oct, Tue–Sat 10–5.*

**8 Kilmarnock**
Dean Castle and Country Park
Dean Road. Tel: 01563 522702.
www.deancastle.com
*Open all year daily: country park dawn to dusk; castle noon–5; visitor centre 11–5 (to 4pm in winter).*

**9 Irvine**
Scottish Maritime Museum
Harbour Street. Tel: 01294 278283.
www.scottishmaritimemuseum.org
*Open Apr–Oct, daily 10–5.*

Glasgow Vennel Museum and Burns Heckling Shop
4 & 10 Glasgow Vennel.
Tel: 01294 275059.
*Open Mon–Sat 10–4.*

Cunninghame House
Friars Croft. Tel: 0845 603 0590.
*Open all year, Mon–Thu 9–4.45, Fri 9–4.30 (may close for lunch, check before visiting).*

Burns Club and Museum
28 Eglinton Street.
Tel: 01294 274511.
www.irvineayrshire.org/burns/
*Open Easter–Sep, Mon–Wed, Fri–Sat 2.30–4.30; Oct–Mar Sat 2.30–4.30.*

**10 Largs**
Skelmorlie Aisle
Tel: 01475 687081.
*Open (pick up key from the museum) Jun–Aug, Mon–Sat 2–5.*

Vikingar
Greenock Road. Tel: 01475 689777.
www.vikingar.co.uk
*Open Apr–Sep, daily 10.30–5.30; Oct, Mar, daily 10.30–3.30; Nov–Feb daily Sat–Sun 10.30–3.30.*

**For Children**
Galleon Centre
99 Titchfield Street, Kilmarnock. Tel: 01563 524014.
www.galleoncentre.com
*Open daily 7am–11pm (to 6pm Sat).*

Loudoun Castle Family Theme Park
Galston. Tel: 01563 822296.
www.loudouncastle.co.uk
*Open Apr–Aug, daily 10–5; Sep–Oct, weekends only 10–5 (later at peak times).*

**For Children**
Magnum Centre
Harbourside, Irvine.
Tel: 01294 278381.
www.themagnum.co.uk
*Open daily, from 9am Fri–Mon, 10am Tue–Thu; closes 10pm weekdays, 6pm weekends.*

## TOUR 2

[i] Dashwood Square, Newton Stewart (seasonal). Tel: 01671 402431.

[i] The Whithorn Trust, Whithorn (seasonal).
Tel: 01988 500508.

[i] 30 Harbour Street, Stranraer. Tel: 01776 702595.

**1 Wigtown**
Bladnoch Distillery
Half mile (1km) south on the A746. Tel: 01988 402605.
www.bladnoch.co.uk
*Open Easter–Oct, Mon–Fri tours 9–5, shop 9–5.30; Nov to mid-Dec, Mon–Fri tours 11–3.30.*

**2 Whithorn**
Whithorn Story Visitor Centre
45–7 George Street.
Tel: 01988 500508.
www.whithorn.com
*Open Apr–Oct, daily 10.30–5.*

**3 Isle of Whithorn**
St Ninian's Chapel
*Open at all times.*

**5 Glenluce**
Glenluce Abbey
2 miles (3km) northwest off the A75. Tel: 01581 300541.
www.dumfriesmuseum.demon.co.uk
*Open Apr–Sep, daily 9.30–6.30; Oct–Mar, Sat 9.30–4.30, Sun 2–4.30.*

**6 Port Logan**
Logan Fish Pond Marine Life Centre
Tel: 01776 860300.
www.loganfishpond.co.uk
*Open Feb–Sep, daily 10–5; Oct–early Nov, daily 10–4.*

Logan Botanic Garden
off B7065. Tel: 01776 860231.
www.rbge.org.uk
*Open Mar–Oct, daily 10–5.*

**7 Portpatrick**
Dunksey Castle
South of Portpatrick along the clifftop footpath.
*Accessible at all times.*

**8 Stranraer**
Stranraer Museum
George Street. Tel: 01776 705088.
www.dumfriesmuseum.demon.co.uk
*Open Mon–Sat 10–5 (closed for lunch between 1 and 2pm on Sat).*

Castle of St John
Tel: 01776 705088.
www.dumfriesmuseum.demon.co.uk
*Open Apr to mid-Sep, Mon–Sat 10–1, 2–5.*

**9 Girvan**
McKechnie Institute
Dalrymple Street.
Tel: 01465 713643.
www.south-ayrshire.gov.uk
*Open Tue, Thu–Fri 1–4, Wed 1.30–4.30, Sat 10.30–4.*

**10 Glen Trool Visitor Centre**
Off A714 at Bargrennan.
Tel: 01671 402420.
*Open late Mar–late Sep, daily 10.30–5; late Sep–Oct, daily 10.30–4.30.*

**For Children**
Monreith Animal World
On A747, 6 miles (10km) west of Whithorn. Tel: 01988 700217.
*Open Mar–Oct, daily 10–5.30.*

**For History Buffs**
Castle Kennedy Gardens
3 miles (5km) east of Stranraer on A75. Tel: 01776 702024. www.castlekennedygardens.co.uk
*Open Apr–Sep, daily 10–5.*

**Back to Nature**
Wood of Cree Nature Reserve
4 miles (6km) north of Newton Stewart. Tel: 01671 402861. www.rspb.org.uk/reserves
*Open at all times.*

## TOUR 3

i Whitesands, Dumfries. Tel: 01387 253862

i Markethill Car Park, Castle Douglas (seasonal). Tel: 01556 502611

i NTS Threave Gardens, Castle Douglas (seasonal). Tel: 01556 502575

i Harbour Square, Kirkcudbright (seasonal). Tel: 01557 330494

i Car Park, Gatehouse of Fleet (seasonal). Tel: 01557 814212

### 1 New Abbey

Sweetheart Abbey
Tel: 01387 850397. www.dumfriesmuseum.demon.co.uk
*Open Apr–Sep, daily 9.30–6.30; Oct–Mar, Mon–Wed, Sat 9.30–4.30, Thu 9.30–12.30, Sun 2–4.30.*

Shambellie House and Museum of Costume
Tel: 01387 850375. www.nms.ac.uk/costume
*Open Apr–Oct, daily 10–5.*

New Abbey Corn Mill
Tel: 01387 850260. www.dumfriesmuseum.demon.co.uk
*Open Apr–Sep, daily 9.30–6.30; Oct–Mar, 9.30–4.30 (closed Thu afternoon, all day Fri–Sun morning).*

### 3 Castle Douglas

Threave Garden
1 mile (1.6km) west off A75. Tel: 01556 502575. www.nts.org.uk
*Open daily 9.30–sunset.*

Threave Castle
3 miles (5km) west on the A75. Tel: 07711 223101. www.dumfriesmuseum.demon.co.uk
*Open Apr–Sep, daily 9.30–6.30.*

### 4 Kirkcudbright

Tolbooth Art Centre
Tel: 01557 331556. www.kirkcudbright.co.uk/oldhighst
*Open Mon–Sat 11–4; also Sun 2–5 Jun–Sep.*

MacLellan's Castle
Tel: 01557 331856. www.kirkcudbright.co.uk/places/castle
*Open Apr–Sep, daily 9.30–6.30.*

Stewartry Museum
St Mary Street. Tel: 01557 331643. www.dumfriesmuseum.demon.co.uk
*Open Mon–Sat 11–4; Jun–Sep also Sun 2–5; Nov–Feb Sat 11–4.*

Broughton House
12 High Street. Tel: 01557 330437. www.kirkcudbright.co.uk/oldhighst
*Open Garden only: Feb–13 Apr, daily 11–4. House and garden: Good Fri–Jun, Sep–Oct, daily noon–5; Jul–Aug, daily 10–5.*

Tongland Hydroelectric Power Station
2 miles (3km) north on A711. Tel: 01557 330114. www.scottishpower.com
*Open May–Sep, Mon–Fri 9.30–5.*

### 5 Gatehouse of Fleet

Cardoness Castle
1 mile (1.6km) southwest on the A75. Tel: 01557 814427. www.historic-scotland.gov.uk
*Open Apr–Sep, daily 9.30–6.30; Oct–Mar, daily 9.30–4.30.*

### 6 Cairnholy

Carsluith.
*Open at all times.*

### 7 Creetown

Gem Rock Museum
Chain Road. Tel: 01671 820357. www.gemrock.net
*Open Easter–Sep, daily 9.30–5.30; Oct–Nov, Mar–Easter, daily 10–4; Dec–Feb, weekends only 10–4.*

Exhibition Centre
91 St John's Street. Tel: 01671 820343. www.creetown-heritage-museum.com
*Open Apr–May, Sep to mid-Oct, Sun–Tue, Thu–Fri 11–4; Jun–Aug, Sun–Fri 11–4. Closed mid-Oct to Mar.*

Carsluith Castle
3½ miles (5.6km) south on A75.
*Open daily 9.30–6.30 (4.30 Oct–Mar).*

### 8 Clatteringshaws Loch

Clatteringshaws Visitor Centre
6 miles (10km) west of New Galloway. Tel: 01644 420285.
*Open late Mar–late Sep, daily 10.30–5; late Sep–Oct, daily 10.30–4.30.*

**Back to Nature**
Wildfowl and Wetlands Trust Caerlaverock
Eastpark Farm, Caerlaverock. Tel: 01387 770200. www.wwt.org.uk/visit/caerlaverock
*Open daily 10–5.*

**For History Buffs**
Caerlaverock Castle
Glencaple. Tel: 01387 770244. www.historic-scotland.gov.uk
*Open Mon–Sat 9.30–6.30, Sun 2–6.30 (closes 4.30pm Oct–Mar).*

**For Children**
Kirkcudbright Wildlife Park
Lochfergus Plantation, 1 mile (1.5km) east on B727. Tel: 01557 331645. www.gallowaywildlife.co.uk
*Open Feb–Nov, daily 10–dusk; Dec–Jan, Sat–Sun 10–4.*

## TOUR 4

i Horsemarket, Ladyacre Road, Lanark. Tel: 01555 661661.

i 155 High Street, Biggar (seasonal). Tel: 01899 221066.

i Service Area, Junction 13, M74 northbound, Abington. Tel: 01864 502436.

i Service Area, M74 northbound, Hamilton. Tel: 01698 285590.

### 1 New Lanark

New Lanark Visitor Centre
Tel: 01555 661345. www.newlanark.org
*Open daily 11–5.*

### 2 Biggar

Biggar Gasworks Museum
Gasworks Road. Tel: 01899 221050.
*Open Jun–Sep, daily 2–5.*

Gladstone Court Museum
Entrance by 113 High Street. Tel: 01899 221050.
*Open Easter to mid-Oct, Mon–Sat 11–4.30, Sun 2–4.30.*

Moat Park Heritage Centre
Kirkstyle. Tel: 01899 221050.
*Open Apr–Oct, Mon–Sat 10.30–5, Sun 2–5; Nov–Feb, weekdays only, during normal office hours.*

### 3 Wanlockhead

Museum of Leadmining
At the north end of the Mennock Pass. Tel: 01659 74387. www.leadminingmuseum.co.uk
*Open Apr–Oct, daily 11–4.30.*

### 4 Sanquhar

Sanquhar Castle
*Open at all times.*

**Tolbooth Museum**
High Street. Tel: 01659 50186.
www.dumfriesmuseum.demon.co.uk
*Open Apr–Sep, Tue–Sat 10–1, 2–5, Sun 2–5.*

**6 Strathaven**
**John Hastie Museum**
Threestanes Road.
Tel: 01357 521257.
*Open Apr–Sep, daily 12.30–4.30.*

**7 Hamilton**
**Low Parks Museum**
129 Muir Street. Tel: 01698 328232.
*Open Mon–Sat 10–5, Sun noon–5.*

**Hamilton Mausoleum**
Tours available from Low Parks Museum only.
*Tours Sat, Sun, Wed, summer 3pm; winter 2pm.*

**Cadzow Castle Ruins**
Hamilton Hyde Park.
*Open at all times.*

**8 Blantyre**
**David Livingstone Centre**
165 Station Road.
Tel: 01698 823140.
*Open Mon–Sat 10–5, Sun 12.30–5 (restricted winter opening).*

**9 Bothwell Castle**
Castle Avenue, Uddingston.
Tel: 01698 816894.
www.historic-scotland.gov.uk
*Open Apr–Sep, daily 9.30–6.30; Oct–Mar, 9.30–4.30 (closed Thu afternoon, all day Fri and Sun morning).*

**10 Craignethan Castle**
5 miles (8km) west of Lanark off A72. Tel: 01555 860364.
www.historic-scotland.gov.uk
*Open Apr–Sep, daily 9.30–6.30; Nov–Mar, Sat 9.30–4.30, Sun 2–4.30.*

**For Children**
**Discover Carmichael Visitor Centre**
Carmichael. Tel: 01899 308169.
www.carmichael.co.uk/visitor
*Open late Mar–early Jan, daily 9.30–5.30.*

**Biggar Little Theatre (International Purves Puppets)**
Broughton Road.
Tel: 01899 220631.
www.purvespuppets.com
*Open on certain days only.*

**Strathclyde Country Park**
Hamilton Road, Motherwell. Tel: 01698 266155.
www.northlan.gov.uk
*Always accessible.*

**M & D's Scotland's Theme Park**
Strathclyde Country Park.
Tel: 01698 333777.
www.scotlandsthemepark.com
*Open summer, daily. Other times phone.*

**Back to Nature**
**Chatelherault**
Ferniegair, southeast of Hamilton on A72.
Tel: 01698 426213.
www.southlanarkshire.gov.uk
*Open: House Mon–Thu, Sat 10–5, Sun noon–5; Visitor Centre Mon–Sat 10–5, Sun 2–5.*

## TOUR 5

[i] Churchgate, Moffat (seasonal).
Tel: 01683 220620.

[i] High Street, Peebles.
Tel: 0870 608 0404.

[i] 3 St John Street, Galashiels (seasonal).
Tel: 0870 608 0404

**1 Dawyck Botanic Garden**
Stobo. Tel: 01721 760254.
www.rbge.org.uk
*Open Apr–Sep, daily 10–6; Mar, Oct, daily 10–5; Feb, Nov, daily 10–4.*

**2 Broughton**
**John Buchan Centre**
South end of Broughton village on the A701.
www.johnbuchansociety.co.uk/centre.htm
*Open Easter and May to mid-Oct, daily 2–5.*

**Broughton Gallery**
North on A701. Tel: 01899 830234.
www.broughtongallery.co.uk
*Open Tue–Sun during exhibitions 10.30–6 (closed Mon).*

**4 Peebles**
**Tweeddale Museum**
Chambers Institute, High Street. Tel: 01721 724820.
*Open Mon–Fri 10–noon, 2–5; Easter–Oct, also Sat 10–1, 2–4.*

**Cornice Museum of Ornamental Plasterwork**
Innerleithen Road.
Tel: 01721 720212.
*Open Mon–Fri 10–noon, 2–4.30.*

**Old Cross Kirk**
Off High Street.
*Open daily (pm only on Sun); Jan–Mar apply to keykeeper.*

**Neidpath Castle**
1 mile (1.5km) west..
Tel: 01721 720333.
*Open Easter, Jun–Sep, Mon–Sat 10.30–4.30, Sun 12.30–4.30.*

**Kailzie Gardens**
2½ miles (4km) south on B7062. Tel: 01721 720007.
www.kailziegardens.com
*Open late Mar–Oct, daily; call for winter opening.*

**5 Innerleithen**
**Robert Smail's Printing Works**
7–9 High Street. Tel: 01896 830206.
www.nts.org.uk
*Open Easter, Jun–Sep, Thu–Mon noon–5 (Sun 1–5).*

**Traquair House**
Traquair, south on B709.
Tel: 01896 830323.
www.traquair.co.uk
*Open Apr–Oct, daily; Nov, Sat–Sun only.*

**6 Galashiels**
**Lochcarron Cashmere Wool of Scotland Visitor Centre**
Waverley Mill, Huddersfield Street. Tel: 01896 752091.
www.galashiels.bordernet.co.uk/lochcarron
*Open all year, Mon–Sat 9–5; Jun–Sep also Sun noon–5; guided tours Mon–Thu at 10.30, 11.30, 1.30 and 2.30 (morning only on Fri).*

**Old Gala House and Christopher Boyd Gallery**
Scott Crescent. Tel: 01750 20096.
www.galashiels.bordernet.co.uk/oldgalahouse
*Open Easter–Sep, Tue–Sat 10–4; Jul–Aug, also Sun 2–4 and Mon 10–4; Oct, Tue–Sat 1–4.*

**7 Yarrowford**
**Bowhill House and Country Park**
3 miles (5km) west of Selkirk. Tel: 01750 22204.
*Open Jul, daily 1–4.30; country park late Apr–Aug, daily noon–5, closed Fri ex Jul.*

## TOUR 6

Telephone enquiries for tourist information in the area should be directed to tel: 0870 608 0404. Information for personal callers is available at:

[i] Abbey House, Abbey Street, Melrose (seasonal).

[i] Murray's Green, Jedburgh.

[i] Drumlanrig's Tower, Tower Knowe, Hawick (seasonal).

[i] Halliwell's House, Selkirk (seasonal).

**1 Dryburgh Abbey**
Dryburgh. Tel: 01835 822381.
www.historic-scotland.gov.uk
*Open daily 9.30–6.30 (to 4.30pm Oct–Mar, Sun 2–4.30).*

**Smailholm Tower**
Northwest of Dryburgh Abbey on B6404.
Tel: 01573 460365.
www.historic-scotland.gov.uk
*Open Apr–Sep, daily 9.30–6.30; Oct–Mar, Sat–Sun only.*

**2 Jedburgh**
Jedburgh Castle Jail and Museum
Castlegate. Tel: 01835 863254.
www.scotborders.gov.uk/outabout/museums
*Open Easter–Oct, Mon–Sat 10–4.30, Sun 1–4.*

Jedburgh Abbey
Tel: 01835 863925.
www.historic-scotland.gov.uk
*Open Apr–Sep, daily 9.30–6.30; Oct–Mar, Mon–Sat 9.30–4.30, Sun 2–4.30.*

Mary, Queen of Scots' House
Queen Street. Tel: 01835 863331.
*Open Mar–Nov, Mon–Sat 10–4.30, Sun noon–4.30*

**3 Hawick**
Peter Scott Woollen Mill
11 Buccleuch Street.
Tel: 01450 372311.
www.peterscott.co.uk
*Open all year, Mon–Fri 10–5, Sat 10–4.*

Wrights of Trowmill Weaving Flat
2½ miles (4km) northwest on A698. Tel: 01450 372555.
*Open Mon–Thu 9–4, Fri 9–11.30; shop daily 9/10–5.*

Hawick Museum and Scott Art Gallery
Wilton Lodge Park.
Tel: 01450 373457.
*Open Apr–Sep, Mon–Fri 10–noon, 1–4.45, Sat–Sun 2–4.45; Oct–Mar, Mon–Fri 1–4, Sun 2–4.*

**4 Hermitage Castle**
Tel: 01387 376222.
www.historic-scotland.gov.uk
*Open Apr–Sep, daily 9.30–6.30.*

**5 Eskdalemuir**
Kagyu Samye Ling Monastery
B709 northeast of Langholm.
www.samyeling.org
Tel: 013873 73232.
*Open daily 9–6.*

**7 Ettrick**
James Hogg Exhibition & Aikwood Tower
On B7009. Tel: 01750 52253.
*Open Easter Sun, May–Sep, Tue, Thu, Sun 2–5.*

**8 Selkirk**
Sir Walter Scott's Courtroom
Market Place. Tel: 01750 20096.
www.scotborders.gov.uk/outabout/museums
*Open Apr–Sep, Mon–Sat 10–4 (from 1pm in Oct); Jun–Aug also Sun 2–4.*

Halliwell's House Museum
Market Place. Tel: 01750 20096.
www.scotborders.gov.uk/outabout/museums
*Open Mar–Jun, Sep, Mon–Sat 10–5, Sun 10–noon; Jul–Aug, Mon–Sat 10–5.30, Sun 10–noon; Oct, Mon–Sat 10–noon.*

**9 Abbotsford**
Tel: 01896 752043.
www.scottsabbotsford.co.uk
*Open mid-Mar to May, Oct, Mon–Sat 9.30–5, Sun 2–5; Jun–Sep, daily 9.30–5.*

**For History Buffs**
Trimontium Exhibition
Ormiston Institute, The Square, Melrose. Tel: 01896 822651 or 822463.
*Open Apr–Oct, daily 10.30–4.30.*

**Back to Nature**
Harestanes Countryside Visitor Centre
Harestanes, Ancrum, 3 miles (5km) north of Jedburgh off A68.
Tel: 01835 830306.
www.scotborders.gov.uk/outabout/museums
*Open Apr–Oct, daily 10–5.*

Priorwood Garden
Adjacent to Melrose Abbey. Tel: 01896 822493.
*Open Apr–24 Dec, Mon–Sat 10–5.30, Sun 1.30–5.30 (to 4pm Oct–24 Dec).*

Harmony Garden
St Mary's Road, Melrose.
Tel: 01721 722502.
*Open Apr–Sep, Mon–Sat 10–5.30, Sun 1.30–5.30.*

**For Children**
Jedforest Deer and Farm Park
Mervfinslaw Estate, Jedburgh. Tel: 01835 840364.
*Open May–Aug, daily 10–5.30; Sep–Oct, daily 11–4.30.*

**For History Buffs**
Drumlanrig's Tower
Tower Knowe, Hawick.
Tel: 01450 377615.
www.scotborders.gov.uk/outabout/museums
*Open Apr–Oct, Mon–Sat 10–5 (to 6 Jul–Aug), also Sun 1–4 Easter–Sep (to 5 Jul–Aug).*

## TOUR 7

[i] 3 Princes Street, Edinburgh. Tel: 0131 473 3800.

[i] Scottish Mining Museum, Lady Victoria Colliery, Newtongrange. Tel: 0131 663 4262.

[i] Quality Street, North Berwick. Tel: 01620 892197.

[i] 143 High Street, Dunbar. Tel: 01368 863353.

[i] Auld Kirk, Manse Road, Eyemouth (seasonal). Tel: 0870 608 0404.

[i] Town Hall, High Street, Coldstream (seasonal). Tel: 0870 608 0404.

[i] Town House, The Square, Kelso. Tel: 0870 608 0404.

**1 Gullane**
Dirleton Castle and Gardens
Dirleton. Tel: 01620 850330.
www.historic-scotland.gov.uk
*Open Apr–Sep, daily 9.30–6.30; Oct–Mar, Mon–Sat 9.30–4.30, Sun 2–4.30.*

**3 Tantallon Castle**
3 miles (5km) east of North Berwick off A198.
Tel: 01620 892727.
www.historic-scotland.gov.uk
*Open Apr–Sep, Mon–Sat 9.30–6.30 (closes 4.30 Oct–Mar.*

**4 Preston**
Preston Mill and Phantassie Doocot
East Linton. Tel: 01620 860426.
www.nts.org.uk
*Open Apr–Sep, Thu–Mon noon–5 (Sun 1–5).*

**7 St Abbs**
Coldingham Priory
www.stebba-coldinghampriory.org.uk
*Open May–Sep, Wed 2–5, Sun all year for services, noon.*

**8 Eyemouth**
Eyemouth Museum
Auld Kirk. Tel: 018907 50678.
www.scotborders.gov.uk/outabout/museums
*Open Easter–Sep, Mon–Sat 10–5, Sun 11–2; Oct, Mon–Sat 1–4.*

**9 Duns**
Jim Clark Room
44 Newtown Street.
Tel: 01361 883960.
www.duns.bordernet.co.uk
*Open Easter–Sep, Mon–Sat 10.30–1, 2–4.30, Sun 2–4; Oct, Mon–Sat 1–4.*

Manderston
A6105, 2 miles (3km) east.
Tel: 01361 883450.
www.manderston.co.uk
*Open mid-May to Sep, Thu, Sun 11.30–5.*

**10 Coldstream**
Coldstream Museum
12 Market Square.
Tel: 01890 882630.
www.scotborders.gov.uk/outabout/museums
*Open Easter–Sep, Mon–Sat 10–4, Sun 2–4; Oct, Mon–Sat 1–4.*

The Hirsel
Tel: 01890 882834.
www.hirselcountrypark.co.uk
*Open daily, daylight hours.*

**11 Kelso**
Floors Castle
Tel: 01573 223333.
www.floorscastle.com
*Open Apr–Oct, daily 11–5.*

Kelso Abbey
Tel: 0131 668 8800.
www.historic-scotland.gov.uk
*Open Apr–Oct, daily (Sun pm only).*

Mellerstain House
Gordon. Tel: 01573 410225.
www.mellerstain.com
*Open Easter, May–Sep, daily (ex Tue and Sat) 12.30–5.*

**11 Lauder**
Thirlestane Castle
Off A68. Tel: 01578 722430.
www.thirlestanecastle.co.uk
*Open Easter–Sep, Mon, Wed–Thu, Sun 10–3; Jul, Sat–Thu.*

**13 Crichton Castle**
Tel: 01875 320017.
www.historic-scotland.gov.uk
*Open Apr–Sep, daily 9.30–6.30.*

**For History Buffs**
Scottish Mining Museum
Lady Victoria Colliery, Newtongrange. Tel: 0131 663 7519.
www.scottishmining museum.com
*Open Mar–Oct, daily 10–5; Nov–Feb, daily 10–4.*

**For History Buffs**
Rosslyn Chapel
Rosslyn. Tel: 0131 440 2159.
www.rosslynchapel.org.uk
*Open Apr–Sep, daily 9.30–6; Oct–Mar, Mon–Sat 9.30–5, Sun noon–4.45.*

**Back to Nature**
St Abbs Head National Nature Reserve
Tel: 01890 771443.
www.nts-seabirds.org.uk
*Open all year; Reserve Centre Apr–Oct, daily 10–5.*

**For Children**
Scottish Seabird Centre
North Berwick. Tel: 01620 890202.
www.seabird.org
*Open Apr–Oct, daily 10–6; Nov–Mar, Mon–Fri 10–4 (5 Feb & Mar), Sat–Sun 10–5.30.*

## TOUR 8

[i] Albany Street, Oban. Tel: 01631 563122.

[i] Lochnell Street, Lochgilphead (seasonal). Tel: 08707 200618.

[i] Front Street, Inveraray. Tel: 08707 200616.

[i] NTS Visitor Centre, Glen Coe (seasonal). Tel: 01855 811307.

[i] Albert Road, Ballachulish (seasonal). Tel: 01855 811866.

**1 Easdale**
Easdale Island Folk Museum
Tel: 01852 300370.
www.slate.org.uk
*Open Apr–Oct, daily 10.30–5.30.*

**2 Kilmartin**
Kilmartin House Centre for Archaeology & Landscape Interpretation
Tel: 01546 510278.
*Open daily 10–5.30.*

Carnassarie Castle
North, beside A816.
*Open at all times.*

**4 Lochgilphead**
Highbank Pottery
Highbank Industrial Estate.
Tel: 01546 602044.
*Open Mon–Fri 9–5, Sat 10–5.*

**5 Crarae Garden**
On A83 near Minard.
Tel: 01546 886614.
www.nts.org.uk
*Open daily during daylight hours.*

**6 Auchindrain Township Open Air Museum**
On A83 6 miles (10km) southwest of Inveraray.
Tel: 01499 500235.
www.auchindrainmuseum.org.uk
*Open Apr–Sep, daily 10–5.*

**7 Inveraray**
Inveraray Jail Museum
Church Square. Tel: 01499 302381.
www.inverarayjail.co.uk
*Open Apr–Oct, daily 9.30–6; Nov–Mar, daily 10–5.*

*Arctic Penguin*
The Pier. Tel: 01499 302213.
www.inveraraypier.com
*Open daily 10–5 (to 6pm Apr–Sep).*

Inveraray Castle
Northern edge of town, on A83. Tel: 01499 302203.
www.inveraray-castle.com
*Open Apr–May, Oct, Mon–Thu, Sat 10–1, 2–5.45; Jun–Sep, Mon–Sat 10–5.45, Sun 1–5.45.*

**8 Loch Awe**
Cruachan Power Station
Dalmally. Tel: 01866 822618.
www.scottishpower.com
*Open Apr–Dec, daily 9.30–5.*

Kilchurn Castle
Head of Locha Awe, south off A85.
*Open at all times.*

**9 Glen Coe**
Glen Coe Visitor Centre
Tel: 01855 811307.
www.glencoe-nts.org.uk
*Open Apr–Oct, daily 10–5 (9.30–5.30 mid-May to Aug).*

Glen Coe and North Lorn Folk Museum
Tel: 01855 811314.
*Open Easter–Sep, Mon–Sat 10–5.*

**10 Scottish Sea Life Sanctuary**
Barcaldine. Tel: 01631 720386.
www.sealsanctuary.co.uk
*Open daily 10–5 (to 6pm in high season).*

**12 Loch Etive**
Bonawe Iron Furnace
Bonawe. Tel: 01866 822432.
www.historic-scotland.gov.uk
*Open Apr–Sep, daily 9.30–6.30.*

**For Children**
Oban Rare Breeds Farm Park
New Barran, Oban.
Tel: 01631 770608.
www.obanrarebreeds.com
*Open Apr–Oct, daily 10–6.*

Argyll Wildlife Park
Inveraray. Tel: 01499 302264.
www.safaripark.co.uk
*Open daily 10–5.*

**For History Buffs**
Dunadd Fort
1 mile (1.5km) west of Kilmichael Glassary.
*Open at all times.*

## TOUR 9

[i] Glasgow International Airport, Paisley. Tel: 0141 848 4440.

[i] Milton, A82 north-bound, Dumbarton. Tel: 01389 742306.

[i] Clock Tower, The Pier, Helensburgh (seasonal). Tel: 08707 200624.

[i] Harbour Street, Tarbert. Tel: 01880 820429.

[i] 7 Alexandra Parade, Dunoon. Tel: 01369 703785.

**1 Dumbarton**
Dumbarton Castle
Tel: 01389 732167.
www.historic-scotland.gov.uk
*Open 9.30–6.30 (to 4.30pm Oct–Mar, and closed Thu pm & Fri).*

**2 Helensburgh**
Hill House
Upper Colquhoun Street.
Tel: 01436 673900.
www.nts.org.uk
*Open Apr–Oct, daily 1.30–5.30.*

**4 Lochgoilhead**
Carrick Castle
On west side of Loch Goil.
*Open at all times.*

**5 Loch Fyne**
Strachur Smiddy
The Clachan. Tel: 01369 860565.
*Open Easter–Sep, daily 1–4.*

**7 Dunoon**
Castle House Museum
Castle Gardens. Tel: 01369 701422.
www.castlehousemuseum.org.uk
*Open Easter–Oct, daily 10.30–4.30, Sun 2–4.30.*

**Cowal Bird Garden**
Lochan Wood, Sandbank Road. Tel: 01369 707999. www.cowal-dunoon.com
*Open Easter–Oct, daily 10.30–6.*

**Younger Botanic Garden**
Benmore. Tel: 01369 706261.
www.rbge.org.uk
*Open Mar–Oct, daily 10–6.*

### 8 Greenock

**Custom House Museum**
Custom House Quay, Greenock. Tel: 01475 881452.
www.greenock-town.co.uk/custom_house_quay.html
*Open Mon–Fri 10–4.*

**McLean Museum and Art Gallery**
15 Kelly Street, Greenock. Tel: 01475 715624.
www.inverclyde.gov.uk
*Open Mon–Sat 10–5.*

**Newark Castle**
On the A8, Port Glasgow. Tel: 01475 741858.
*Open Apr–Sep, Mon–Sat 9.30–6.30, Sun 2–6.30.*

### 2 Kilbarchan

**Weaver's Cottage**
The Cross. Tel: 01505 705588.
www.nts.org.uk
*Open Easter–Sep, daily 1.30–5.30; Oct weekends.*

### For Children

**Helensburgh Pier**
Pier Car Park, West Clyde Street. Tel: 01436 671552.
*Open Apr–May, Sep Sat–Sun; Jun–Aug, daily, 1.30–10.*

### For History Buffs

**Castle Toward**
End of the A815 south of Dunoon.
*Open at all times.*

### Special To...

**PS *Waverley* cruises**
Anderston Quay, Glasgow. Tel: 0845 130 4647.
www.waverleyexcursions.co.uk
*Cruises Jul–Aug, daily.*

## TOUR 10

[i] 11 George Square, Glasgow. Tel: 0141 204 4400.

[i] Drymen Library, The Square, Drymen (seasonal). Tel: 01360 660068.

[i] Breadalbane Folklore Centre, Falls of Dochart, Killin (seasonal). Tel: 08707 200627.

[i] The Square, Aberfeldy. Tel: 01887 820276.

[i] High Street, Crieff. Tel: 01764 652578.

[i] Rob Roy and Trossachs Visitor Centre, Ancaster Square, Callander. Tel: 01877 330342.

[i] Trossachs Discovery Centre, Main Street, Aberfoyle (seasonal). Tel: 08707 200604.

### 1 Gartocharn

**Balloch Castle Country Park**
Old Station, Balloch Road, Balloch. Tel: 01389 758216.
*Open all year, 8–dusk; visitor centre Apr–Oct, daily 10–5.45.*

### 2 Luss

**National Park Centre**
Tel: 01389 722199.
*Open daily.*

**Thistle Bagpipe Works**
Tel: 01436 860250.
www.kiltsandbagpipes.co.uk
*Open daily 9–5.30 (later in summer).*

### 3 Killin

**Ben Lawers Visitor Centre**
Lynedoch, Main Street. Tel: 01567 820397.
www.nts.orh.uk
*Open Apr–Sep, daily 10–5 (may close for lunch).*

**Breadalbane Folklore Centre**
St Fillan's Mill. Tel: 01567 820254.
www.breadalbanefolklorecentre.com
*Open Mar–May, Oct, daily 10–5; Jun, Sep, daily 10–6; Jul–Aug, daily 9.30–6.30.*

### 5 Aberfeldy

**Watermill**
Mill Street. Tel: 01887 822896.
*Call for information.*

**Castle Menzies**
Weem. Tel: 01887 820982.
www.menzies.org/castle/
*Open Apr to mid-Oct, Mon–Sat 10.30–5, Sun 2–5.*

### 6 Crieff

**Thistle Pottery**
Visitor Centre, Muthill Road. Tel: 01764 655081.
www.buchanthistlepottery.co.uk
*Open Apr–Oct, daily 9–5.30; Nov–Mar daily 10–4.*

**Glenturret Distillery**
Northwest off the A85.
Tel: 01764 656565.
www.famousgrouse.co.uk/experience
*Open daily 9–6.*

### 8 Callander

**Rob Roy and Trossachs Visitor Centre**
Ancaster Square. Tel: 01887 330342.
www.robroyvisitorcentre.com
*Open Jan–Feb, weekends 11–4.30; Mar–May, Oct–Dec, daily 10–5; Jun, daily 9.30–6; Jul–Aug, daily 9–8; Sep, daily 10–6.*

### 9 Loch Katrine

***Sir Walter Scott* cruises**
Trossachs Pier, by Callander.
Tel: 01877 376316.
*Open Apr–Oct daily, sailings 11, 1.45 & 3.15.*

### 10 Aberfoyle

**Scottish Wool Centre**
Off Main Street. Tel: 01877 382850.
www.scottishsheepdogschool.com/woolcentre.htm
*Open daily 9.30–5.30 (to 6pm Sat–Sun).*

### Recommended Walks

**Queen Elizabeth Forest Park Visitor Centre**
North of Aberfoyle on the A821. Tel: 01877 382258.
*Open Easter–Oct, daily 10–6; Nov–Dec, daily 11–4.*

### For History Buffs

**Inchmahome Priory**
Accessible by ferry from Port of Menteith.
Tel: 01877 385294.
www.historic-scotland.gov.uk
*Open Apr–Sep, daily 9.30–6.30.*

## TOUR 11

[i] 41 Dumbarton Road, Stirling. Tel: 08707 200620.

[i] Royal Burgh of Stirling Visitor Centre, Castle Esplanade, Stirling.
Tel: 08707 200622.

[i] Pirnhall Motorway Service Area, M9/M80 Junction 9 (seasonal).
Tel: 08707 200621.

[i] Stirling Road, Dunblane (seasonal). Tel: 08707 200613.

[i] Mill Trail Visitor Centre, West Stirling Street, Alva.
Tel: 08707 200605.

[i] 1 High Street, Dunfermline (seasonal).
Tel: 01383 720999.

[i] Burgh Halls, The Cross, Linlithgow (seasonal).
Tel: 01506 844600.

[i] Car Park, Seaview Place, Bo'ness (seasonal).
Tel: 08707 200608.

[i] NTS Visitor Centre, Bannockburn. Tel: 01786 812664.

### 1 Causewayhead

**Wallace Monument**
Abbey Craig. Tel: 01786 472140.
www.nationalwallacemonument.com
*Open all year daily.*

### 2 Dunblane

**Doune Castle**
Tel: 01786 841742.
www.historic-scotland.gov.uk
*Open Apr–Sep, daily 9.30–6.30; Oct–Mar, 9.30–4.30 closed Thu afternoon, all day Fri and Sun morning.*

[i] Tourist Information Office
**12** Number on tour

Dunblane Museum
The Cross.
www.dunblanemuseum.org.uk
*Open early May–early Oct, Mon–Sat 10.30–4.30.*

**3 Dollar**
Castle Campbell
Off A91 at head of Dollar Glen. Tel: 01259 742408.
www.historic-scotland.gov.uk
*Open daily 9.30–6.30 (to 4.30pm Oct–Mar, closed Thu pm, Fri, and Sun am).*

Mill Trail Visitor Centre
Glentana Mill, Alva.
Tel: 01259 769696.
*Open all year daily.*

**4 Culross**
Culross Palace, Town House and The Study
West Green House.
Tel: 01383 880359.
www.culross.org/palace.htm
*Open Apr–Sep. daily noon–5; Town House and Study open at 1.30, and weekends in Oct noon–5.*

**5 Dunfermline**
Dunfermline Abbey
Pittencrieff Park. Tel: 01383 739026.
www.dunfermlineabbey.co.uk
*Open Mon–Sat 9.30–6.30, Sun 2–6.30 (to 4.30pm Oct–Mar, closed Thu pm).*

Abbot House Museum
The Maygate. Tel: 01383 733266.
*Open daily 10–5.*

Pittencrieff House Museum and Art Gallery
Pittencrieff Park. Tel: 01383 722935 & 313838.
*Open daily 11–4 or 5.*

Andrew Carnegie Birthplace Museum
Moodie Street. Tel: 01383 724302.
www.carnegiebirthplace.com
*Open Apr–Oct, Mon–Sat 11–5 (from 10am Jun–Aug), Sun 2–5.*

**6 Blackness**
Blackness Castle
Tel: 01506 834807.
*Open Apr–Sep, Mon–Sat 9.30–6.30, Sun 2–6.30; Oct–Mar, 9.30–4.30 closed Thu afternoon, all day Fri and Sun morning).*

**7 Linlithgow**
Linlithgow Palace
Tel: 01506 842896.
www.historic-scotland.gov.uk
*Open Mon–Sat 9.30–6.30, Sun 2–6.30 (4.30 Oct–Mar).*

Burgh Halls Visitor Centre
The Cross. Tel: 01506 844600.
*Open Easter–Oct, daily 10–5.*

House of the Binns
Tel: 01506 834255.
www.nts.org.uk
*Open May–Sep, Sat–Thu 1.30–5.30; parkland Apr–Oct, daily 10–7; Nov–Mar, daily 10–4.*

The Linlithgow Story
High Street. Tel: 01506 670677.
www.linlithgowstory.org.uk
*Open mid-Apr to Oct, daily 11–5 (1–4 on Sun).*

Canal Museum
Manse Road Basin.
Tel: 01506 671215.
www.lucs.org.uk
*Open Easter–Oct, weekends 2–5 (daily Jul–Aug).*

**8 Bo'ness**
Bo'ness & Kinneil Railway and Birkhill Clay Mine
Bo'ness Station, Union Street. Tel: 01506 822298.
www.srps.org.uk/railway
*Open Apr–Oct, weekends and bank hols; Jul–Aug, Tue–Sun.*

**9 Bannockburn**
Heritage Centre
Glasgow Road, Stirling.
Tel: 01786 812664.
www.nts.org.uk
*Heritage Centre: open Apr–Oct, daily 10–5.30; Mar, Nov–23 Dec, daily 11–4.30; the site is open all year daily.*

**For Children**
**Blair Drummond Safari and Leisure Park**
Blair Drummond.
Tel: 01786 841456.
www.safari-park.co.uk
*Open late Apr–early Oct, daily 10–5.30.*

## TOUR 12

[i] Lower City Mills, West Mill Street, Perth. Tel: 01738 450600.

[i] Caithness Glass, Inveralmond, by the A9.
Tel: 01738 492320.

[i] The Cross, Dunkeld.
Tel: 01350 727688.

[i] 26 Wellmeadow, Blairgowrie. Tel: 01250 872960.

[i] Brechin Castle Centre, Haughmuir, Brechin (seasonal). Tel: 01356 623050.

[i] Bridge Street, Montrose (seasonal).
Tel: 01674 672000.

[i] Market Place, Arbroath.
Tel: 01241 872609.

[i] 1B High Street, Carnoustie (seasonal).
Tel: 01241 852258.

[i] 21 Castle Street, Dundee. Tel: 01382 527527.

**1 Dunkeld**
The Ell Shop
The Cross. Tel: 01350 727460.
*Open Apr–Sep, Mon–Sat 10.30–5.30 (also Sun from 12.30 Jun–Aug); Oct–23 Dec, Mon–Sat 10–4.30.*

**3 Meigle**
Sculptured Stone Museum
Tel: 01828 640612.
www.historic-scotland.gov.uk
*Open daily 9.30–6.30 (to 4.30pm Oct–Nov); may close for lunch on weekdays.*

**4 Glamis**
Glamis Castle
Tel: 01307 840393.
www.glamis-castle.co.uk
*Open late Mar–late Oct, daily 10–6 (last admission 4.30).*

Angus Folk Museum
Kirkwynd, Glamis.
Tel: 01307 840288.
www.nts.org.uk
*Open Easter, May–Sep, Sat–Wed noon–5.*

**6 House of Dun**
Montrose. Tel: 01674 810264.
www.nts.org.uk
*Open Easter, May–Sep, Fri–Tue 12.30–5; grounds all year, 9.30–sunset.*

**10 Dundee**
Discovery Point Visitor Centre
Discovery Quay, Riverside Drive. Tel: 01382 201245.
www.city-of-dundee.info
*Open Mon–Sat 10–6, Sun 11–6 (to 5pm Nov–Mar).*

Frigate *Unicorn*
Victoria Dock. Tel: 01382 200900.
www.frigateunicorn.org
*Open Easter–Oct, daily 10–5; Nov–Easter, Mon–Fri 10–4.*

McManus Galleries
Albert Square. Tel: 01382 432350.
www.mcmanus.co.uk
*Call for details.*

Broughty Castle Museum
Castle Approach, Broughty Ferry. Tel: 01382 436916.
www.dundeecity.gov.uk/broughtycastle
*Open Apr–Sep, Mon–Sat 10–4, Sun 12.30–4; Oct–Mar, Tue–Sat 10–4, Sun 12.30–4.*

**Back to Nature**
Loch of the Lowes Visitor Centre
Dunkeld. Tel: 01350 727337.
www.swt.org.uk/wildlife/lochoflowes.asp
*Open Apr–Sep, daily 10–5.*

## TOUR 13

[i] 70 Market Street, St Andrews. Tel: 01334 472021.

[i] Museum and Heritage Centre, Crail (seasonal).
Tel: 01333 450869.

[i] Scottish Fisheries Museum, Harbourhead, Anstruther (seasonal). Tel: 01333 311073.

[i] Kinross Service Area, off Junc 6, M90. Tel: 01577 863680.

**1 Crail**
Museum and Heritage Centre
62–4 Marketgate.
Tel: 01333 450869.
www.crailmuseum.org.uk
*Open May, Sat–Sun 10–1, 2–5; Jun–Sep, Mon–Sat 10–1, 2–5, Sun 2–5.*

Crail Pottery
75 Nethergate. Tel: 01333 451212.
www.crailpottery.com
*Open Mon–Fri 9–5, Sat–Sun 10–5.*

**2 Anstruther**
Scottish Fisheries Museum
St Ayles, Harbourhead.
Tel: 01333 310628.
www.scotfishmuseum.org
*Open Apr–Sep, Mon–Sat 10–5.30, Sun 11–5; Oct–Mar, Mon–Sat 10–4.30, Sun noon–4.30.*

Scotland's Secret Bunker
4 miles (6.5km) north on B940. Tel: 01333 310301.
www.secretbunker.co.uk
*Open Apr–Oct, daily 10–5.*

**3 Pittenweem**
St Fillan's Cave
Tel: 01333 311495.
*Open all year (get key from 9 High Street).*

Kellie Castle
3 miles (5km) northwest of Pittenweem. Tel: 01333 720271.
www.nts.org.uk
*Open Easter, Jun–Sep, daily 1–5; weekends in Oct 1.30–5.30; grounds all year daily 9.30–sunset.*

**4 St Monans**
St Monans Windmill
Coal Farm, St Monans.
Tel: 01334 412690.
*Open late Jun–Sep, daily noon–4.*

**6 Falkland**
Falkland Palace
Tel: 01337 857397.
www.nts.org.uk
*Open Apr–Oct, Mon–Sat 11–5.30, Sun 1.30–5.30.*

**8 Kinross**
Loch Leven Castle
Ferry from Kirkgate Park.
Tel: 07778 040483.
www.historic-scotland.gov.uk
*Open Apr–Oct from 9.30 (last ferry off the island departs at 6pm, or 4pm in Oct). Closed Tue, Fri in Oct..*

Kinross House Gardens
Tel: 01577 863467.
www.kinrosshouse.com
*Open Apr–Sep, daily.*

**10 Cupar**
Hill of Tarvit
Ceres. Tel: 01334 653127.
www.nts.org.uk
*Open Apr–Sep, daily 1–5; Oct, Sat–Sun 1–5.*

Scotstarvit Tower
Ceres.
*Open Apr–Oct, daily noon–5 (key from Hill of Tarvit).*

**For Children**
Scottish Deer Centre and Raptor World
Rankeilour Park, Bow of Fife, by Cupar. Tel: 01337 810391 (Deer); 07976 227699 (Raptors).
www.thedeercentre.co.uk
*Open daily from 10am; closes at 5 or 6, depending on the season.*

## TOUR 14

[i] Castle Wynd, Inverness. Tel: 01463 234353.

[i] 62 King Street, Nairn (seasonal). Tel: 01667 452753.

[i] 116 High Street, Forres (seasonal). Tel: 01309 672938.

[i] 54 High Street, Grantown-on-Spey (seasonal). Tel: 01479 872773.

[i] Picnic Area, Daviot Wood, on the A9, by Inverness (seasonal). Tel: 01463 772203.

**1 Fort George**
11 miles (18km) northeast of Inverness. Tel: 01667 462777.
www.historic-scotland.gov.uk
*Open Apr–Sep, daily 9.30–6.30; Oct–Mar, daily 9.30–4.30.*

**2 Cawdor Castle**
Tel: 01667 404401.
www.cawdorcastle.com
*Open May to mid-Oct daily 10–5.30.*

Kilravock Castle
6 miles (10km) south of Nairn off B9090. Tel: 01667 493258.
www.kilravockcastle.com
*Open Wed–Thu 2.30–4.*

**3 Nairn**
Nairn Museum
Viewfield House. Tel: 01667 456791.
www.visitnairn.com/nairnmuseum
*Open late Mar–Oct, daily 1–4.30; Nov, Sat–Sun 1–4.30.*

**4 Brodie Castle**
Brodie, near Forres.
Tel: 01309 641371.
www.nts.org.uk
*Open Apr, Jul–Aug, daily noon–4; May–Jun, Sep, Sun–Thu noon–4; grounds: all year daily 9.30–sunset.*

**5 Forres**
Falconer Museum
Tolbooth Street. Tel: 01309 673701.
*Open Apr–Oct, Mon–Sat 10–5; Nov–Mar, Mon–Thu 11–12.30, 1–3.30.*

Sueno's Stone
Findhorn Road, east of Forres. Tel: 01667 460232.
*Open at all times.*

**7 Grantown-on-Spey**
Grantown Museum & Heritage Trust
Burnfield House, Burnfield Avenue. Tel: 01479 872478.
www.grantownmuseum.co.uk
*Open Mar–Dec, Mon–Sat 10–4.*

**8 Carrbridge**
Landmark Forest Heritage and Adventure Park
Tel: 0800 731 3446.
www.landmark-centre.co.uk
*Open daily 10–5 (later in summer). May close in winter due to bad weather.*

**9 Culloden**
Battlefield and Visitor Centre
Culloden Moor. Tel: 01463 790607.
www.nts.org.uk
*Site always accessible; visitor centre open Feb–Dec, daily 10–4; (9–6 Apr–Oct).*

Clava Cairns
On B9006. Tel: 0131 668 8800.
*Open at all times.*

**Special To...**
Speyside Heather Centre
Skye of Curr, Dulnain Bridge. Tel: 01479 851359.
www.heathercentre.com
*Open Feb–Dec, daily 9–6.*

## TOUR 15

[i] 17 High Street, Elgin. Tel: 01343 542666/543388.

[i] Clock Tower, The Square, Dufftown (seasonal). Tel: 01340 820501.

**1 Lossiemouth**
Lossiemouth Fisheries and Community Museum
Bitgavney Quay. Tel: 01343 543221.
*Open Easter–Oct, Mon–Sat 10.30–5.*

Palace of Spynie
2 miles (3km) north of Elgin off A941. Tel: 01343 546358.
www.historic-scotland.gov.uk
*Open Apr–Sep, daily 9.30–6.30; Oct, Sat–Wed 9.30–4.30; Nov–Dec, Sat–Sun 9.30–4.30; Jan–Mar, daily 9.30–4.30, (pm only Sat–Sun).*

**2 Fochabers**
Baxters Factory Tours and Visitor Centre
1 mile (1.5km) west of Fochabers on A96.
Tel: 01343 820666.
www.baxters.com
*Open all year.*

Fochabers Folk Museum
High Street. Tel: 01343 821204.
*Open May–Sep, daily 10.30–4.*

**3 Spey Bay**
Tugnet Ice-House Museum
Tugnet. Tel: 01309 673701.
*Open Apr–Sep, daily 1–5 (to 7pm Jul–Aug).*

Moray Firth Wildlife Centre
Tugnet. Tel: 01343 820339.
*Open Apr–Oct, daily 10.30–5; Feb–Mar, Sat–Sun 10.30–5.*

**4 Buckie**
Buckie Drifter Maritime Heritage Centre
Freuchny Road. Tel: 01542 834646.
*Open Apr–Oct, Mon–Sat 10–5, Sun noon–5.*

**5 Cullen**
Findlater Castle
By Sandend.
www.findlater.org.uk
*Open at all times.*

**6 Portsoy**
Portsoy Marble Workshop
Shorehead. Tel: 01261 842404.
*Open Fri–Sat afternoons.*

**7 Keith**
Strathisla Distillery
Seafield Avenue. Tel: 01542 783044.
www.maltwhiskytrail.com
*Open Apr–Oct, Mon–Sat 10–4, Sun 12.30–4.*

**8 Dufftown**
Keith & Dufftown Railway
Dufftown Station.
Tel: 01340 821181.
www.keith-dufftown.org.uk
*Open Easter to mid-Oct, Sat–Sun 10–5.*

Glenfiddich Distillery
Tel: 01340 820373.
http://uk.glenfiddich.com
*Open all year Mon–Fri 9.30–4.30; also Easter to mid-Oct., Sat 9.30–4.30, Sun noon–4.30.*

Balvenie Castle
Tel: 01340 820121.
www.historic-scotland.gov.uk
*Open Apr–Sep, daily 9.30–6.30.*

**9 Rothes**
Glen Grant Distillery
Elgin Road. Tel: 01542 783318.
www.maltwhiskytrail.com
*Open Apr–Oct, Mon–Sat 10–4, Sun 12.30–4.*

**Back to Nature**
Dolphin Cruises
Shore Street Quay, Inverness. Tel: 01463 717900.
www.inverness-dolphin-cruises.co.uk
*Open Mar–Oct, daily.*

**Special To...**
Speyside Cooperage
Dufftown Road, Craigellachie. Tel: 01340 871108.
www.speysidecooperage.co.uk
*Open Mon–Fri 9.30–4.*

## TOUR 16

[i] Collie Lodge, Banff (seasonal). Tel: 01261 812419.

[i] 3 Saltoun Square, Fraserburgh (seasonal). Tel: 01346 518315.

[i] 18 High Street, Inverurie. Tel: 01467 625800.

[i] 9A The Square, Huntly (seasonal). Tel: 01466 792255.

**4 Fraserburgh**
Scotland's Lighthouse Museum
Kinnaird Head. Tel: 01346 511022.
www.lighthousemuseum.org.uk
*Open Mon–Sat 11–5 (to 6pm Jul–Aug; 4pm Nov–Mar), Sun noon–5 (to 6pm Jul–Aug; 4pm Nov–Mar).*

**5 Peterhead**
Maritime Heritage
The Lido, South Road.
Tel: 01779 473000.
www.zincweb.co.uk
*Open Jun–Aug, Mon–Sat 10.30–5, Sun 11.30–5.*

Arbuthnot Museum and Art Gallery
St Peter Street. Tel: 01779 477778.
*Open Mon–Sat 11–4.30 (to 1pm Wed; closed 1–2 Sun and public holidays).*

**7 Ellon**
Haddo House
Tel: 01651 851440.
www.nts.org.uk
*Open, House: Jun, Fri–Mon 11–4.30; Jul–Aug, daily 11–4.30; Garden all year, daily 9.30–6.*

**8 Pitmedden Garden**
On A920 1 mile (1.5km) west of Pitmedden village.
Tel: 01651 842352.
www.nts.org.uk
*Open May–Sep, daily 10–5.30.*

**10 Inverurie**
Archaeolink Prehistory Park
Oyne, off A96 8 miles (13km) northwest of Inverurie. Tel: 01464 851500.
www.archaeolink.co.uk
*Open Apr–Oct, daily 10–5; Nov–Mar, daily 11–4.*

**11 Huntly**
Huntly Castle
Tel: 01466 793191.
www.historic-scotland.gov.uk
*Open summer: daily; winter: closed Thu pm, Fri, Sun am.*

**Recommended Walks**
Duff House
Banff. Tel: 01261 818181.
www.duffhouse.com
*Open daily 11–5.*

**For Children**
Northfield Farm Museum
New Pitsligo, Fraserburgh.
Tel: 01771 653504.
*Open May–Sep, daily 11–5.30.*

**Back to Nature**
Sands of Forvie National Nature Reserve
Collieston. Tel: 01358 751330.
www.nnr-scotland.org.uk
*Open at all times.*

**For History Buffs**
Fyvie Castle
Fyvie. Tel: 01651 891266.
www.nts.org.uk
*Open Apr–Jun, Sep, Fri–Tue noon–5; Jul–Aug, daily 11–5.*

## TOUR 17

[i] 22 Atholl Road, Pitlochry. Tel: 01796 472215/472751.

[i] NTS Visitor Centre, Killiecrankie (seasonal). Tel: 01796 473233.

[i] Ralia, on the A9 near Newtonmore (seasonal). Tel: 01540 673253.

[i] Grampian Road, Aviemore. Tel: 01479 810363.

[i] The Square, Tomintoul (seasonal). Tel: 01807 580285.

[i] Old Royal Station, Station Square, Ballater. Tel: 013397 55306.

**2 Blair Atholl**
Blair Castle
Tel: 01796 481207.
www.blair-castle.co.uk
*Open Apr–Oct, daily 9.30–4.30; Nov–Mar, Tue 9.30–12.30.*

**3 Dalwhinnie**
Distillery
Tel: 01540 672219.
*Open Mar–Dec, Mon–Fri 9.30–4.30 (also Sat Jun–Oct; also Sun 12.30–4.30 Jul–Aug).*

**4 Kingussie**
Highland Folk Museum
Duke Street. Tel: 01540 661307.
www.highlandfolk.com
*Open Apr–Aug, Mon–Sat 9.30–5.30; Sep–Oct, Mon–Fri 9.30–4.30.*

Ruthven Barracks
www.historic-scotland.gov.uk
*Open at all times.*

**5 Kincraig**
Highland Wildlife Park
3 miles (5km) south on B9152. Tel: 01540 651270.
www.highlandwildlifepark.org
*Open daily 10–6 (to 7pm Jun–Aug; to 4pm Nov–Mar).*

**6 Aviemore**
Strathspey Steam Railway
Aviemore Speyside Station, Dalfaber Road. Tel: 01479 810725.
www.strathspeyrailway.co.uk
*Open late May–Sep, daily; Easter, Apr–late May, Oct, Dec, trains run less frequently.*

**9 Tomintoul**
Tomintoul Museum
The Square. Tel: 01309 673701.
*Open Apr–Oct, Mon–Fri 9.30–noon, 2–4 (to 4.30 Jun–Aug; also Sat Jun–Sep).*

Glenlivet Distillery
Glenlivet, Ballindalloch. Tel: 01340 821720.
www.scotchwhisky.net/distilleries/glenlivet.htm
*Open mid-Mar to Oct, Mon–Sat 10–4, Sun 12.30–4 (to 6pm Jul–Sep).*

**10 The Lecht**
Corgarff Castle
8 miles (13km) west of Strathdon on the A939. Tel: 01975 651460.
www.historic-scotland.gov.uk
*Open Apr–Sep, daily 9.30–6.30; Oct–Mar daily 9.30–4.40.*

**11 Ballater**
Balmoral Castle
Tel: 013397 42534.
www.balmoralcastle.com
*Open Apr–Jul, daily 10–5.*

**12 Braemar**
Braemar Castle
Tel: 013397 4122.
www.braemarcastle.co.uk
*Phone for opening times.*

## TOUR 18

[i] Provost Ross's House, Shiprow, Aberdeen. Tel: 01224 288828.

[i] 66 Allardice Street, Stonehaven (seasonal). Tel: 01569 762806.

[i] Bridge Street, Banchory. Tel: 01330 822000.

[i] Railway Museum, Station Yard, Alford (seasonal). Tel: 019755 62052.

**1 Stonehaven**
Tolbooth Museum
The Harbour. Tel: 01771 622906.
*Open May–Oct, Wed–Mon 1.30–4.30.*

Dunnottar Castle
2 miles (3km) south. Tel: 01569 762173.
*Open Easter–Oct, Mon–Sat 9–6, Sun 2–5.*

**2 Fettercairn**
Fettercairn Distillery
Tel: 01561 340205.
www.scotchwhisky.net/distilleries.htm
*Open May–Sep, Mon–Sat 10–2.30.*

Fasque House
Tel: 01561 340569.
*Open May–Sep, daily 11–5.30.*

**3 Drum Castle**
Drumoak. Tel: 01330 811204.
www.drum-castle.org.uk
*Open: castle Easter, May–Sep, daily 1.30–5.30; Oct weekends; garden Easter, May–Sep, daily 10–6; grounds all year, daily 9.30–sunset.*

Garlogie Mill Power House Museum
Garlogie, Skene. Tel: 01771 622906.
*Open by appointment.*

**4 Crathes Castle and Gardens**
Crathes, by Banchory. Tel: 01330 844525.
www.nts.org.uk
*Open Apr–Oct, daily 10.30–5.30; garden and grounds all year daily 9–sunset.*

**5 Banchory**
Banchory Museum
Bridge Street. Tel: 01771 622906.
www.aberdeenshire.gov.uk/museums/banchory.asp
*Open May–Jun, Mon, Fri, Sat 11–1, 2–4; Jul–Aug, Mon–Wed, Fri–Sat 11–1, 2–4; Sep–Oct, Mon, Fri–Sat 11–1, 2–4.*

**8 Kildrummy Castle**
Kildrummy. Tel: 01975 571331.
www.historic-scotland.gov.uk
*Open Apr–Sep, daily 9.30–6.30.*

**9 Alford**
Grampian Transport Museum
Tel: 019755 62292.
www.gtm.org.uk
*Open Apr–Oct, daily 10–5.*

Alford Valley Railway
Alford Station. Tel: 07871 797360.
*Trains run Apr–May, Sep, Sat–Sun 1–4.30, every half hour; Jun–Aug, daily 1–4.30, every half hour.*

Haughton House Country Park
*Open all year dawn–dusk.*

Alford Heritage Centre
Mart Road. Tel: 019755 62906.
*Open Apr–Oct, Mon–Sat 10–5, Sun 1–5.*

**11 Castle Fraser**
Sauchen, Inverurie. Tel: 01330 833463.
www.nts.org.uk
*Open Apr–Sep, Fri–Tue noon–5.30 (Jun–Aug, daily from 11); grounds open all year daily 9.30–sunset.*

**Back to Nature**
Fowlsheugh RSPB Seabird Colony
Crawton, by Stonehaven. Tel: 01224 624824.
*Open at all times.*

**For Children**
Satrosphere
The Tramsheds, 179 Constitution Street, Aberdeen. Tel: 01224 640340.
www.satrosphere.net
*Open daily 9–5.*

Storybook Glen
Maryculter. Tel: 01224 732941.
www.storybookglenaberdeen.co.uk
*Open Mar–Oct, daily 10–6; Nov–Feb, daily 11–4.*

Doonies Farm
Nigg, Aberdeen. Tel: 01224 875879.
*Open all year 10–4.*

## TOUR 19

[i] Cameron Centre, Cameron Square, Fort William. Tel: 01397 703781.

[i] NTS Visitor Centre, Glenfinnan (seasonal). Tel: 01397 722250.

[i] Pier Road, Kilchoan (seasonal). Tel: 01972 510222.

[i] Strontian (seasonal). Tel: 01967 402381.

**1 Banavie**
Inverlochy Castle
On Fort William road.
www.historic-scotland.gov.uk
*Open at all times.*

Treasures of the Earth
On A830, Corpach. Tel: 01397 772283.
*Open daily, summer 9.30–7; winter 10–5.*

**2 Glenfinnan**
Glenfinnan Monument and NTS Visitor Centre
Tel: 01397 722250.
www.nts.org.uk
*Open all year; visitor centre Apr–Oct, daily 10–5 (9.30–6 mid-May to Aug).*

Railway Museum
Glenfinnan Railway Station. Tel: 01397 722295.
www.road-to-the-isles.org.uk/glenfinnan-station.html
*Open Jun–Sep, daily.*

**5 Mallaig**
Marine World Aquarium
The Harbour. Tel: 01687 462292.
www.mallaigmarineworld.com
*Open daily 9–6 (or later).*

[i] Tourist Information Office
**12** Number on tour

Heritage Centre
Station Road. Tel: 01687 462085.
www.mallaigheritage.org.uk
*Open Easter–Nov, Christmas/New Year, daily.*

**8 Acharacle**
Castle Tioram
4 miles (6.5km) north.
*Always open, subject to tides.*

**9 Glenbeg**
RSPB Glenborrodale
1 mile (1.5km) southeast of Glenbeg off B8007.
www.rspb.org.net/reserves
*Open all year daily.*

**11 Strontian**
Ariundle Oakwood Nature Reserve
Tel: 01967 402279.
*Open all year daily.*

**12 Lochaline**
Ardtornish House Gardens
Tel: 01967 421643.
www.ardtornish.co.uk
*Open Mar–Nov, daily 8–8.*

**For Children**
Lochaber Leisure Centre
Belford Road, Fort William.
Tel: 01397 704359.
*Open all year daily.*

## TOUR 20

[i] Car Park, Fort Augustus (seasonal). Tel: 01320 366367.

[i] Car Park, Kyle of Lochalsh (seasonal). Tel: 01599 534276.

[i] Main Street, Lochcarron (seasonal). Tel: 01520 722357.

[i] NTS Centre, Torridon (seasonal). Tel: 01445 791221.

[i] Achtercairn, Gairloch (seasonal). Tel: 01445 712130.

[i] NTS Centre, Inverewe (seasonal). Tel: 01445 781200.

[i] The Square, Strathpeffer (seasonal). Tel: 01997 421415.

**1 Invergarry**
Invergarry Castle
Glengarry Castle Hotel.
Tel: 01809 501254.
www.invergarrycastle.co.uk
*Open at all times.*

**2 Shiel Bridge**
Eilean Donan Castle
Dornie. Tel: 01599 555202.
www.eileandonancastle.co.uk
*Open Apr–Oct, daily 10–5.30.*

**3 Kyle of Lochalsh**
Balmacara Estate and Lochalsh House Woodland Garden
Tel: 01599 566325.
www.nts.org.uk
*Open daily 9–sunset.*

**5 Lochcarron**
Strome Castle
4 miles (6.5km) southwest, off A896.
www.nts.org.uk
*Open all year daily.*

**8 Torridon**
NTS Countryside Centre and Deer Museum
The Mains. Tel: 01445 791221.
www.nts.org.uk
*Open Easter–Sep, daily 10–6; estate park and deer museum all year daily.*

**9 Kinlochewe**
Aultroy Visitor Centre and Beinn Eighe National Nature Reserve
Tel: 01445 760254.
*Open May–Sep, daily 10–5; nature reserve always open.*

**10 Gairloch**
Gairloch Heritage Museum
Auchtercairn. Tel: 01445 712287.
www.gairlochheritagemuseum.org.uk
*Open Easter–Sep, Mon–Sat 10–5; Oct, Mon–Sat 10–1.30.*

**11 Inverewe Gardens**
Poolewe. Tel: 01445 781200.
www.nts.org.uk
*Open daily 9.30–5 (to 9pm mid-Mar–Oct).*

**14 Beauly**
Beauly Priory
Tel: 01667 460232.
www.historic-scotland.gov.uk
*Open mid-Jun to Sep, daily 9.30–6.30.*

Moniack Castle
On the A862. Tel: 01463 831283.
www.moniackcastle.co.uk
*Open all year, Mon–Sat, summer 11–5; winter 11–4.*

**16 Drumnadrochit**
Official Loch Ness 2000
Tel: 01456 450573.
www.loch-ness-scotland.com
*Open all year daily.*

The Original Loch Ness Visitor Centre
Loch Ness Lodge Hotel.
Tel: 01456 450342.
www.lochness-centre.com
*Open all year daily.*

Urquhart Castle
On the A82. Tel: 01456 450551.
*Open all year daily.*

**For Children**
Gairloch Leisure Centre
Gairloch. Tel: 01445 712345.
*Open all year daily.*

## TOUR 21

[i] Kirk Lane, Lochinver (seasonal). Tel: 01571 844330.

[i] Ferrycroft Countryside Centre, Lairg (seasonal). Tel: 01549 402160.

**1 Knockan Cliff**
Inverpolly National Nature Reserve
Off A835.
www.inverpolly.com
*Open May–Sep, most days.*

**2 Inchnadamph**
Ardvreck Castle
Loch Assynt, Lochinver.
*Open at all times.*

**3 Lochinver**
Assynt Visitor Centre
Kirk Lane. Tel: 01571 844330.
www.assynt.info
*Open Easter–Oct, Mon–Sat 10–5 (longer hours Jun–Aug); also Sun 11–4 in Aug.*

Highland Stoneware
Assynt. Tel: 01571 844376.
www.highlandstoneware.com
*Open Mon–Fri 9–6; also Sat 9–5 Easter–Oct.*

**7 Lairg**
Ferrycroft Countryside Centre
Tel: 01549 402160.
www.highland.gov.uk/leisure/tourism/visitorcentres/ferrycroft.htm
*Open Apr–Oct, daily 10–5 (to 4pm on Sun).*

Falls of Shin Visitor Centre
Achany. Tel: 01549 402231
www.fallsofshin.co.uk.
*Open Mar–Dec, daily.*

## TOUR 22

[i] The Square, Dornoch. Tel: 01862 810400.

[i] Durine, Durness (seasonal). Tel: 01971 511259.

[i] Clachan, Bettyhill (seasonal). Tel: 01641 521342.

[i] Riverside, Thurso (seasonal). Tel: 01847 892371.

[i] County Road, John o'Groats (seasonal). Tel: 01955 611373.

[i] Whitechapel Road, Wick. Tel: 01955 602596.

**3 Durness**
Balnakeil Craft Village
www.durness.org
*Open Apr–Oct, daily 10–6.*

**4 Bettyhill**
Strathnaver Museum
Tel: 01641 521418.
www.strathnavermuseum.org
*Open Apr–Oct, Mon–Sat 10–1, 2–5.*

Invernaver Nature Reserve
*Open at all times.*

**5 Reay**
UKAEA Exhibition Centre
Dounreay. Tel: 01847 806086.
www.ukaea.org.uk
*Open Apr–Oct, daily 10–4.*

**6 Thurso**
Thurso Heritage Museum
Town Hall. Tel: 01847 892692.
www.caithnesshorizons.co.uk
*Undergoing refurbishment. Telephone for details.*

Castle of Mey
Tel: 01847 851473.
www.castleofmey.org.uk
*Open mid-May to Jul, mid-Aug to Sep, Tue–Sat 11–4.30, Sun 2–5 (dates may vary).*

**8 Wick**
Castle of Old Wick
*Open at all times, unless adjoining rifle range is in use.*

Wick Heritage Centre
Tel: 01955 605393.
www.caithness.org/history/wickheritagecentre/newwickheritage
*Open Easter–Oct, daily 10–5.*

**10 Dunbeath**
Heritage Centre
Old School. Tel: 01593 731233.
www.dunbeath-heritage.org.uk
*Open Easter–Oct, daily 10–5.*

Laidhay Croft Museum
1 mile (1.5km) north on the A9. Tel: 01593 731244.
*Open Easter–Oct, daily 10–6.*

**11 Helmsdale**
Timespan Heritage Centre
Dunrobin Street. Tel: 01431 821327.
www.timespan.org.uk
*Open Mar–Oct, Mon–Sat 10–5, Sun noon–5.*

**12 Brora**
Clynelish Distillery
Tel: 01408 623000.
www.scotchwhisky.net/distilleries/clynelish.htm
*Open Mar–Oct, Mon–Fri 9.30–5.*

**13 Golspie**
Orcadian Stone Company
Main Street. Tel: 01408 633483.
www.orcadianstone.co.uk
*Open Easter–Oct, Mon–Sat 9–5.30.*

Dunrobin Castle and Gardens
Tel: 01408 633177.
*Open Apr to mid-Oct, daily (ex Sun am) 10.30–4.30.*

## TOUR 23

[i] The Square, Dornoch.
Tel: 01862 810400.

**1 Evanton**
Storehouse of Foulis
Foulis Ferry Point.
Tel: 01349 830038.
ww.storehouseoffoulis.co.uk
*Open Mon–Sat 9–6, Sun 10–5.*

**2 Tain**
Tain Through Time
Tower Street. Tel: 01862 894089.
www.tainmuseum.org.uk
*Open Apr–Oct, Mon–Sat 10–5 (6 in Jul–Aug).*

Glenmorangie Distillery
Outskirts of Tain. Tel: 01862 892477.
www.glenmorangie.com
*Open all year daily.*

**5 Cromarty**
Cromarty Courthouse Museum
Church Street. Tel: 01381 600418.
www.cromarty-courthouse.org.uk
*Open Apr–Oct, daily 10–5.*

Hugh Miller's Cottage
Church Street. Tel: 01381 600245.
www.nts.org.uk
*Open Easter–Oct, daily noon–5 (closed Mon–Tue in Oct).*

**6 Rosemarkie**
Groam House Museum
Tel: 01381 620961.
*Telephone for opening times.*

## TOUR 24

[i] The Car Park, Broadford (seasonal).
Tel: 01471 822361.

[i] Bayfield House, Bayfield Road, Portree. Tel: 01478 612137.

[i] 2 Lochside, Dunvegan (seasonal). Tel: 01470 521581.

**6 Kilmuir**
Museum of Island Life
Tel: 01470 552206.
www.skyemuseum.co.uk
*Open Apr–Oct, Mon–Sat (phone for times).*

**8 Dunvegan Castle**
Tel: 01470 521206.
www.dunvegancastle.com
*Open late Mar–Oct, Mon–Sat 10–5.30, Sun 1–5.30 (gardens open from 10.30am); Nov–Mar, daily 11–4.*

**9 Colbost**
Croft Museum
Next to the Three Chimneys, near Dunvegan.
Tel: 01470 521296.
*Open Easter–Oct, daily 9.30–6.*

**10 Carbost**
Talisker Distillery
Tel: 01478 614308.
*Open Apr–Oct, Mon–Fri 9–4.30 (also Sat in Jul–Aug); Nov–Mar, Mon–Fri 2–4.30.*

**15 Armadale**
Clan Donald Centre and Armadale Castle
Tel: 01471 844305.
www.clandonald.com
*Open Apr–Oct, daily 9.30–5.30.*

## TOUR 25

[i] The Pier, Main Street, Tobermory (seasonal).
Tel: 01688 302182.

**1 Craignure**
Torosay Castle and Gardens
Tel: 01680 812421.
www.torosay.com
*Open Easter–Oct, daily 10.30–5; gardens all year.*

Mull & West Highland Narrow Gauge Railway
Craignure (Old Pier) Station. Tel: 01680 812494.
www.mullrail.co.uk
*Open Easter to mid-Oct, daily 11–5.*

Duart Castle
Tel: 01680 812309.
www.duartcastle.com
*Open May to mid-Oct, daily 10.30–6.*

**3 Iona**
Iona Abbey
Tel: 01681 700512.
www.isle-of-iona.com/abbey.htm
*Open at all times.*

Iona Heritage Centre
Tel: 01681 700328.
*Open Apr–Oct, Mon–Sat 10.30–4.30.*

**7 Dervaig**
Old Byre Heritage Centre
Tel: 01688 400229.
www.old-byre.co.uk
*Open Easter–Oct, Wed–Sun 10.30–6.30.*

**Opening times**
The opening times of museums and other attractions are subject to change and, in addition to opening and closing times given in the text, are usually closed on some public holidays. Some may be open by appointment outside the stated times. Visitors are advised to check locally to avoid disappointment.

Statue of Robert the Bruce on the Gatehouse, Edinburgh Castle

# INDEX

**The Automobile Association**
wishes to thank the following libraries and photographers for their assistance in the preparation of this book.

PICTURES COLOUR LIBRARY 4
SPECTRUM COLOUR LIBRARY 5

The remaining photographs are held in the Association's own photo library (AA PHOTO LIBRARY) and were taken by the following photographers:

M ALEXANDER 6, 12, 22, 30B, 36B, 40, 41, 42, 44B, 45, 46A, 50A, 50B, 76B; A BAKER 67A, 82; J BEAZLEY 10, 16, 17, 19, 20, 24/5, 26A, 26B, 30A, 42/3, 46B, 51, 61A, 61B, 77, 87B, 88, 109, 128; J CARNIE 7, 33, 56B, 62, 64, 67B, 71B, 78, 90, 104, 107B, 120, 212A, 121B, 144; D CORRANCE i34, 38, 65, 75A, 76A, 118; S DAY 52, 57B, 58, 59A, 66, 68, 70, 72, 73A, 73B, 75B, 79, 83B, 85, 86, 105A, 119A, 119B, 122; E ELLINGTON 87A, 93, 94/5, 97, 98A, 99, 103A, 110, 113, 115, 125, 132/3, 136B, 139A, 139B, 147A, 148, 154; R ELLIOTT 48, 53, 117A, 123, 126/7; D FORSS 55A, 55B, 157; S GIBSON PHOTOGRAPHY 14, 28, 29, 60; A GREELEY 150B; D HARDLEY 57A, 116; J HENDERSON 36A, 89, 106A, 107A, 111B, 114B, 132, 134A, 140, 142, 143, 150A, 151, 153; C LEES 25, 35, 44A; S & O MATTHEWS 18/9; K PATERSON 8, 11, 21, 32, 37, 49A, 49B, 56A, 62/3, 69, 81, 84, 111A, 112, 130B, 145A, 145B, 164, 178/9; P SHARPE 9, 13, 23, 31, 59B, 92; J SMITH 124, 192; M TAYLOR 74, 83A, 101B, 103B, 130A, 134B, 136A, 138, 146, 147B; R WEIR 80, 91, 96/7, 100, 101A, 102, 105B, 108, 112/3, 114A, 135, 137, 141, 149, 152, 155A, 156; S WHITEHORNE 131 H WILLIAMS 27, 39, 106B.

**Contributors**
**Verifier:** Hugh Taylor **Copy editor:** Dilys Jones **Indexer:** Marie Lorimer

# Atlas

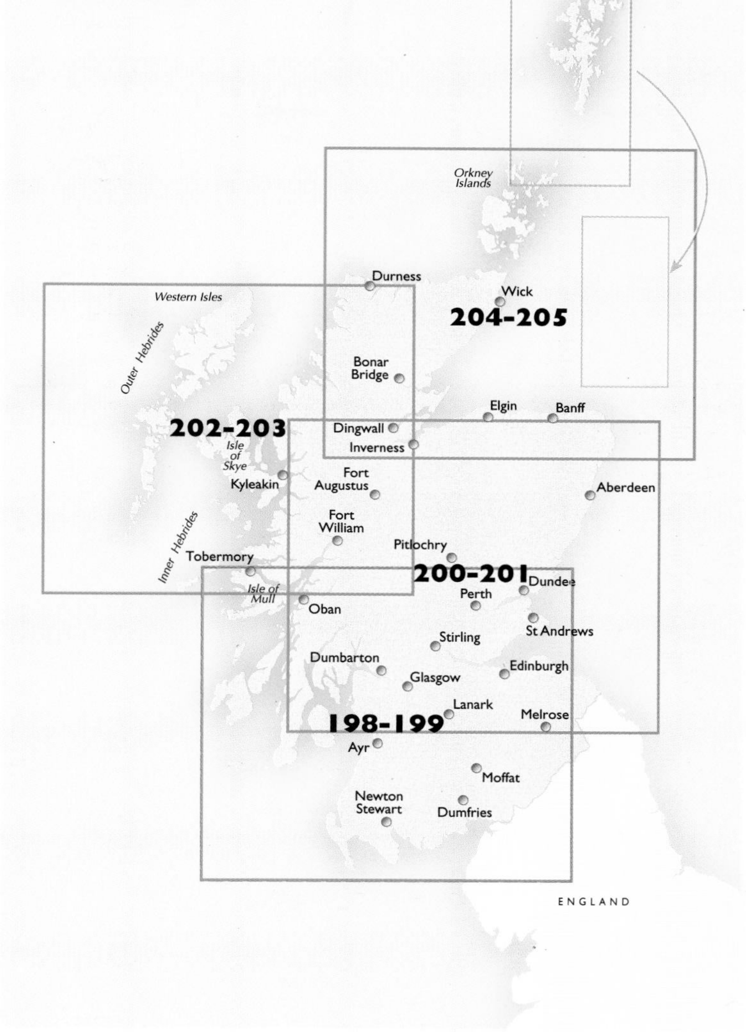

Shetland Islands
Orkney Islands
Western Isles
Outer Hebrides
Inner Hebrides
Isle of Skye
Isle of Mull
Durness
Wick
204-205
Bonar Bridge
Elgin
Banff
202-203
Dingwall
Inverness
Kyleakin
Fort Augustus
Aberdeen
Fort William
Pitlochry
Tobermory
200-201
Dundee
Perth
Oban
St Andrews
Stirling
Dumbarton
Edinburgh
Glasgow
Lanark
Melrose
198-199
Ayr
Moffat
Newton Stewart
Dumfries
ENGLAND

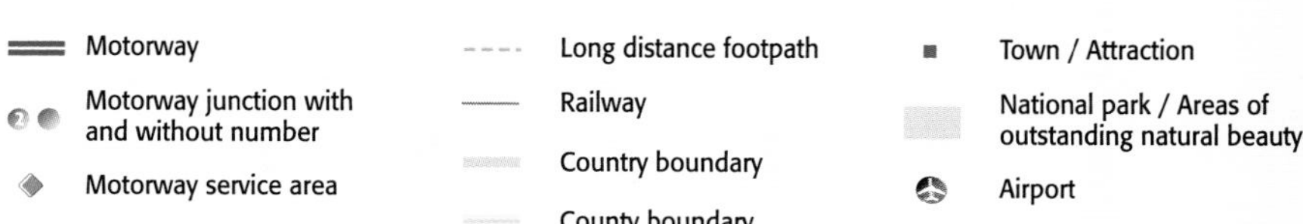


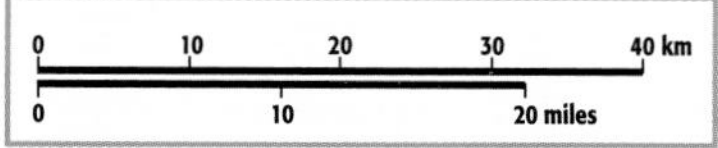


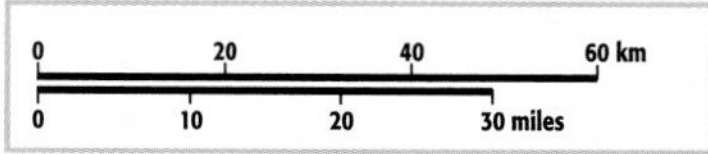

203
A
B
C
5
4
3
2
1
Sound of Mull
Lochaline
Loch Linnhe
A828
Bidean Nam Bian
Ben Nevis & Glen Coe
Loch na Keal, Isle of Mull
Mull
Ulva
966 Ben More
A849
Lynn of Lorne
1079 Ben Starav
1074 Ben Dorain
Tyndrum
A85
Oban
1124 Ben Cruachan
Dalmally
1130 Ben Lui
Crianlarich
1171 Ben More
A82
Iona
Fionnphort
Firth of Lorne
A816
Seil
Loch Awe
A819
Loch Katrine
Loch Lomond & The Trossachs National Park
Luing
ARGYLL & BUTE
Inveraray
Scarba, Lunga & The Garvellachs
Scarba
973 Ben Lomond
A83
Argyll Forest Park
A815
A814
Colonsay
Scalasaig
Jura
Oronsay
Sound of Jura
Lochgilphead
Knapdale
A886
Loch Lomond
A817
Helensburgh
A880
A8003
Kyles of Bute
Dunoon
784 Beinn An Oir
A846
Colintraive
Greenock
A8
Dumbarton
WEST DUNBARTONSHIRE
INVERCLYDE
Port Askaig
Tarbert
Glasgow
A761
Paisley
RENFREWSHIRE
A847
Kennacraig
Rothesay
Bute
Islay
Claonaig
Sound of Bute
Largs
A760
A737
A736
Kilbirnie
Beith
A844
A78
Portnahaven
Islay
Gigha
Kintyre
Kilbrannan Sound
NORTH AYRSHIRE
Stewarton
A735
Port Ellen
North Arran
874 Goat Fell
Kilwinning
A736
Ardrossan
Irvine
A71
Mull of Oa
A841
Brodick
Firth of Clyde
A759
A77
Lamlash
Holy Island
Clyde
Troon
Isle of Arran
Prestwick
Ayr
Campbeltown
A70
A719
A713
Maybole
Doon
Mull of Kintyre
Ailsa Craig
Girvan
SOUTH AYRSHIRE
A714
842 Merrick
Galloway Forest Park
Ballantrae
North Channel
Loch Ryan
A718
Southern Upland Way
Newton Stewart
Stranraer
A75
Portpatrick
A716
Wigtown
A747
A746
Luce Bay
Drummore
Mull of Galloway

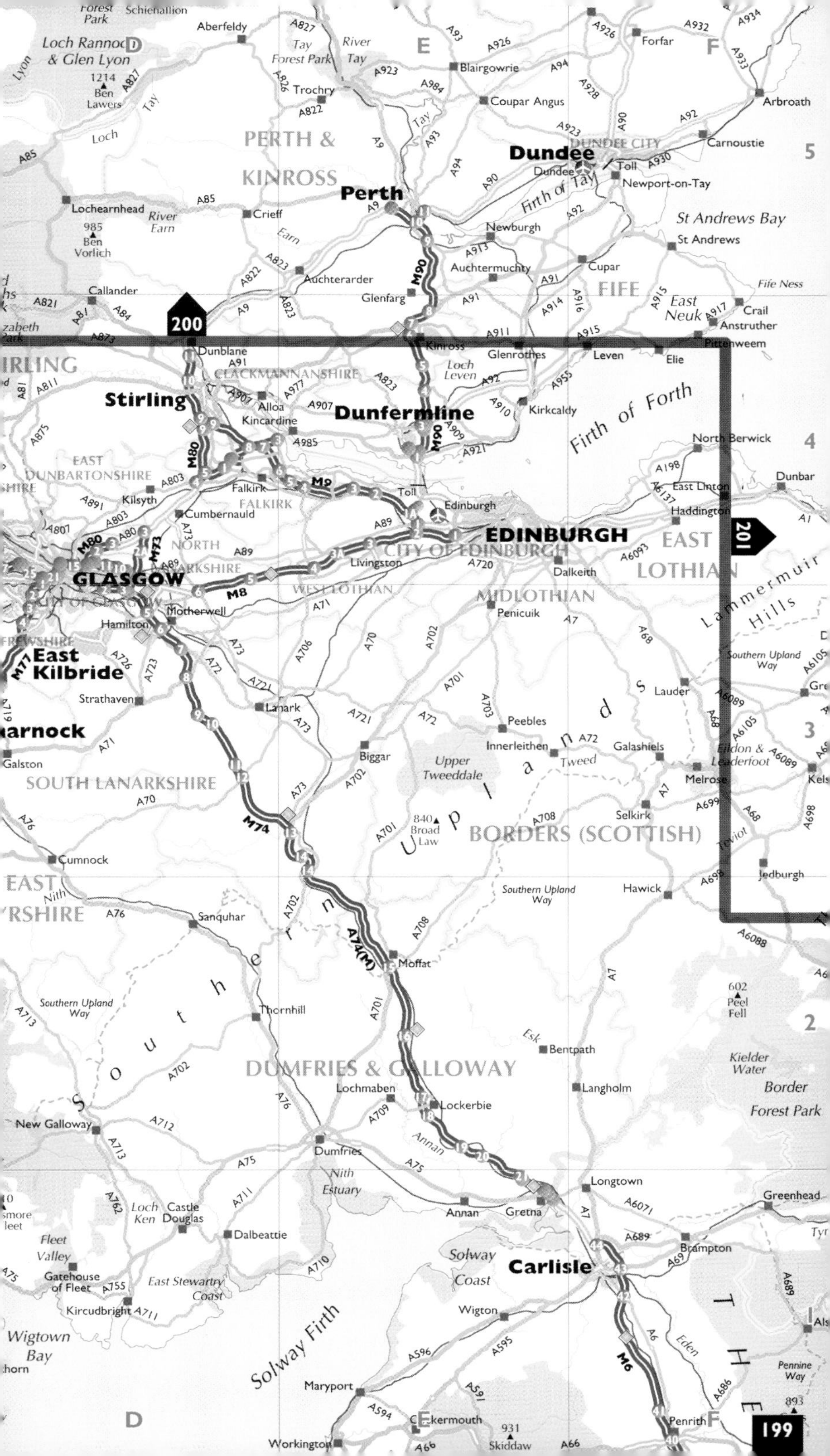
Perth
Dundee
Stirling
Dunfermline
Edinburgh
EDINBURGH
GLASGOW
East Kilbride
Carlisle
PERTH & KINROSS
FIFE
CLACKMANNANSHIRE
EAST DUNBARTONSHIRE
FALKIRK
NORTH LANARKSHIRE
CITY OF EDINBURGH
WEST LOTHIAN
MIDLOTHIAN
EAST LOTHIAN
SOUTH LANARKSHIRE
BORDERS (SCOTTISH)
DUMFRIES & GALLOWAY
Southern Uplands
Lammermuir Hills
Firth of Forth
Firth of Tay
Solway Firth
Solway Coast
St Andrews Bay
Southern Upland Way
Kielder Water
Border Forest Park
200
201

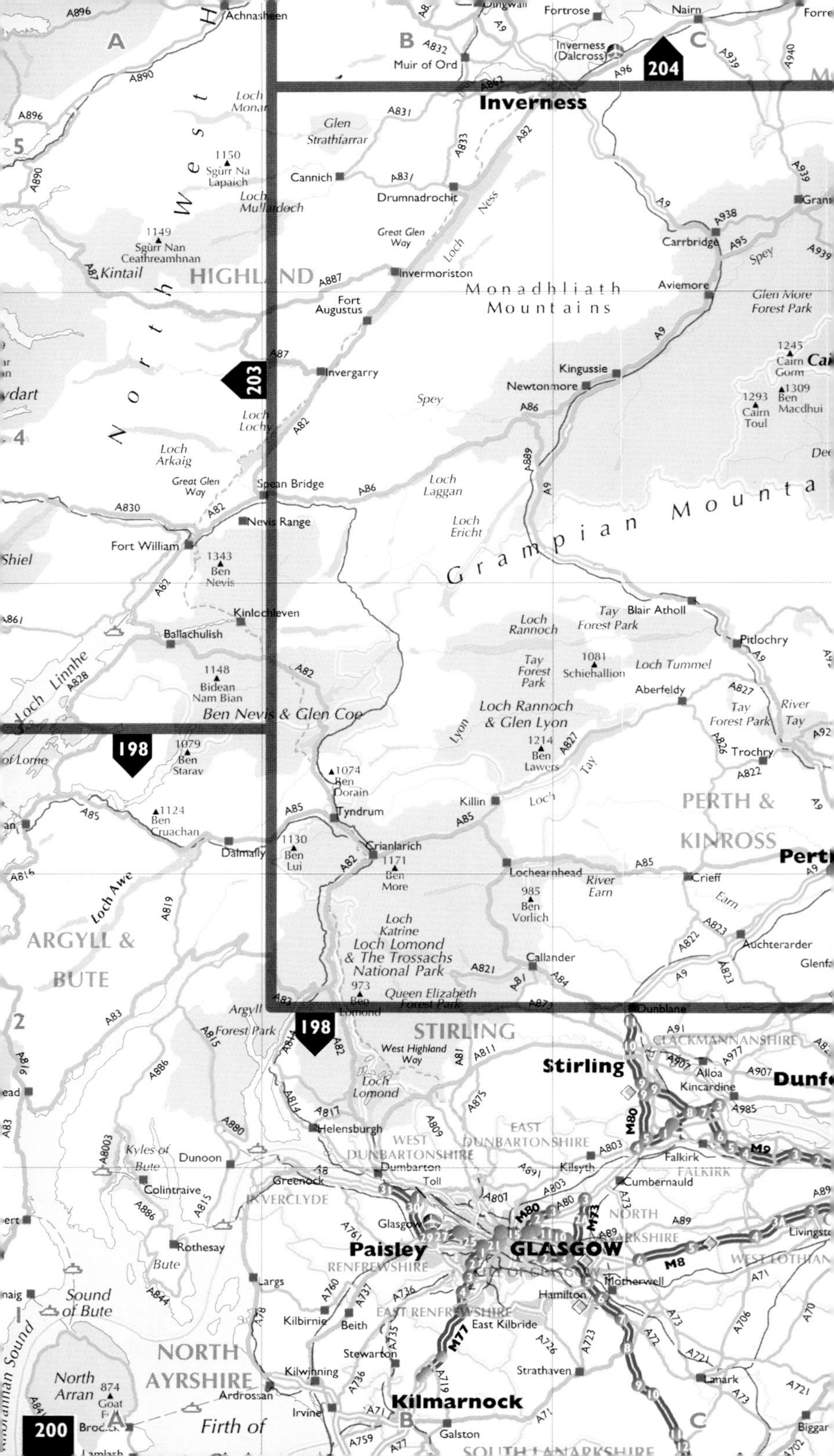

A
B
C
5
4
3
2
1
204
203
198
198
Achnasheen
Dingwall
Fortrose
Nairn
Forres
Muir of Ord
Inverness (Dalcross)
Inverness
Glen Strathfarrar
Loch Monar
1150 Sgùrr Na Lapaich
Loch Mullardoch
Cannich
Drumnadrochit
Loch Ness
Great Glen Way
1149 Sgùrr Nan Ceathreamhnan
Kintail
HIGHLAND
North West H
Invermoriston
Fort Augustus
Monadhliath Mountains
Carrbridge
Aviemore
Spey
Glen More Forest Park
Grantown
Invergarry
Kingussie
Newtonmore
1245 Cairn Gorm
1309 Ben Macdhui
1293 Cairn Toul
Dee
Loch Lochy
Loch Arkaig
Great Glen Way
Spean Bridge
Loch Laggan
Loch Ericht
Grampian Mountains
Nevis Range
Fort William
1343 Ben Nevis
Shiel
Kinlochleven
Ballachulish
Loch Linnhe
1148 Bidean Nam Bian
Ben Nevis & Glen Coe
Blair Atholl
Tay Forest Park
Loch Rannoch
Pitlochry
Tay Forest Park
1081 Schiehallion
Loch Tummel
Aberfeldy
Loch Rannoch & Glen Lyon
Lyon
River Tay
Tay Forest Park
1214 Ben Lawers
Trochry
1079 Ben Starav
of Lorne
1074 Ben Dorain
Tyndrum
Killin
Loch Tay
PERTH & KINROSS
Perth
1124 Ben Cruachan
Dalmally
1130 Ben Lui
Crianlarich
1171 Ben More
Lochearnhead
River Earn
Crieff
985 Ben Vorlich
Loch Awe
ARGYLL & BUTE
Loch Katrine
Loch Lomond & The Trossachs National Park
Callander
Auchterarder
973 Ben Lomond
Queen Elizabeth Forest Park
Dunblane
Argyll Forest Park
STIRLING
CLACKMANNANSHIRE
West Highland Way
Stirling
Alloa
Kincardine
Dunfermline
Loch Lomond
Helensburgh
EAST DUNBARTONSHIRE
WEST DUNBARTONSHIRE
Falkirk
FALKIRK
Kyles of Bute
Dunoon
Dumbarton
Kilsyth
Cumbernauld
Colintraive
Greenock
INVERCLYDE
NORTH LANARKSHIRE
Glasgow
Livingston
Rothesay
Bute
Paisley
GLASGOW
RENFREWSHIRE
CITY OF GLASGOW
WEST LOTHIAN
Largs
Motherwell
Hamilton
Sound of Bute
Kilbirnie
Beith
EAST RENFREWSHIRE
East Kilbride
NORTH AYRSHIRE
Stewarton
Kilwinning
Strathaven
Lanark
North Arran
874 Goat Fell
Ardrossan
Irvine
Kilmarnock
Firth of Clyde
Brodick
Lamlash
Galston
SOUTH LANARKSHIRE
Biggar
Kilbrannan Sound
M8
M9
M73
M77
M80
A9
A82
A85
A86

D
E
F
205
Rothes
Keith
Aberchirder
Turriff
Peterhead
Aberlour
Dufftown
Huntly
Speyside Way
Ellon
Oldmeldrum
Inverurie
Tomintoul
Kintore
Alford
Aberdeen
Dyce
KIRKWALL
LERWICK
ABERDEEN
ABERDEENSHIRE
ABERDEEN CITY
Aboyne
Banchory
Ballater
Dee
Don
Muick
1154
Lochnagar
1067
Glas Maol
Stonehaven
Laurencekirk
Inverbervie
ANGUS
Brechin
Montrose
Kirriemuir
Forfar
Blairgowrie
Coupar Angus
Arbroath
Carnoustie
DUNDEE CITY
Dundee
Toll
Newport-on-Tay
Firth of Tay
St Andrews Bay
Newburgh
St Andrews
Auchtermuchty
Cupar
FIFE
Fife Ness
East Neuk
Falkland
Crail
Anstruther
Pittenweem
Kinross
Leven
Elie
199
Loch Leven
Kirkcaldy
Firth of Forth
Dunbar
East Linton
Edinburgh
EDINBURGH
EAST LOTHIAN
Dalkeith
MIDLOTHIAN
Penicuik
Lammermuir Hills
St Abb's Head
Eyemouth
Berwick-upon-Tweed
Duns
Southern Upland Way
Greenlaw
Lauder
Tweed
Coldstream
Peebles
Innerleithen
Galashiels
Eildon & Leaderfoot
Melrose
Upper Tweeddale
Farne Islands
5
4
3
2
1

A
B
C
5
4
3
2
1
Outer Hebrides
Oiseval Gallery
A858
Carloway (Carlabh
Storno
(Steorr
Lewis (Leodhais)
WESTERN ISLES
Scarp
South Lewis, Harris & North Uist
A859
Kilda
Taransay
Tarbert (Tairbeart)
Harris (Hearadh)
Pabbay
Sound of Harris
Berneray
North Uist (Uibhist a Tuath)
Lochmaddy (Loch nam Madadh)
A865
A867
The Little Minch
Benbecula
Benbecula (Beinn Na Faoghla)
Dunvegan
A863
South Uist (Uibhist a Deas)
South Uist Machair
Lochboisdale (Loch Baghasdail)
Sound of Barra
Eriskay (Eiriosgaigh)
Barra
Barra (Barraigh)
Castlebay (Bagh a Chaisteil)
Canna
Sandray
Pabbay
Mingulay
Berneray
Inner Hebrides
The Small Is
Coll
Arinagour
Tiree
Scarinish
Tiree

Port of Ness
(Port Nis)
Broad Bay
Stornoway
The Minch
Shiant Islands
Scourie
North-west Sutherland
Tongue
Kyle of Tongue
Altnaharra
Loch Naver
Lochinver
Inchnadamph
Assynt - Coigach
998
Ben More Assynt
Loch Shin
Lairg
Ullapool
Bonar Bridge
Dornoch
Gairloch
Loch Maree
Benn Dearg
Loch Fannich
1045
Ben Wyvis
Alness
Trotternish
Uig
Rona
Wester Ross
Kinlochewe
Achnasheen
Dingwall
Torridon
Muir of Ord
Portree
Sound of Raasay
Inner Sound
Raasay
Scalpay
Loch Monar
Glen Strathfarrar
Cannich
Drumnadrochit
1150
Sgùrr Na Lapaich
Kyle of Lochalsh
Loch Mullardoch
The Cuillin Hills
1009
Sgùrr Alasdair
1149
Sgùrr Nan Ceathreamhnan
Great Glen Way
Loch Ness
Kintail
HIGHLAND
Invermoriston
Fort Augustus
North West Highlands
Cuillin
Sound of Sleat
Ardvasar
1019
Ladhar Bheinn
Knoydart
Invergarry
Mallaig
Rùm
Sound
Loch Morar
Loch Lochy
Spey
Newtonmore
Eigg
Loch Arkaig
Glenfinnan
Spean Bridge
Loch Laggan
Sound of Arisaig
Loch Ericht
Morar, Moidart & Ardnamurchan
Loch Shiel
Fort William
1343
Ben Nevis
Acharacle
Kinlochleven
Ballachulish
Glencoe
1148
Bidean Nam Bian
Tobermory
Loch Linnhe
Sound of Mull
Tay Forest Park
Ben Nevis & Glen Coe
Loch Rannoch
Lynn of Lorne
och na Keal, Isle of Mull
1079
Ben
204
200
198
203

A
B
C
5
4
3
2
Hoy &
West Mainland
Stromness
Hoy
Pentland
Cape Wrath
Durness
Scrabster
Thurso
A836
A838
Bettyhill
Melvich
A9
Tongue
A882
Kyle of Tongue
Loch
Loyal
North-west
Sutherland
Naver
A897
A99
A894
Thurso
Altnaharra
Loch
Naver
Lybster
Dunbeath
A837
A836
Inchnadamph
998
Ben More
Assynt
Assynt - Coigach
Loch
Shin
Helmsdale
Lairg
A839
A835
203
A837
Golspie
Brora
Carron
Bonar
Bridge
A949
Dornoch
A832
Dornoch Firth
Tain
1081
Benn
Dearg
Moray Firth
Alness
Invergordon
Loch
Fannich
1045
Ben
Wyvis
Cromarty
Firth
Cromarty
Lossiemouth
A941
A862
A96
Elgin
Dingwall
Fortrose
Nairn
Forres
Achnasheen
A834
Inverness
(Dalcross)
A939
A940
Muir of Ord
Rothes
MORAY
Spey
Loch
Monar
A831
Inverness
200
Aberlour
Glen
Strathfarrar
A833
A82
A95
Dufftown
Speyside
204

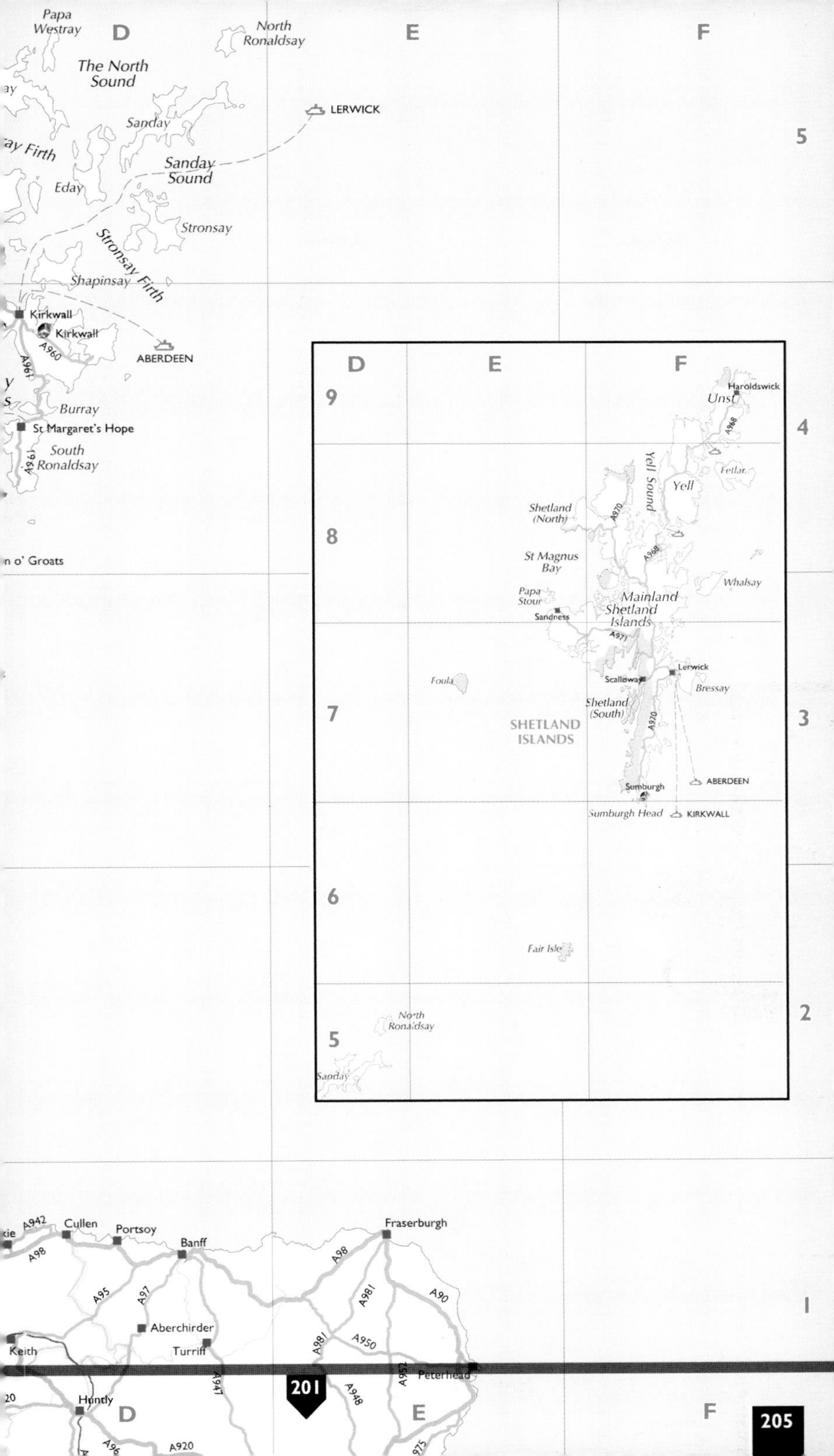

D
E
F
Papa Westray
North Ronaldsay
The North Sound
Sanday
Sanday Sound
LERWICK
Eday
Stronsay
Stronsay Firth
Shapinsay
Kirkwall
Kirkwall
A960
A961
ABERDEEN
Burray
St Margaret's Hope
South Ronaldsay
A961
n o' Groats
5
4
3
2
1
D
E
F
9
8
7
6
5
Haroldswick
Unst
A968
Fetlar
Yell
Yell Sound
Shetland (North)
A970
St Magnus Bay
A968
Whalsay
Papa Stour
Sandness
Mainland Shetland Islands
A971
Lerwick
Bressay
Foula
Scalloway
Shetland (South)
A970
SHETLAND ISLANDS
Sumburgh
ABERDEEN
Sumburgh Head
KIRKWALL
Fair Isle
North Ronaldsay
Sanday
Cullen
Portsoy
A942
A98
Banff
Fraserburgh
A98
A95
A97
A981
A90
Aberchirder
Keith
Turriff
A981
A950
A947
A952
Peterhead
201
A948
Huntly
D
E
F
A96
A920
975

# ATLAS INDEX